D1416881

Journeys

Autobiographical
Writings by Women

A Publication in Women's Studies

Barbara Haber, Series Editor

"Marcia Paints a Self-Portrait," from *De claris mulieribus* of Boccaccio, French translation, ca. 1402 *(Permission of Bibliotèque Nationale, Paris, from MS Fr. 12420)*

Edited by
Mary Grimley Mason and
Carol Hurd Green

Journeys
Autobiographical Writings by Women

G. K. Hall & Co.   Boston, Massachusetts

Library of Congress Cataloging in Publication Data

Main entry under title:
Journeys: autobiographical writings by women.

  CONTENTS: Julian, of Norwich. Revelations of divine love.—Kempe, M. The book of Margery Kempe.—Bradstreet, A. Spiritual autobiography. Selected poems.—Newcastle, M. C., Duchess of. The true relation of my birth, breeding, and life. Life of William Cavendish, Duke of Newcastle. The blazing world. [etc]
  1. Women—Biography. I. Mason, Mary Grimley. II. Green, Carol Hurd.
HQ1123.J68   301.41'2'0922 [B]   79-10726
ISBN 0-8161-8310-4

Publ. 14.95 9 20 79

This publication is printed on permanent/durable acid-free paper
MANUFACTURED IN THE UNITED STATES OF AMERICA

Contents

Preface

The autobiographies of women throughout the centuries provide a valuable record of their inner lives, of their images of themselves, and of society's expectations for them. Autobiographies reveal as well the kinds of choices women have been able to make.

We are focusing in this anthology on a particular kind of choice, the decision to make a journey—actual or metaphorical—beyond individual concerns toward involvement or commitment, to a creed, to an institution, to a leader, to another culture. The selections chosen represent stages on the journey as well as goals, failures as well as successes.

The journeys included here range from the medieval religious pilgrimage to the twentieth-century political pilgrimage to Hanoi. Between the two comes a wide range of explorations—intellectual, spiritual, psychological, and emotional. Some of the women represented here are well known, others are only now becoming part of history. We have restricted our selections to work originally written in English to avoid the risks inherent in translation and to suggest most clearly the connections and affinites among the women.

By linking together the autobiographies of such a varied group of women around the idea of the journey, we hope to underline two implications of that metaphor: journey as action and movement, implying freedom and the will to choose, and journey as direction, implying a goal beyond the self. We believe that these documents provide vivid proof that the journey beyond self leads not to obliteration but to self-discovery and self-realization. Within these widely scattered times and places, these women are adventurers—some are even heroes in ways that suggest the variety of forms heroism may take.

Women have always written autobiography; the selections given here demonstrate as well the unique contribution women have made to the genre. Like its male counterpart, women's autobiography had its origins in religious writings. We have included two selections in this tradition from the fourteenth and fifteenth centuries, the work of the only two women who wrote in this genre in English, Julian of Norwich (1342-1416) and Margery Kempe (1373-1438). From seventeenth-century Puritan spiritual testimonies, we have included the spiritual autobiography of Anne Bradstreet, the first American woman poet, written about 1656. The account of her life by Margaret Cavendish, the Duchess of Newcastle, *A True Relation of My Birth, Breeding, and Life* (1656), represents a woman's contribution to the increasingly popular seventeenth-century form of secular autobiography, the memoir. Our selection from Lady Mary Wortley Montagu (1689-1762) illustrates one of the popular autobiographical forms of the eighteenth century, the travel memoir, an outgrowth of the epistolatory genre. Further developments of the travel memoir in the nineteenth century are here represented by Lady Anne Blunt's *Pilgrimage to Nejd* (1881), which shows the enthusiasm of the scholar and linguist discovering another culture. Anna Cooper's journey to France similarly represents the scholar's response to another culture, but it has a significance beyond that, representing as well the black woman's determination to educate herself and others.

In contrast with important male writers of the nineteenth century, major women writers of that time, such as Charlotte Brontë and George Eliot, seldom chose to write their autobiographies except in fictional form. Sara Coleridge's *Memoirs* and selections from her letters are included here because they reflect important cultural currents while revealing a strong sense of self-identity.

The spiritual concerns of the women of the medieval and Puritan times, and the meaning of a life directed by religious imperatives, are reflected in several later selections. Jarena Lee, the first woman preacher of the African Methodist Episcopal Church, travels indefatigably to carry her message of conversion, as Mira Behn almost one hundred years later travelled with confidence to join Gandhi and later to spread his teachings. The quests of Vida Scudder, Beatrice Webb, and Dorothy Day for a creed that would satisfy both spiritual and political needs adds a further dimension. Hilda Doolittle, too, is seeking for an explanation for chaos, especially the chaos of war; she turns to Freud and to psychoanalysis for the clarity that will allow her to integrate her spiritual and visionary experiences with the realities of the threat of war.

The moral implications of political life, seen in Scudder and Day, are central to the final selections. The work of Susan Sontag and Denise Levertov represents two of the many journeys to Hanoi made by American opponents of the war in Vietnam. Their sensitivity to the Vietnamese culture, and their self-awareness in its presence, make their work a suitable conclusion for the volume.

The collection is far from inclusive: many more pieces of autobiography might be here. For example, the writings of leaders of movements for women's rights, the creators of new beliefs and institutions, are omitted because they are otherwise available. The volume has a double purpose: to outline the history of women's autobiographical writing and to provide an introduction to the history of religious and political ideas as they appear in this writing.

MGM
CHG

November, 1978

Acknowledgments

We are grateful to the Moorland-Spingarn Research Center, Howard University, for permission to reprint from their collection of Anna Julia Haywood Cooper Papers, to The Society of the Companions of the Holy Cross for permission to reprint material from Vida Scudder's *My Quest for Reality,* to Denise Levertov for permission to use a selection from her essay "With the Seabrook Natural Guard" and for the use of her photographs taken in Vietnam, and to Sister Anna Maria Reynolds, C.P., for permission to use her translation *A Shewing of God's Love,* the shorter version of Julian of Norwich's *Revelations.* Some of the research for this book was done during a Mellon Faculty Development Grant from The Wellesley Center for Research on Women to Mary Grimley Mason.

Introduction

Part I

A reading of the autobiographical writings of women from medieval to modern times makes it clear that women have made an important contribution to the genre. The way in which women have written about their lives is often distinct from the way men have written. The often-cited archetypal models of male autobiography—Saint Augustine's *Confessions* as religious autobiography and Rousseau's *Confessions* as modern secular autobiography—are not representative of models for women's autobiographical writing. Women usually do not present the "self" on a dramatic scale where a battle of opposing forces is played out and a victory of one force over another—the spirit over the flesh, in the case of Saint Augustine—completes the drama. Nor do women use a Rousseauean version of the confession which changes the dramatic presentation of a spiritual battle to the story of an evolving secular consciousness in which characters and events exist only to become part of the landscape of the hero's self-discovery. In women's autobiographical writing, the self-portrait often includes the real presence and recognition of another consciousness. We can call this real presence "the other," borrowing Simone de Beauvoir's phrase in *The Second Sex*. While de Beauvoir argues that men have cast women into the role of "the other" existing only in relation to the male identity, women, as revealed in our selections, seem to recognize the full autonomy of the "other" (in this case the male) without destroying their own sense of self. They achieve the "reciprocity" that de Beauvoir seeks in human relationships.

Our four early models of women's autobiography in the middle ages and the seventeenth century suggest appropriate prototypes for women's lifestories:

Julian of Norwich's *Revelations* (1373, 1393) is the first example of women's self-disclosure that we have in English. She gives an account of an interior religious experience but she does not dramatize the self in the classical mode of Augustine. Julian's writing, growing from the Anglo-Saxon prose tradition and the small but important English mystical tradition, is committed to the simple recording of human experience and to the mystic's personal relationship with the divine "other" who in the conventional medieval terms of her day was the Creator, the Father, the Lover. The "I" of the narrative is not the heroic victor in the battle of spiritual forces but the intense perceiver of the "moment." Her poetic distillation of experience is characteristic of later English autobiographical poetry written by both men and women, but the singleness of her focus and her unsentimental self-scrutiny are patterns for later autobiographical writing particularly by women. The autobiographical poetry, for instance, of Emile Brontë and Christina Rossetti, suggests some of the intensity and self-knowledge of Julian's religious account. Her whole life pattern is strikingly paralleled in our own century by the French writer, Simone Weil, a religious contemplative and a radical activist who wrote autobiographical narratives that are scrupulously self-revealing but nondramatic. Of our selections, Dorothy Day's account most closely echoes the chosen loneliness of Julian.

Our second archetypal model, Margery Kempe's autobiography, *The Book of Margery Kempe* (1436-38), is more self-dramatizing. It places the author against the medieval world stage and it maintains a double focus. Margery Kempe is both the wife-mother and the pilgrim-mystic almost continuously throughout her life, representing a more common pattern of a woman's journey, which often discloses two equally demanding identities. Margery was obliged to fulfill domestic roles though she felt an equally strong call to a religious vocation and a compelling need to use her energies to establish a unique identity. *The Book of Margery Kempe* narrates her conflicts, her strategies, and her confrontations. It includes the account of her meeting with Julian about 1413 when she sought spiritual advice from the renowned anchoress. In the narration of her life, Margery is as vivid and panoramic in her accounts of her visions as she is in the retelling of her travels and adventures. Our selections from Jarena Lee's journal of an itinerant preacher in nineteenth-century America with its picaresque account of her life evokes the journey of Margery Kempe. In her secular travel memoirs Lady Mary Wortley Montagu in the eighteenth century shows the way a woman of a different class and era maintained a similar double focus in her life.

Our third model, the spiritual autobiography of Anne Bradstreet (1613-1672), written for her children when she was in her forties, is self-revealing when we place it in the context of her autobiographical poetry. Her Puritan spiritual testimony records a restrained and disciplined review of her religious development which seems to admit of very little individual self-realization, but her personal poetry shows a free and self-reliant spirit. In her poetry, for instance, she openly celebrates her passionate and worldly love for her husband, and she admits in her poem "In Reference to her Children" that although she will miss her offspring as they leave her nest, she will also rejoice in her freedom to spend her days "in tune." Placing her autobiography in the context of her other work, we realize that she achieved a sense of self-identification not through a sublimation of herself within Puritan religion but through an identification with a total community which included and unified her emotional, social, political, and religious life. Out of such unity she was able to develop a very individual talent as a poet while maintaining an active role in a demanding and rigid communal society. The harmony of public and private life that she discloses has no doubt been duplicated in other women's lives but seldom has it been recorded by them. The quest for harmony in public and private commitments is, of course, still a major concern for contemporary women writers.

Margaret Cavendish (1623-1672) gives us a model for the secularization of women's autobiographical writing, using the increasingly popular seventeenth-century form of the memoir. She published her memoir, *A True Relation of My Birth, Breeding, and Life,* in 1656 about the time when Anne Bradstreet was writing her spiritual legacy for her children. Accepting the conventions of her day, the Duchess at first sought self-realization through her relationship to her husband, although she had a passionate commitment in her life to her own development as a writer. Her dependence on her husband soon became an equal partnership in which she established her own identity as an author. In her biography of the Duke, for instance, in 1667, she says clearly in her preface that though she celebrates her husband as a classical, heroic warrior, she sees herself beside him as the heroic and worthy bard. And she writes: "The Great God, that hath hitherto blessed both your grace and me, will I question not, preserve both our fames to after ages." Other "partnerships" reflected in our selections include Lady Anne Blunt and her husband, Wilfred Scawen Blunt, and the "partnership" of Beatrice and Sidney Webb.

These four early autobiographical models offer some compelling patterns for women's self-disclosure of their interior journeys and their outer commitments. The other selections show rich variations of these patterns and new directions as women are confronted more and more with complexities of choice in their life commitments.

MARY GRIMLEY MASON

Part II

As one traces the history and evolution of the genre of women's autobiography, one is seeing at the same time the evolution of religious and social ideas and, in later centuries, of the problems of belief. These parallel histories necessarily influence the way in which we read. In the medieval and Puritan worlds one can discern harmony, even identity, between religious belief and social structure; this harmony in turn created a clearly defined literary form for any personal document. For the medieval women writers, as for Anne

Bradstreet, therefore, the expression of individuality and the establishment of an individual voice is more of an accomplishment than it is for the modern writer. Striking, too, is the ability to create, as Bradstreet does, an expression of orthodoxy which allows for the possibility of disbelief while affirming the strength of individual faith.

For the modern woman, the choice of belief itself, and of the forms which belief will take, is much more complicated. These are, as Vida Scudder said, "terrible choices," and the risks involved—for men as well as for women—are great. To have such choices, however, means to have greater freedom of self-expression in both words and action than the women of earlier centuries. One must, therefore, look at the writings included here from a double perspective: as documenting both the increasing difficulties and complexities involved in making acts of faith, and the increasing possibilities and complexities of choice for women. In formal terms, the progression may be seen as moving from the attempt to individualize given literary forms to the search for new forms adequate to the task of accommodating paradox and ambiguity.

But to choose belief in the twentieth century—to choose to direct one's actions in accordance with a creed, religious or political, may be to sacrifice freedom. A woman, especially, who chooses this route runs the risk of being seen as having abandoned her individuality for the easier option of letting someone else tell her what to do. The lives of Vida Scudder, Dorothy Day, or Denise Levertov, different as they are, offer clear refutations of that charge. Their allegiances, to religious belief and to political action, come in response to their own analysis of the world in which each lives, and the ideas they embrace are chosen because they serve the individual woman's needs, rather than the reverse. As they translate these ideas into words and actions they in turn affect, even restructure, the institutions of which they become a part. The existence within the American Catholic Church of a Dorothy Day presents a constant challenge to the church's potential social complacency; Levertov's refusal to separate political commitment from commitment to her poetry and to her students challenges the traditional structures of the university.

More problematic, perhaps, is the case of Mira Behn, who details her devotion to Gandhi in her autobiography in a way that some readers will see as submission, even destruction, of the self. But for her, as for large numbers then and since, Gandhi was more than an individual. To join Gandhi, and to share his belief in the necessity of suppressing individual needs and desires, was to become a force in history, transforming the evils of an imperialist society into a truly human community.

The autobiographies of Beatrice Webb and of the poet H. D. (Hilda Doolittle), although very different in detail, offer other very interesting cases of the relation of a woman and a man. In both cases the man represents, as did Gandhi, a modern answer to the problems of individual and social existence. The marriage of Beatrice Potter and Sidney Webb in 1892 came after a long period of refusal on her part even to consider marrying him. Her refusal stemmed in part from class differences (her father was a wealthy industrialist, his parents were of a lower class), and in part from a fear that marriage would result in a sacrifice of her hard-won individuality and of the importance of her work. It seemed that way to others too, but the evidence of her later accomplishments and of the recently published Webb letters demonstrates the rightness of Beatrice Potter's decision that her work and convictions, as well as his, would benefit from their union. In her coolly objective fashion she noted that they were both "second-class minds" and so accepted his argument that one and one close together made eleven; she saw to it that the figure never became merely two.

By 1933, when H. D. traveled to Vienna, Freud was internationally known, It is not at all surprising that a poet drawn to the mysteries of the mind and aware of the contradictions of her own behavior would turn to someone whose doctrine seemed to offer answers as religion had for earlier generations. Keeping skepticism and respect equally alive, H. D. in her tribute to Freud records her submission to the power of the "great man" but also her refusal to accept his explanation of women's motives. It was Freud who made it possible for her to concentrate on the central experience of the writings on the wall, but it is her interpretation of the experience, not his, with which she concludes.

Choosing the writings of this group of women, and emphasizing that for them self-identity was in some important part defined by already existing forms, may be seen as an argument for the liberating possibilities of such forms. An analogy might be made with the poet who chooses rhyme and traditional patterns over "free" verse. It is possible to say that the acceptance of traditional verse forms frees the poet to concentrate on ideas and images. It may also be claimed that the challenge involved in maintaining the individual voice within the strictures of traditional form adds value to the work which results. That, essentially, is the argument this book makes.

CAROL HURD GREEN

Woman Scribe, pictured in annonymous *Flemish Hours,* fourteenth century
(Permission of The Master and Fellows of Trinity College, Cambridge, from MS B.11.22)

Julian of Norwich, 1342–1416?

Revelations of Divine Love
Shorter Version, probably 1373.
Longer version, 1393

We know little of the author of *Revelations of Divine Love* except that she was well educated, perhaps by Benedictine nuns at Carrow where she later might have become a nun herself. She is the first English woman of letters, and her *Revelations* are considered not only the "crown" of the English mystical tradition, which included Richard Rolle of Hampole (c. 1295-1349), another mystic known only as the author of *The Cloud of Unknowing,* and Walter Hilton (d. 1396), but it is also described as "a major literary expression of the Gothic spirit." At about thirty she had a severe illness and after three days she experienced a vision of Christ and fifteen "shewings" the next night. Her account of this mystical experience and her gradual understanding of it over twenty years survives in two main versions: a brief account written soon after the event in 1373—composed with "every detail fresh in Julian's mind" as one of her editors has said—and a longer version finished after years of study and meditation.

In 1413, Julian, who had become well known as a spiritual counselor after becoming an anchoress, met Margery Kempe, whose autobiographical selections are included elsewhere in this volume. Margery came to ask Julian for spiritual advice, and she no doubt spoke to the recluse through one of the three windows of the cell of her anchorage at Saint Julian's church in Conisford, Norwich. The two women spent several days together, and Margery was much comforted by the older woman's counsel.

After a long obscurity—there was only one early edition of Revelations, in the seventeenth century—Julian's writings were rediscovered in the nineteenth century. Another revival occurred after the Second World War when the bombed church at Norwich was rebuilt and rededicated to her. Recently a definitive edition of both texts has been published. Her *Revelations* have influenced writers, artists, intellectuals, and activists: Florence Nightingale read her in the Crimea, T. S. Eliot quoted her in "Little Gidding," and her words have been set to music and used in fiction. Although she lived six hundred years ago, her language has a contemporary quality. She can use the rhetoric of traditional self-effacement, calling herself "a simple creature," but she can also ask: "But because I am a woman must I therefore believe I should not tell you the goodness of God." She reminds us that despite the rigid codifying of roles and life patterns in the fourteenth century, there was a remarkable breadth of consciousness in her perceptions.

In the selections included here, which are primarily from the shorter, more autobiographical version, we can appreciate the depth and range of her observations: her awe at her role in God's creation through the poetic image of "the hazel nut," her detached, almost clinical, record of her physical and mental changes during her illness and mystical experience, and later her sudden revelation of the unity and harmony of all things. We can also marvel, as we read the selection from the later version, at the breadth of her grasp of theological questions. She was unique in her day in perceiving a feminine principle in the Divine Nature, and she combined this innovative teaching with the more traditional perception of the "motherhood" of Christ. Julian has been praised as a "professional" theologian and as a great teacher of the Church; her "Showings" also give us a vivid autobiographical record of the stages of her own spiritual growth and a remarkable analysis of the psychological as well as the religious experience she witnessed.

EDITIONS USED:

A Shewing of God's Love: the shorter version of Sixteen Revelations of Divine Love. Edited by Sister Anna Maria Reynolds. London: Longmans, Green, 1958.
XVI Revelations of Divine Love. Published by R. F. S. Cressy, 1670.

SUGGESTED READINGS:

Julian of Norwich. *Showings.* Translated from the critical text with an introduction by Edmund Colledge, O.S.A., and James Walsh, S.J. Preface by Jean LeClerq, O.S.B.; in The Classics of Western Spirituality. New York: Paulist Press, 1978.
Knowles, David. *The English Mystical Tradition.* New York: Harper, 1961.
Molinari, Paul, S.J. *The Teaching of a Fourteenth Century English Mystic.* London: Longmans Green, 1958.
Sayer, Frank Dale, ed. *Commemorative Essays and Handbook to the Exhibition "Revelations of Divine Love."* Norwich: Julian of Norwich Celebration Committee, 1973.
Stone, Robert Karl. *Middle English Prose Style: Margery Kempe and Julian of Norwich.* The Hague: Mouton, 1970.

A Shewing of God's Love

PROLOGUE BY THE SCRIBE

PROLOGUE BY THE SCRIBE

Here is a vision shewn by the goodness of God to a devout woman whose name is Julian. She is a recluse at Norwich and is living yet in this year of our Lord 1413. In this vision are full many comfortable and most moving words unto all those who desire to be Christ's lovers.

. . . .

II.
Sickness and the Last
Rites

And when I was thirty winters old and a half God sent me a bodily sickness, in the which I lay for three days and three nights. On the fourth night I received all the rites of Holy Church and thought not to be alive at daybreak. After this I languished for two days and two nights more, and on the third night I thought often times to have passed away and so too thought they who were about me. But in this I was right sorry and loath to die (though not for anything that was on earth that me liked to live for, nor for anything that I was afeared for; for I trusted in God). But it was because I would have lived on to have loved God better and for a longer time—that I might, by the grace of that living, have the more knowing and loving of God in the bliss of heaven, for methought all the time that I had lived here so little and so short in the regard of endless bliss. I thought thus: 'Good Lord, may my living be no longer to Thy worship?' And I was answered in my reason and by the feeling of my pains that I should die; and I assented fully, with all the will of my heart, to God's will.

Thus I endured till day and by then was my body dead from the middle downwards, as to feeling. Then was I moved to be set upright, leaning back, with cloths to my head, in order to have the more freedom of heart to be one with God's will, thinking on Him whilst my life would last.

They who were with me sent for the priest, my curate, to be at my ending. He came and a child with him, and brought a cross. By that time my eyes were set in my head and I could not speak. The priest set the cross before my face and said: 'Daughter, I have brought thee the image of thy Saviour. Look thereupon and comfort thee therewith in reverencing of Him who died for thee and me.' Methought that I was well as it was, for my eyes were set upwards, towards heaven whither I trusted to come. But nevertheless I assented to set my eyes upon the face of the crucifix if I could, to be able to endure the longer unto the time of mine ending. For methought I might longer endure to look straight forward than straight upward. After this my sight began to fail and it was all dark about me in the chamber, and murky as if it were night, except that on the image of the cross there remained the ordinary light. And, I knew not how, all that was beside the cross was as ugly to me as if it had been crowded with fiends.

After this the upper half of my body began to die as to feeling; my hands fell down on either side and also, from weakness, my head sank to one side. The most pain that I felt was shortness of breath and the failing of life. Then thought I truly that was at the point of death.

And in this, suddenly all my pain was away from me: I was all whole as ever I was before or afterwards, and especially in the upper part of my body. I marvelled at this change, for methought it was a secret working of God and not of nature: yet, by the feeling of this ease I did not trust any the more that I should live, and the feeling of this ease was no true ease to me; for methought I had liefer been delivered of this world, and my heart was set thereon.

III.
Comfort Against
Temptation

Suddenly it came to my mind that I should desire the second wound, of our Lord's gift and of His grace: that He would fill my body with mind and feeling of this blessed Passion, as I had before prayed. For I would that His pains were my pains, with compassion and then with longing for God. Thus methought that I might with His grace have His wounds that I had before desired. But in this I desired never of God either bodily sight or any manner of shewing, but compassion such as methought a kind soul might have towards our Lord Jesus, that for love willed to become a mortal man. With Him I desired to suffer whilst I lived in this mortal body, as God would give me grace.

In this, suddenly I saw the red blood trickle down from under the garland of thorns, all hot, freshly, plentifully, and lifelike, right as me thought that it was at that time when the garland of thorns was thrust on His blessed Head. Right so, both God and Man, the same suffered for me. I conceived truly and mightily that it was Himself that showed it me without any intermediary, and then I said: *Benedicite! Dominus.* This I said with reverence as my meaning, with a mighty voice. Full greatly I was astonished, for the wonder and marvel that I had, that He would be so homely with a sinful creature living in this wretched mortal life.

I took it thus, that for that time our Lord Jesus in His courteous love would shew me comfort before the time of my temptation—for methought it might be well that I should, by the sufferance of God and with His keeping, be tempted by fiends before I died—and with this sight of His blessed Passion, with the Godhead that I saw in my understanding, I saw that this was strength enough for me, yea, for all creatures living that should be saved, against all the fiends of hell and against all ghostly enemies.

IV.
God: The Maker,
the Lover, the Keeper

In this same time that I saw this bodily sight, our Lord shewed me a ghostly sight of His homely loving. I saw that He is to us all-thing that is good and comfortable for our help. He is our clothing, for love; He enwraps us and envelops us, embraces us and encloses us; He hovers over us, for tender love, that He may never leave us. And so in this sight I saw truly that He is everything that is good, as to mine understanding.

In this He shewed me a little thing, the quantity of a hazel nut, lying in the palm of my hand, and to my understanding it was as round as any ball. I looked thereupon and thought: 'What may this be?' And I was answered in a general way, thus: 'It is all that is made.' I marvelled how it could last, for methought it might fall suddenly to naught for littleness. And I was answered in my understanding: 'It lasts and ever shall last because God loves it, and so hath all-thing its being through the love of God.'

In this little thing I saw three parts. The first is that God made it; the second is that He loves it; the third is that God keeps it. But what is that to me? In sooth, the Maker, the Lover, the Keeper. For until I am substantially oned to Him I may never have love, rest, nor very bliss; that is to say, until I be so fastened unto Him that there be right naught that is made between my God and me. And who shall do this deed? In sooth, Himself, by His mercy and His grace, because He has made me for this and blessedfully restored me thereto.

In this, God brought our Lady to my understanding. I saw her ghostly, in bodily likeness, a simple maiden and meek, young of age, in the stature that she was when she conceived. Also God shewed me in part the wisdom and the truth of her soul, wherein I understood the reverent beholding where-with she beheld her God that is her Maker, marvelling with great reverence that He that was her Maker would be born of her. For this was her marvelling: that He that was her Maker would be born of her who was a simple creature of His making. And this wisdom of truth, this knowing the greatness of her Maker and the littleness of herself that is made, made her to say meekly to the Angel Gabriel: 'Lo me here, God's handmaiden!' In this sight I saw truly that she is greater than all that God made beneath her in worthiness and in fulness of grace. For above her is nothing that is made but the blessed Manhood of Christ.

This little thing that is made, that is beneath our Lady, Saint Mary, God shewed it unto me as little as if it had been a hazel nut. Methought it might have fallen to nothing because of its littleness.

In this blessed revelation God shewed me three naughts, of which naughts this is the first that was shewed me; of this needs every man and woman who desires to live contemplatively to have knowing, that they should like to naught all things that are made for to have the love of God who is unmade. For this is the cause why they that are preoccupied wilfully with earthly business and ever more seek after wordly weal are not His in heart and in soul here: they love and seek their rest in this thing that is so little, wherein is no rest, and know not God who is All-Mighty, All-Wise and All-Good. For He is very rest.

God wills to be known and it pleaseth Him that we rest us in Him. For all that is beneath Him sufficeth not to us; and this is the cause why that no soul is rested until all that is made be as naught to him. When he is fully emptied, for love, to have Him who is all that is good, then is he able to receive ghostly rest.

.   .   .   .

VIII.
All-Thing that is Done,
is Done Well

After this I saw with my bodily sight the Face of the crucifix that hung before me, in which I beheld continually a part of the Passion: contempt, spitting on, defiling of His body, buffeting His blessed Face and many languors and pains—more than I can tell; and oft changing of colour. At one time all His blessed Face was covered with dried blood. This I saw bodily, but dimly and darkly; and I desired more bodily light in order to have seen more clearly, and I was answered in my reason that if God willed to shew me more, He would, but that I needed no light but Him.

And after this I saw God in a point, that is, in my understanding, by which sight I saw that He is in all-thing. I gazed intently, perceiving and knowing in that sight that He does all that is done. I marvelled at this sight, with a soft dread, and thought, 'What is sin?' For I saw truly that God doth all thing, be it ever so little; nor is anything done by mere chance, but by the endless foresight of the wisdom of God; therefore it behoved me to grant that all-thing that is done is well done. And I was certain that God does no sin, therefore it seemed to me that sin is naught. For in all this sin was not shewed me. And I would no longer marvel at this but beheld our Lord and what He would shew me. In another time God shewed me what sin is, nakedly, by itself, as I shall tell afterwards.

And after this I saw, beholding, the body plenteously bleeding, hotly, freshly and in a lifelike way, just as I saw before in the head. This was shewed in the furrows of the scourging; the blood ran down so plenteously as to my sight, that methought it would have covered the bed and have spread all about if it had been so in reality for that time. God has made waters plenteous on earth for our service and for ease of our bodies, out of the tender love he has for us. Yet it pleaseth Him better that we betake us wholly to His Blessed Blood to wash us therewith from sin. For there is no drink that is made that He likes so well to give us—it is so plenteous and of our nature.

After this, ere God shewed me any wounds, He allowed me to behold longer both all that I had seen and all that was contained therin. And then, without voice or opening of lips this word was formed in my soul: 'Herewith is the fiend overcome.' This word said our Lord meaning His Passion, as He had shewn me before. In this our Lord brought unto my mind and shewed me a part of the fiend's malice and the whole of his unmight. Though He shewed me that His Passion is the overcoming of the fiend, God shewed that the fiend has now the same malice that he had before the Incarnation and as sorely he travails and as continually he sees that all chosen souls worshipfully escape him: that is all his sorrow. For all that God suffers him to do turns to our joy and to his pain and shame. And he has a great sorrow when God gives him leave to work as when he works not, and that because he may never do so great evil as he wills, for his might is all locked in God's hand. Also I saw our Lord scorning his malice and setting him at naught, and He wills that we do the same. At this sight I laughed mightily and that made those who were about me to laugh too, and their laughing was joy to me. I thought: 'I would that my fellow-Christians had seen what I saw, and then would they all have laughed with me.' But I saw not Christ laughing. Nevertheless it pleaseth Him that we laugh in comforting of ourselves and in joyfulness in God that the fiend is overcome.

After this I fell into a more serious mood and said: 'I see! I see three things: game, scorn and earnest. I see game in that the fiend is overcome; I see scorn for that God scorns him and he shall be scorned; and I see earnest—that he is overcome by the Passion of our Lord Jesus Christ and by His death that was done full earnestly and with grievous travail.'

. . . .

XXI.
'Wretch that I Am!'

Soon after this, I came to myself and returned to my bodily sickness, understanding that I should live. And as a wretch I heaved and moaned over the bodily pains that I felt, and thought it great irksomeness that I should longer live. I was as barren and dry as if I had had but little comfort before, because of falling again into pain, and for failing of ghostly feeling.

Then came a religious person to me and asked me how I fared. And I said that I had raved that day, and he laughed loud and heartily. I said: 'The cross that stood at my bed's foot it bled fast.' And with this word, the person that I spoke to became all serious, marvelling. And anon I was sore ashamed of my recklessness and I thought thus: 'This man takes seriously the least word that I might say, since he says nothing thereto.' And when I saw that he took it in this way and with such great reverence, I became right greatly ashamed and would have been shiriven. But I could tell it to no priest, for I thought 'How should a priest believe me? I believed not our Lord God.' At the time when I saw Him I believed it firmly, and it was then my will and my meaning to continue to believe without end. But as a fool I allowed it to pass from my mind, wretch that I am. This was a great sin, a great want of filial love, that I, out of vexation at feeling bodily pain, so unwisely left aside for the time the comfort of all this blessed shewing of our Lord.

Here may you see what I am of myself. But herein would not our courteous Lord leave me. I lay until night, trusting in His mercy, and then I began to sleep.

In my sleep, at the beginning, methought the fiend seized me by the throat and would have strangled me; but he could not. Scarcely alive, I woke out of my sleep. The persons who were with me saw this, and bathed my temples; and my heart began to take comfort. Soon a little smoke came in at the door, with a great heat and a foul stench. I said: *'Benedicite! Dominus*—Is everything here on fire?' And I thought it was a bodily fire that would burn us to death. I asked them that were with me if they noticed any stench; they said no, they noticed nothing. I said: 'Blessed be God!' for then knew I well that it was the fiend which was come to tempest me; and once more I received that which our Lord had shewed me that same day with all the faith of Holy Church (for I hold both as one), and fled thereto as to my comfort. And very soon all vanished away and I was brought to great rest and peace, without sickness of body or dread of conscience.

.   .   .   .

XXIII.
Ever He Longs to Have
Our Love

After this the fiend came again with his heat and with his stench, and made me full restless—the stench was so vile and so painful, and the bodily heat so dreadful and oppressive. Also I heard a bodily jangling and speaking as if it had been of two people (and both, to my thinking, jangled at once, with great earnestness, as though they were holding a parliament); all was soft muttering, and I understood not what they said. And all this was to stir me to despair, as methought, but I trusted earnestly in God and comforted myself with bodily speech, as I would have done any other person that had been so travailed.

Methought this busy-ness might be likened to no bodily busy-ness. My bodily eyes I fixed upon the same cross that I had seen comfort in before that time; my tongue I occupied with speech about Christ's Passion and rehearsing of the faith of Holy Church; and my heart I fastened on God, with all the trust and all the might that was in me. And I thought to myself, meaning: 'Thou hast now great busy-ness. If thou wouldst now from this time evermore be so busy to keep thee from sin, this were a sovereign and a good occupation.' For I believe truly, were I safe from sin I were full safe from all the fiends of hell and enemies of my soul.

Thus they kept me occupied all the night, and on the morrow till it was about the hour of prime. Then anon they were all gone and past, and there remained nothing but the stench and that lasted still a while. And I scorned them. In this way was I delivered of them by the virtue of Christ's Passion, 'for therewith is the fiend overcome', as Christ said before to me.

'Ah, wretched sin! What art thou? Thou art naught. For I saw that God is all thing—I saw not thee. And when I saw that God has made all thing I saw thee not, and when I saw that God is in all thing I saw thee not, and when I saw that God does all thing that is done, small and great, I saw thee not. And when I saw our Lord sit in our soul so worshipfully and love and like, rule and care for all that He has made, I saw not thee. Thus I am sure that thou art naught, and all those who love thee and like thee and follow thee and wilfully end in thee—I am sure they shall be brought to naught with thee and endlessly confounded. God shield us all from thee! So be it, for God's love.'

XVI Revelation of Divine Love

The Fifty-eighth Chapter

God the blessedful Trinity which is everlasting being, right as he is endless from without beginning; right so it was in his purpose endless to make mankind. Which fair kind was first dight to his own Son the Second Person; and when he would by full accord of all the Trinity, he made us all at ones. And in our making he knit us, and oned us to himself: by which oning, we be kept as clean, and as noble as we were made; by the vertue of that each precious oning, we love our Maker, and like him, praise him, and thank him, and endlesly enjoy in him. And this is the working which is wrought continually in each soul that shall be saved: which is the godly will before said. And thus in our making God Almighty is our kindly Father. And God all wisdom is our kindly mother, with the love and the goodness of the Holy Ghost, which is all one God, one Lord. And in the knitting, and in the oning he is our very true spouse, and we his loved wife, and his fair maiden; with which wife he was never displeased, for he saith, *'I love thee, and thou lovest me, and our love shall never part in two.'* I beheld the working of all the blessed Trinity. In which beholding, I saw and understood these *three* properties; the property of the father-head, and the property of the mother-head, and the property of the lordship in one God. In our Father Almighty we have our keeping, and our bliss. And aneynst our kindly substance, which is to us by our making fro without beginning. And in the Second Person, in wit and wisdom we have our keeping: and aneynst our sensuality, our restoring, and our saving; for he is our Mother, Brother, and Saviour. And in our good Lord the Holy Ghost we have our rewarding, and our yielding for our living and our travel, and endlesly over-passing all that we desire in his marvellous courtesie of his high plentuous grace; for all our life is in *three:* in the *first* our being: and in the *second,* we have our encreasing: and in the *third,* we have our fulfilling. The *first* is kind; the *second* is mercy; the *third* is grace. For the *first,* I saw and understood, that the high might of the Trinity is our Father, and the deep wisdom of the Trinity is our Mother, and the great love of the Trinity is our Lord. And all these have we in kind, and in our substantial making. And furthermore, I saw that the Second Person which is our Mother substancially, the same deer worthy person is now become our mother sensual; for we be double of Gods making; that is to say, substancial and sensual. Our substance is the higher party which we have in our Father God Almighty: and the Second Person of the Trinity is our Mother in kind, in our substancial making, in whom we be grounded and rooted: and he is our Mother of mercy, in our sensuality taking. And thus our Mother is to us diverse manner working, in whom our parts be kept undeparted: for in our Mother Christ we profit and encrease; and in mercy he reformeth us and restoreth. And by the vertue of his passion, his death, and his uprising oned us to our substance. This worketh our Mother in mercy to all his beloved children, which be to him buxom and obedient: and grace worketh with mercy, and namely in *two* properties, as it was shewed. Which working longeth to the Third Person the Holy Ghost; he worketh rewarding and giving. Rewarding is a gift of trust that the Lord doth to them that hath traveled. And giving is a courteous working which he doth freely of grace, fulfilling and over-passing all that is deserved of creatures. Thus in our Father God Almighty we have our being. And in our Mother of mercy Jesu Christ, we have our reforming, and our restoring, in whom our parts be oned, and all made perfect man: and by yielding and giving in grace of the Holy Ghost we be fulfilled, and our substance is in our Father, God Almighty: and our substance is in our Mother God all wisdom: and our substance is in our Lord God the Holy Ghost, all goodness; for our substance is whole in each person of the Trinity, which is one God. And our sensuality is only in the Second Person, Christ Jesu, in whom is the Father and the Holy Ghost. And in him, and by him, we be mightily taken out of hell, and out of the wretchedness in earth; and worshipfully brought up into heaven, and blessedfully oned to our substance; encreased in riches and nobly, by all the vertue of Christ, and by the grace and working of the Holy Ghost.

Self-portrait signed by "Claricia," from a Psalter, Germany, late twelfth century *(Permission of the Walters Art Gallery, Baltimore, from MS 10.26)*

Margery Kempe, 1373–1438?

The Book of Margery Kempe (1436–38)

Margery Burnham, daughter of the mayor of Lynn, married John Kempe in 1393. After the birth of her first child, she had a nervous collapse and experienced a spiritual crisis, which convinced her that she had a special religious vocation. She was given "the gift of tears"—an affliction of hysterical weeping spells deriving from a close identification with Christ's Passion—and she experienced mystical visions and voices. Her autobiography records her attempts to reconcile her religious vocation of pilgrimage with her role as wife, mother, and townswoman.

Margery Kempe was part of a strong tide of feminine spirituality in Europe, originating on the continent between the twelfth and fifteenth centuries. Famous saints, such as Saint Catherine of Siena, Saint Bridget of Sweden, and Saint Joan of Arc, as well as lesser known women, many of them in religious orders, were part of this tradition. Many of these women recorded their spiritual autobiographies although some of them left the composing of their testimonies to their confessors. The medieval scholar, Hope Emily Allen, has argued that Margery's *Book* shares "the common form" of the continental tradition of spiritual autobiography, though Margery was probably unaware of much of the tradition, with the exception of the writings of Bridget of Sweden (d. 1373) and, perhaps, Blessed Dorothea of Prussia (d. 1394).

Margery's *Book* is the first extant autobiography in English and in it she gives us a vivid account of her domestic, marital life, and of her conversion from a worldly burgess's wife to a religious enthusiast and reformer. Like Saint Bridget, she suffered from the conflict between her marital vows and her desire to take vows of chastity. Her husband, who was at first bewildered by her determination, became reconciled to her religious vocation and loyally supported her against suspicious townspeople and hostile officials of church and state. He accompanied her to her audiences with the renowned Biship of Lincoln and the Archbishop of Canterbury, who were both convinced that she was genuinely inspired. Despite official ecclesiastical approval, Margery was frequently persecuted by the civil authorities and by local clergy and religious, who did not understand her vocation. Events at that time, in the reign of Henry IV, made the church and state suspicious of eccentric behavior, particularly from a woman who travelled about freely and who claimed to have special "voices" from God. Margery was accused of being one of the "Lollards"—followers of John Wycliffe, some of whom had been burned as heretics. Even her fellow pilgrims to Jerusalem and to Spain distrusted her outlandish behavior and often ostracized her.

Her visit in 1413 to the revered anchoress, Julian of Norwich, was a high point in her life. Julian urged her to be patient with the world, which, she assured her, would misunderstand her vocation. After this reassurance and advice, Margery went on pilgrimages and became a witness of compassion and penance for the next twenty-five years of her life. In one of her dialogues with Christ, she is told: "I have ordained thee to be a miror amonst them [mankind], to have great sorrow, so that they should take example of thee." Her book mirrors her as a model of human compassion and an agent of intercession but it also mirrors for us the broad canvas of the medieval social, religious, and political world seen from a woman's point of view.

In 1432 her husband died after a lengthy illness during which she faithfully returned to care for him. Her son, who had gone through both profligacy and a religious conversion, died the same year. Margery, who was then about sixty years old, accompanied her daughter-in-law and grandchild home to Germany and made her last pilgrimage. Her final years were devoted to working on her autobiography with a priest, who transcribed it from the original copy that the illiterate Margery had dictated to a townsman about four years previously. Not until 1938 was the complete manuscript of *The Book of Margery Kempe* discovered and identified by Colonel W. Butler-Bowden. In the full text now available, Margery emerges as an intriguing woman who, with Julian of Norwich, broke the long "feminine silence in England."

EDITION USED:

The Book of Margery Kempe: A Modernized Version. Edited by W. Butler-
  Bowden. With introduction by R. W. Chambers. New York: The Devin-
  Adair Co., 1944.

SUGGESTED READINGS:

Collis, Louise. *The Apprentice Saint.* London: Michael Joseph, 1964.
Gies, Frances and Joseph. *Women in the Middle Ages.* New York: Thomas Y.
  Crowell Co., 1978.
Meech, Sandford Brown, ed. *The Book of Margery Kempe.* With prefatory
  note by Hope Emily Allen. London: Early English Text Society, 1940.
  [Transcription of Butler-Bowden Ms.]
Power, Eileen. *Medieval Women.* Edited by M. M. Poston. London: Cambridge
  University Press, 1975.
Stuard, Susan Mosher, ed. *Women in Medieval Society.* University of
  Pennsylvania Press, 1976.
Walsh, James, ed. *Pre-Reformation English Spirituality.* New York: Fordham
  University Press, n.d.

The Book of Margery Kempe

Chapter 1. Her Marriage and Illness after Childbirth. She Recovers.

When this creature was twenty years of age, or some deal more, she was married to a worshipful burgess (of Lynne) and was with child within a short time, as nature would. And after she had conceived, she was belaboured with great accesses till the child was born and then, what with the labour she had in childing, and the sickness going before, she despaired of her life, weening she might not live. And then she sent for her ghostly father, for she had a thing on her conscience which she had never shewn before that time in all her life. For she was ever hindered by her enemy, the devil, evermore saying to her that whilst she was in good health she needed no confession, but to do penance by herself alone and all should be forgiven, for God is merciful enough. And therefore this creature oftentimes did great penance in fasting on bread and water, and other deeds of alms with devout prayers, save she would not shew that in confession.

And when she was at any time sick or dis-eased, the devil said in her mind that she should be damned because she was not shriven of that default. Wherefore after her child was born, she, not trusting to live, sent for her ghostly father, as is said before, in full will to be shriven of all her lifetime, as near as she could. And when she came to the point for to say that thing which she had so long concealed, her confessor was a little too hasty and began sharply to reprove her, before she had fully said her intent, and so she would no more say for aught he might do. Anon, for the dread she had of damnation on the one side, and his sharp reproving of her on the other side, this creature went out of her mind and was wondrously vexed and laboured with spirits for half a year, eight weeks and odd days.

And in this time she saw, as she thought, devils opening their mouths all inflamed with burning waves of fire, as if they would have swallowed her in, sometimes ramping at her, sometimes threatening her, pulling her and hauling her, night and day during the aforesaid time. Also the devils cried upon her with great threatenings, and bade her that she should forsake Christendom, her faith, and deny her God, His Mother and all the Saints in Heaven, her good works and all good virtues, her father, her mother and all her friends. And so she did. She slandered her husband, her friends and her own self. She said many a wicked word, and many a cruel word; she knew no virtue nor goodness; she desired all wickedness; like as the spirits tempted her to say and do, so she said and did. She would have destroyed herself many a time at their stirrings and have been damned with them in Hell, and in witness thereof, she bit her own hand so violently, that the mark was seen all her life after.

And also she rived the skin on her body against her heart with her nails spitefully, for she had no other instruments, and worse she would have done, but that she was bound and kept with strength day and night so that she might not have her will. And when she had long been laboured in these and many other temptations, so that men weened she should never have escaped or lived, then on a time as she lay alone and her keepers were from her, Our Merciful Lord Jesus Christ, ever to be trusted, worshipped be His Name, never forsaking His servant in time of need, appeared to His creature who had forsaken Him, in the likeness of a man, most seemly, most beauteous and most amiable that ever might be seen with man's eye, clad in a mantle of purple silk, sitting upon her bedside, looking upon her with so blessed a face that she was strengthened in all her spirit, and said to her these words:—

'Daughter, why hast thou forsaken Me, and I forsook never thee?'

And anon, as He said these words, she saw verily how the air opened as bright as any lightning. And He rose up into the air, not right hastily and quickly, but fair and easily, so that she might well behold Him in the air till it was closed again.

And anon this creature became calmed in her wits and reason, as well as ever she was before, and prayed her husband as soon as he came to her, that she might have the keys of the buttery to take her meat and drink as she had done before. Her maidens and her keepers counselled him that he should deliver her no keys, as they said she would but give away such goods as there were, for she knew not what she said, as they weened.

Nevertheless, her husband ever having tenderness and compassion for her, commanded that they should deliver to her the keys; and she took her meat and drink as her bodily strength would serve her, and knew her friends and her household and all others that came to see how Our Lord Jesus Christ had wrought His grace in her, so blessed may He be, Who ever is near in tribulation. When men think He is far from them, He is full near by His grace. Afterwards, this creature did all other occupations as fell to her to do, wisely and soberly enough, save she knew not verily the call of Our Lord.

Chapter 2. Her Worldly Pride. Her Attempt at Brewing and Milling,
and Failure at Both. She Amends her Ways

When this creature had thus graciously come again to her mind, she thought
that she was bound to God and that she would be His servant. Nevertheless,
she would not leave her pride or her pompous array, which she had used
beforetime, either for her husband, or for any other man's counsel. Yet she
knew full well that men said of her full much villainy, for she wore gold pipes
on her head, and her hoods, with the tippets, were slashed. Her cloaks also
were slashed and laid with divers colours between the slashes, so that they
should be the more staring to men's sight, and herself the more worshipped.

And when her husband spoke to her to leave her pride, she answered
shrewdly and shortly, and said that she was come of worthy kindred—he
should never have wedded her—for her father was sometime Mayor of the
town of N . . .[1] and afterwards he was alderman of the High Guild of the
Trinity in N . . . And therefore she would keep the worship of her kindred
whatever any man said.

She had full great envy of her neighbours, that they should be as well
arrayed as she. All her desire was to be worshipped by the people. She would
not take heed of any chastisement, nor be content with the goods that God
had sent her, as her husband was, but ever desired more and more.

Then for pure covetousness, and to maintain her pride, she began to brew,
and was one of the greatest brewers in the town of N . . . for three years or
four, till she lost much money, for she had never been used thereto. For,
though she had ever such good servants, cunning in brewing, yet it would
never succeed with them. For when the ale was fair standing under barm as
any man might see, suddenly the barm would fall down, so that all the ale
was lost, one brewing after another, so that her servants were ashamed and
would not dwell with her.

Then this creature thought how God had punished her aforetime—and she
could not take heed—and how again, by the loss of her goods. Then she left
and brewed no more.

Then she asked her husband's mercy because she would not follow his
counsel aforetime, and she said that her pride and sin were the cause of all her
punishing, and that she would amend and that she had trespassed with good
will.

Yet she left not the world altogether, for she now bethought herself of a
new housewifery. She had a horse-mill. She got herself two good horses and a
man to grind men's corn, and thus she trusted to get her living. This
enterprise lasted not long, for in a short time after, on Corpus Christi Eve,

1. Lynne, now King's Lynn, is evidently referred to. This anonymity is
dropped later on.

befell this marvel. This man, being in good health of body, and his two horses sturdy and gentle, had pulled well in the mill beforetime, and now he took one of these horses and put him in the mill as he had done before, and this horse would draw no draught in the mill for anything the man might do. The man was sorry and essayed with all his wits how he should make this horse pull. Sometimes he led him by the head, sometimes he beat him, sometimes he cherished him and all availed not, for he would rather go backward than forward. Then this man set a sharp pair of spurs on his heels and rode on the horse's back to make him pull, and it was never the better. When the man saw it would work in no way, he set up this horse again in the stable, and gave him corn, and he ate well and freshly. And later he took the other horse and put him in the mill, and like his fellow did, so did he, for he would not draw for anything the man might do. Then the man forsook his service and would no longer remain with the aforesaid creature. Anon, it was noised about the town of N . . . that neither man nor beast would serve the said creature.

Then some said she was accursed; some said God took open vengeance on her; some said one thing and some said another. Some wise men, whose minds were more grounded in the love of Our Lord, said that it was the high mercy of Our Lord Jesus Christ that called her from the pride and vanity of the wretched world.

Then this creature, seeing all these adversities coming on every side, thought they were the scourges of Our Lord that would chastise her for her sin. Then she asked God's mercy, and forsook her pride, her covetousness, and the desire that she had for the worship of the world, and did great bodily penance, and began to enter the way of everlasting life as shall be told hereafter.

.   .   .   .

Chapter 11. On the Way Back from York, she and her Husband Argue as to Their Carnal Relationship to Each Other

It befell on a Friday on Midsummer Eve in right hot weather, as this creature was coming from York-ward carrying a bottle with beer in her hand, and her husband a cake in his bosom, that he asked his wife this question:—

'Margery, if there came a man with a sword, who would strike off my head, unless I should commune naturally with you as I have done before, tell me on your conscience—for ye say ye will not lie—whether ye would suffer my head to be smitten off, or whether ye would suffer me to meddle with you again, as I did at one time?'

'Alas, sir,' said she, 'why raise this matter, when we have been chaste these eight weeks?'

'For I will know the truth of your heart.'

And then she said with great sorrow:—'Forsooth, I would rather

see you being slain, than that we should turn again to our uncleanness."
And he replied:—'Ye are no good wife.'

She then asked her husband what was the cause that he had not meddled
with her for eight weeks, since she lay with him every night in his bed. He
said he was made so afraid when he would have touched her, that he dare do
no more.

'Now, good sir, amend your ways, and ask God's mercy, for I told you
nearly three years ago that ye [1] should be slain suddenly, and now is this the
third year, and so I hope I shall have my desire. Good sir, I pray you grant me
what I ask, and I will pray for you that ye shall be saved through the mercy
of Our Lord Jesus Christ, and ye shall have more reward in Heaven than if ye
wore a hair-cloth or a habergeon.[2] I pray you, suffer me to make a vow of
chastity at what bishop's hand God wills.'

'Nay,' he said, 'that I will not grant you, for now may I use you without
deadly sin, and then might I not do so.'

Then she said to him:—'If it be the will of the Holy Ghost to fulfil what I
have said, I pray God that ye may consent thereto; and if it be not the will of
the Holy Ghost, I pray God ye never consent to it.'

Then they went forth towards Bridlington in right hot weather, the
creature having great sorrow and dread for her chastity. As they came by a
cross, her husband sat down under the cross, calling his wife to him and
saying these words unto her:—'Margery, grant me my desire, and I shall grant
you your desire. My first desire is that we shall lie together in bed as we have
done before; the second, that ye shall pay my debts, ere ye go to Jerusalem;
and the third, that ye shall eat and drink with me on the Friday as ye were
wont to do.'

'Nay, sir,' said she, 'to break the Friday, I will never grant you whilst I live.'

'Well,' said he, 'then I shall meddle with you again.'

She prayed him that he would give her leave to say her prayers, and he
granted it kindly. Then she knelt down beside a cross in the field and prayed
in this manner, with a great abundance of tears:—

'Lord God, Thou knowest all things. Thou knowest what sorrow I have had
to be chaste in my body to Thee all these three years, and now might I have
my will, and dare not for love of Thee. For if I should break that manner of
fasting which Thou commandest me to keep on the Friday, without meat or
drink, I should now have my desire. But, Blessed Lord, Thou knowest that I
will not contravene Thy will, and much now is my sorrow unless I find
comfort in Thee. Now, Blessed Jesus, make Thy will known to me unworthy,
that I may follow it thereafter and fulfil it with all my might.'

1. I.e. 'your lust.'
2. A habergeon, or coat of mail, was worn as a penance, in addition to its
primary purpose of bodily protection.

Then Our Lord Jesus Christ with great sweetness, spoke to her, commanding her to go again to her husband, and pray him to grant her what she desired, 'And he shall have what he desireth. For, my dearworthy daughter, this was the cause that I bade thee fast, so that thou shouldst the sooner obtain and get thy desire, and now it is granted to thee. I will no longer that thou fast. Therefore I bid thee in the Name of Jesus, eat and drink as thy husband doth.'

.   .   .   .

Chapter 16. She and her Husband go to Lambeth to Visit the Archbishop of Canterbury, Whom she Reproves for the Bad Behaviour of his Clergy and Household

Then went this creature forth to London with her husband unto Lambeth, where the Archbishop lay at that time; and as they came into the hall in the afternoon, there were many of the Archbishop's clerks and other reckless men, both squires and yeomen, who swore many great oaths and spoke many reckless words, and this creature boldly reprehended them, and said they would be damned unless they left off their swearing and other sins that they used.

And with that, there came forth another woman of the same town in a furred cloak, who forswore this creature, banned her, and spoke full cursedly to her in this manner:—

'I would thou wert in Smithfield, and I would bring a faggot to burn thee with. It is a pity thou art alive.'

This creature stood still and answered not, and her husband suffered it with great pain, and was full sorry to hear his wife so rebuked.

Then the Archbishop sent for this creature into his garden. When she came into his presence, she saluted him as best she could, praying him of his gracious lordship to grant her authority to choose her confessor and to be houselled [1] every Sunday, if God would dispose her thereto, under his letter and his seal through all his province. And he granted her full benignly all her desire without any silver or gold, nor would he let his clerks take anything for the writing or the sealing of the letter.

When this creature found this grace in his sight, she was well comforted and strengthened in her soul, and so she showed this worshipful lord her manner of life, and such grace as God wrought in her mind and in her soul, to find out what he would say thereto, and whether he found any default either in her contemplation or in her weeping.

And she told him also the cause of her weeping, and the manner of dalliance that Our Lord spoke to her soul; and he found no default in her, but

1. To go to Holy Communion.

praised her manner of living, and was right glad that Our Merciful Lord Christ Jesus showed such grace in our days, blessed may He be.

Then this creature boldly spoke to him for the correction of his household, saying with reverence: —

'My lord, Our Lord of all, Almighty God has not given you your benefice and great worldly wealth to keep His traitors and them that slay Him every day by great oaths swearing. Ye shall answer for them, unless ye correct them, or else put them out of your service.'

Full benignly and meekly he suffered her to speak her intent, and gave her a fair answer, she supposing it would then be better. And so their dalliance continued till stars appeared in the firmament. Then she took her leave, and her husband also.

Afterwards they came again to London, and many worthy men desired to hear her dalliances and communication, for her communication was so much in the love of God that her hearers were often stirred thereby to weep right sadly.

And so she had there right great cheer, and her husband because of her, as long as they remained in the city.

Afterwards they came again to Lynne, and then went this creature to the anchorite at the Preaching Friars in Lynne and told him what cheer she had had, and how she had sped whilst she was in the country. And he was right glad of her coming home, and held it was a great miracle, her coming and going to and fro.

And he said to her: —'I have heard much evil language of you since ye went out, and I have been sore counselled to leave you and no more to associate with you, and there are promised me great friendships, on condition that I leave you. And I answered for you thus: —

' "If ye were in the same plight as ye were when we parted asunder, I durst well say that ye were a good woman, a lover of God, and highly inspired by the Holy Ghost. And I will not forsake her for any lady in this realm, if speaking with the lady means leaving her. Rather would I leave the lady and speak with her, if I might not do both, than do the contrary".'

.   .   .   .

Chapter 18. At Norwich she Visits a White Friar, William Sowth-feld, and an Anchoress, Dame Jelyan

This creature was charged and commanded in her soul that she should go to a White Friar, in the same city of Norwich, called William Sowthfeld, a good man and a holy liver, to shew him the grace that God wrought in her, as she had done to the good Vicar before. She did as she was commanded and came to the friar on a forenoon, and was with him in a chapel a long time, and shewed him her meditations, and what God had wrought in her soul, to findout if she were deceived by any illusion or not.

This good man, the White Friar, ever whilst she told him her feelings, holding up his hands, said:—'Jesu Mercy and gramercy.'

'Sister,' he said, 'dread not for your manner of living, for it is the Holy Ghost working plenteously His grace in your soul. Thank Him highly for His goodness, for we all be bound to Thank Him highly for His goodness, for we all be bound to thank Him for you, Who now in our days will inspire His grace in you, to the help and comfort of us all, who are supported by your prayers and by such others as ye be. And we are preserved from many mischiefs and diseases which we should suffer, and worthily, for our trespass. Never were such good creatures amongst us. Blessed be Almighty God for His goodness. And therefore, sister, I counsel you that ye dispose yourself to receive the gifts of God as lowly and meekly as ye can, and put no obstacle or objection against the goodness of the Holy Ghost, for He may give His gifts where He will, and of unworthy He maketh worthy, of sinful He maketh rightful. His mercy is ever ready unto us, unless the fault be in ourselves, for He dwelleth not in a body subject to sin. He flieth all false feigning and falsehood: He asketh of us a lowly, a meek and a contrite heart, with a good will. Our Lord sayeth Himself:—"My Spirit shall rest upon a meek man, a contrite man, and one dreading My words."

'Sister, I trust to Our Lord that ye have these conditions either in your will or your affection, or else in both, and I believe not that Our Lord suffereth them to be deceived endlessly, that set all their trust in Him, and seek and desire nothing but Him only, as I hope ye do. And therefore believe fully that Our Lord loveth you and worketh His grace in you. I pray God to increase it and continue it to His everlasting worship, for His mercy.'

The aforesaid creature was much comforted both in body and in soul by this good man's words, and greatly strengthened in her faith.

Then she was bidden by Our Lord to go to an anchoress in the same city, named Dame Jelyan, and so she did, and showed her the grace that God put into her soul, of compunction, contrition, sweetness and devotion, compassion with holy meditation and high contemplation, and full many holy speeches and dalliance that Our Lord spake to her soul; and many wonderful revelations, which she shewed to the anchoress to find out if there were any deceit in them, for the anchoress was expert in such things, and good counsel could give.

The anchoress, hearing the marvellous goodness of Our Lord, highly thanked God with all her heart for His visitation, counselling this creature to be obedient to the will of Our Lord God and to fulfil with all her might whatever He put into her soul, if it were not against the worship of God, and profit of her fellow Christians, for if it were, then it were not the moving of a good spirit, but rather of an evil spirit. 'The Holy Ghost moveth ne'er a thing against charity, for if He did, He would be contrary to His own self for He is all charity. Also He moveth a soul to all chasteness, for chaste livers are called the Temple of the Holy Ghost, and the Holy Ghost maketh a soul stable and steadfast in the right faith, an the right belief.

'And a double man in soul is ever unstable and unsteadfast in all his ways. He that is ever doubting is like the flood of the sea which is moved and born about with the wind, and that man is not likely to receive the gifts of God.

'Any creature that hath these tokens may steadfastly believe that the Holy Ghost dwelleth in his soul. And much more when God visiteth a creature with tears of contrition, devotion, and compassion, he may and ought to believe that the Holy Ghost is in his soul. Saint Paul saith that the Holy Ghost asketh for us with mourning and weeping unspeakable, that is to say, He maketh us to ask and pray with mourning and weeping so plenteously that the tears may not be numbered. No evil spirit may give these tokens, for Saint Jerome saith that tears torment more the devil than do the pains of Hell. God and the devil are ever at odds and they shall never dwell together in one place, and the devil hath no power in a man's soul.

'Holy Writ saith that the soul of a rightful man is the seat of God, and so I trust, sister, that he be. I pray God grant you perseverance. Set all your trust in God and fear not the language of the world, for the more despite, shame and reproof that ye have in the world, the more is your merit in the sight of God. Patience is necessary to you, for in that shall ye keep your soul.'

Much was the holy dalliance that the anchoress and this creature had by communing in the love of Our Lord Jesus Christ the many days that they were together.

. . . .

Chapter 26

When the time came that this creature should visit those holy places where Our Lord was quick and dead, as she had by revelation years before, she prayed the parish priest of the town where she was dwelling, to say for her in the pulpit, that, if any man or woman claimed any debt from her husband or herself, they should come and speak with her ere she went, and she, with the help of God would make a settlement with each of them, so that they should hold themselves content. And so she did.

Afterwards, she took her leave of her husband and of the holy anchorite, who had told her, before the process of her going and the great dis-ease that she would suffer by the way, and when all her fellowship forsook her, how a broken-backed man would lead her forth in safety, through the help of Our Lord.

And so it befell indeed, as shall be written afterward.

Then she took her leave of Master Robert, and prayed him for his blessing, and so, forth of other friends. Then she went forth to Norwich, and offered at the Trinity, and afterwards she went to Yarmouth and offered at an image of Our Lady, and there she took her ship.

And next day they came to a great town called Zierikzee, where Our Lord of His high goodness visited this creature with abundant tears of contrition for her own sins, and sometime for other men's sins also. And especially she had tears of compassion in mind of Our Lord's Passion. And she was houselled each Sunday where there was time and place convenient thereto, with great weeping and boisterous sobbing, so that many men marvelled and wondered at the great grace that God had wrought in His creature.

This creature had eaten no flesh and drunk no wine for four years ere she went out of England, and so now her ghostly father charged her, by virtue of obedience, that she should both eat flesh and drink wine. And so she did a little while; afterwards she prayed her confessor that he would hold her excused if she ate no flesh, and suffer her to do as she would for such time as pleased him.

And soon after, through the moving of some of her company, her confessor was displeased because she ate no flesh, and so were many of the company. And they were most displeased because she wept so much and spoke always of the love and goodness of Our Lord, as much at the table as in other places. And therefore shamefully they reproved her, and severely chid her, and said they would not put up with her as her husband did when she was at home and in England.

And she answered meekly to them:—'Our Lord, Almighty God, is as great a Lord here as in England, and as good cause have I to love Him here as there, blessed may He be.'

At these words, her fellowship was angrier than before, and their wrath and unkindness to this creature was a matter of great grief, for they were held right good men and she desired greatly their love, if she might have it to the pleasure of God.

And then she said to one of them specially:—'Ye cause me much shame and great grievance.'

He answered her anon:—'I pray God that the devil's death may overcome thee soon and quickly,' and many more cruel words he said to her than she could repeat.

And soon after some of the company in whom she trusted best, and her own maiden also, said she could no longer go in their fellowship. And they said that they would take away her maiden from her, so that she should no strumpet be, in her company. And then one of them, who had her gold in keeping, left her a noble with great anger and vexation to go where she would and help herself as she might, for with them, they said, she should no longer abide; and they forsook her that night.

Then, on the next morning, there came to her one of their company, a man who loved her well, praying her that she would go to his fellows and meeken herself to them, and pray them that she might go still in their company till she came to Constance.

And so she did, and sent forth with them till she came to Constance with great discomfort and great trouble, for they did her much shame and much reproof as they went, in divers places. They cut her gown so short that it came but little beneath her knee, and made her put on a white canvas, in the manner of a sacken apron, so that she should be held a fool and the people should not make much of her or hold her in repute. They made her sit at the table's end, below all the others, so that she ill durst speak a word.

And, notwithstanding all their malice, she was held in more worship than they were, wherever they went.

And the good man of the house where they were hostelled, though she sat lowest at the table's end, would always help her before them all as well as he could, and sent her from his own table such service as he had, and that annoyed her fellowship full evil.

As they went by the way Constance-ward, it was told them that they would be robbed and have great discomfort unless they had great grace.

Then this creature came to a church and went in to make her prayer, and she prayed with all her heart, with great weeping and many tears, for help and succour against their enemies.

Then Our Lord said to her mind:—'Dread thee naught, daughter, thy fellowship shall come to no harm whilst thou art in their company.'

And so, blessed may Our Lord be in all His works, they went forth in safety to Constance.

.   .   .   .

Chapter 89. On her Feelings. The end of the Treatise Through the Death of the First Writer of it

Also, while the aforesaid creature was occupied about the writing of this treatise, she had many holy tears and weeping, and oftentimes there came a flame of fire about her breast, full hot and delectable; and also he that was her writer could not sometimes keep himself from weeping.

And often in the meantime, when the creature was in church, Our Lord Jesus Christ with His Glorious Mother and many saints also came into her soul and thanked her, saying that they were well pleased with the writing of this book. And also she heard many times a voice of a sweet bird singing in her ear, and oftentimes she heard sweet sounds and melodies that passed her wit to tell of. And she was many times sick while this treatise was in writing, and, as soon as she would go about the writing of this treatise, she was hale and whole suddenly, in a manner; and often she was commanded to make herself ready in all haste.

And, on a time, as she lay in her prayers in the church at the time of Advent before Christmas, she thought in her heart she would that God of His goodness would make Master Aleyn to say a sermon as well as he could; and as quickly as she had thought thus, she heard Our Sovereign Lord Christ Jesus saying in her soul:—

'Daughter, I wot right well what thou thinkest now of Master Aleyn, and I tell thee truly that he shall say a right holy sermon; and look that thou believest steadfastly the words that he shall preach, as though I preached them Myself, for they shall be words of great solace and comfort to thee, for I shall speak in him.'

When she heard this answer, she went and told it to her confessor and to two other priests that she trusted much on; and when the had told them her feeling, she was full sorry for dread whether he should speak as well as he had felt or not, for revelations be hard sometimes to understand.

And sometimes those that men think were revelations, are deceits and illusions, and therefore it is not expedient to give readily credence to every stirring, but soberly abide, and pray if it be sent of God. Nevertheless, as to this feeling of this creature, it was very truth, shewn in experience, and her dread and her gloom turned into great ghostly comfort and gladness.

Sometimes she was in a great gloom for her feelings, when she knew not how they should be understood, for many days together, for dread that she had of deceits and illusions, so that she thought she would that her head had been smitten from her body till God of His goodness declared them to her mind.

For sometimes, what she understood bodily was to be understood ghostly, and the dread that she had of her feelings was the greatest scourge that she had on earth; and especially when she had her first feelings; and that dread made her full meek, for she had no joy in the feeling till she knew by experience whether it was true or not.

But ever blessed may God be, for He made her always more mighty and more strong in His love and in His dread, and gave her increase of virtue with perseverance.

Here endeth this treatsie, for God took him to His mercy, that wrote the copy[1] of this book, and, though he wrote it not clearly nor open to our manner of speaking, he, in his manner of writing and spelling made true sense, which, through the help of God and of herself that had all this treatise in feeling and working, is truly drawn out of the copy into this little book.

1. By 'copy', Margery means the original ill-written book that they have just finished copying here.

ANNE BRADSTREET

Anne Bradstreet, from a stained-glass window, St. Botolph's Church, Boston, England (*Courtesy of Elizabeth Wade White and St. Botolph's Church*)

Anne Bradstreet, 1612/1613–1672

Spiritual Autobiography (ca. 1656); Selected Poems (1650, 1678)

Anne Bradstreet arrived in New England in July, 1630, with her father, Thomas Dudley, deputy governor of the new Massachusetts Bay Company, her mother, Dorothy Yorke Dudley, and her husband, Simon Bradstreet. She was eighteen years old and she had been married for two years. Both she and her husband had been brought up in the household of the Earl of Lincoln, who employed her father as steward over his vast estates. While Simon Bradstreet was sent to Cambridge University for his education, Anne received her education at home with private tutors, and with full access to the impressive library of the Earl in an atmosphere of intellectual stimulation and Non-conformist zeal.

In the New World, first at Cambridge, then Ipswich, and finally Andover, she had a secure and dignified position as the governor's daughter and as the wife of an influential member of the Commonweal, but like the other colonists she had to endure the hardships of pioneer life: the severe climate and solitude of winters, the hazards of giving birth to eight children, the difficulties of contending with severe illnesses, and the terrors of natural disasters such as the fire which destroyed her house in Andover and her possessions—including some of her writings. The Puritan community had little toleration for deviant behavior, as the case and exile of Anne Hutchinson was shown us. Other women in the settlement had broken under the strain of isolation and rigidity. One woman, Anne Hopkins, had "suffered a loss of her understanding and reason," and the community had blamed it on her "giving herself wholly to reading and writing." It is surprising, therefore, that the same community encouraged Anne Bradstreet in her literary aspirations. Her brother-in-law took her first collection of poems, *The Tenth Muse,* to London in 1650 (without her knowledge) to be published as a testament to the achievements of the colonists. Clearly, she was considered an exemplary representative of the "New Jerusalem."

When we read her spiritual autobiography, written about 1656, after she had been living in New England about twenty-five years, we wonder how a woman with the natural gifts and inclination to be a poet was able to submit to the confining and exacting Puritan consciousness that she reflects in her autobiography. However, when we place the autobiography in the context of the other personal poetry that she had been writing or was about to write, we can see that she was able to reconcile her public and private consciousness by personalizing her relationshp to the community. For instance, in her elegy to her father in 1653 (not included here), we see that to her he is both governor and magistrate as well as her loving parent and spiritual companion. Her husband, who played the traditional role of authority in the Puritan family, is addressed in her poems to him, as her lover. "If ever two were one, then surely we," she says of their relationship. Her private family community of eight children to watch she wrote "In Reference to her Children" (1659) represented a collective identity for her but one that still left her independent when they had grown up and left her "nest." The harmony of public and private consciousness that much of her personal poetry reveals enables Anne Bradstreet to strip away the individual details in her life when she writes her spiritual autobiography so that she can provide a testimony of faith and a record of her spiritual growth for her children in the tradition of her Puritan congregation. Although she closes her autobiographical account with a prayer, she characteristically adds a personal note: "This was written in much sickness and weakness . . . but, if you can pick any Benefitt out of it, it is the mark which I amied at." Further record of her spiritual life is in the poems and entries in the notebook in which the autobiography was written (1656-57 and 1661), in her poem "The Flesh and the Spirit" (1660-1670?), and in a prose collection, *Meditations Divine and Morall* (begun in 1664 in response to the request of her son, Simon). "Contemplations," composed ten years after she wrote her autobiography and now considered her finest work, is further evidence of her individuality and her self-realization as a poet within the context of family and community.

Her second volume, *Several Poems,* the first collection printed in America, came out in 1678, six years after her death. It includes her revisions of early poems and most of her later work and is the edition on which John Harvard Ellis based his collection (with some additions) in 1867. By 1678 Anne Bradstreet had achieved considerable note in England, and by 1702 in America Cotton Mather wrote in *Magnalia Christi Americana* that she was one of the "learned women" and that her poems were a "Monument to her Memory beyond the Stateliest Marbles." In our own century, after a period of neglect, the same kind of appreciation and praise have been given to Anne Bradstreet, including that of John Berryman in *Homage to Mistress Bradstreet* (1956), and of the poet, Adrienne Rich, in the Preface to the most recent edition of Bradstreet's works (1967).

EDITION USED:

The Works of Anne Bradstreet in Prose and Verse. Edited by John Harvard
 Ellis. Charlestown: Abram F. Cutter, 1867.

SUGGESTED READINGS:

The Works of Anne Bradstreet. Edited by Jeannine Hensley. Preface by
 Adrienne Rich. Cambridge, Mass.: Harvard University Press, 1967.
Piercy, Josephine. *Anne Bradstreet.* New York: Twayne, 1965.
Stanford, Ann. *Anne Bradstreet: The Worldly Puritan, an Introduction to her
 Poetry.* New York: Burt Franklin, 1974.
White, Elizabeth Wade. *Anne Bradstreet: The Tenth Muse.* New York:
 Oxford University Press, 1971.

Spiritual Autobiography

To my Dear Children.

This Book by Any yet unread,
I leave for you when I am dead,
That, being gone, here you may find
What was your liveing mother's mind.
Make use of what I leave in Love
And God shall blesse you from above.

A.B.

MY DEAR CHILDREN,—

I, knowing by experience that the exhortations of parents take most effect when the speakers leave to speak, and those especially sink deepest which are spoke latest—and being ignorant whether on my death bed I shall have opportunity to speak to any of you, much lesse to All—thought it be best, whilst I was able to compose some short matters, (for what else to call them I know not) and bequeath to you, that when I am no more with you, yet I may bee dayly in your remembrance, (Although that is the least in my aim in what I now doe) but that you may gain some spiritual Advantage by my experience. I have not studyed in this you read to show my skill, but to declare the Truth—not to sett forth myself, but the Glory of God. If I had minded the former, it had been perhaps better pleasing to you,—but seing the last is the best, let it bee best pleasing to you.

The method I will observe shall bee this—I will begin with God's dealing with me from my childhood to this Day. In my young years, about 6 or 7 as I take it, I began to make conscience of my wayes, and what I knew was sinfull, as lying, disobedience to Parents, &c. I avoided it. If at any time I was overtaken with the like evills, it was a great Trouble. I could not be at rest till by prayer I had confest it unto God. I was also troubled at the neglect of Private Dutyes, tho: too often tardy that way. I also found much comfort in reading the Scriptures, especially those places I thought most concerned my Condition, and as I grew to have more understanding, so the more solace I took in them.

In a long fitt of sicknes which I had on my bed I often communed with my heart, and made my supplication to the most High who sett me free from that affliction.

But as I grew up to bee about 14 or 15 I found my heart more carnall, and sitting loose from God, vanity and the follyes of youth take hold of me.

About 16, the Lord layd his hand sore upon me and smott mee with the small pox. When I was in my affliction, I besought the Lord, and confessed my Pride and Vanity and he was entreated of me, and again restored me. But I rendered not to him according to the benefitt received.

After a short time I changed my condition and was marryed, and came into this Country, where I found a new world and new manners, at which my heart rose. But after I was convinced it was the way of God, I submitted to it and joined to the church at Boston.

After some time I fell into a lingering sickness like a consumption, together with a lamenesse, which correction I saw the Lord sent to humble and try me and doe mee Good: and it was not altogether ineffectuall.

It pleased God to keep me a long time without a child, which was a great grief to me, and cost mee many prayers and tears before I obtaind one, and after him gave mee many more, of whom I now take the care, that as I have brought you into the world, and with great paines, weaknes, cares, and feares brought you to this, I now travail in birth again of you till Christ bee formed in you.

Among all my experiences of God's gratious Dealings with me I have constantly observed this, that he hath never suffered me long to sitt loose from him, but by one affliction or other hath made me look home, and search what was amisse—so usually thus it hath been with me that I have no sooner felt my heart out of order, but I have expected correction for it, which most commonly hath been upon my own person, in sicknesse, weaknes, paines, sometimes on my soul, in Doubts and feares of God's displeasure, and my sincerity towards him, sometimes he hath smott a child with sicknes, sometimes chasstened by losses in estate,—and these Times (thro: his great mercy) have been the times of my greatest Getting and Advantage, yea I have found them the Times when the Lord hath manifested the most Love to me. Then have I gone to searching, and have said with David, Lord search me and try me, see what wayes of wickednes are in me, and lead me in the way everlasting: and seldome or never but I have found either some sin I lay under which God would have reformed, or some duty neglected which he would have performed. And by his help I have layd Vowes and Bonds upon my Soul to perform his righteous commands.

If at any time you are chastened of God, take it as thankfully and Joyfully as in greatest mercyes, for if yee bee his yee shall reap the greatest benefitt by it. It hath been no small support to me in times of Darkness when the Almighty hath hid his face from me, that yet I have had abundance of sweetnes and refreshment after affliction, and more circumspection in my walking after I have been afflicted. I have been with God like an untoward child, that no longer then the rod has been on my back (or at least in sight) but I have been apt to forgett him and myself too. Before I was afflicted I went astray, but now I keep thy statutes.

I have had great experience of God's hearing my Prayers, and returning comfortable Answers to me, either in granting the Thing I prayed for, or else in satisfying my mind without it; and I have been confident it hath been from him, because I have found my heart through his goodnes enlarged in Thankfullnes to him.

I have often been perplexed that I have not found that constant Joy in my Pilgrimage and refreshing which I supposed most of the servants of God have; although he hath not left me altogether without the wittnes of his holy spirit, who hath oft given mee his word and sett to his Seal that it shall bee well with me. I have sometimes tasted of that hidden Manna that the world knowes not, and have sett up my Ebenezer, and have resolved with myself that against such a promis, such tasts of sweetnes, the Gates of Hell shall never prevail. Yet have I many Times sinkings and droopings, and not enjoyed that felicity that sometimes I have done. But when I have been in darkness and seen no light, yet have I desired to stay my self upon the Lord.

And, when I have been in sicknes and pain, I have thought if the Lord would but lift up the light of his Countenance upon me, altho: he ground me to powder, it would bee but light to me; yea, oft have I thought were it hell itself, and could there find the Love of God toward me, it would bee a Heaven. And, could I have been in Heaven without the Love of God, it would have been a Hell to me; for, in Truth, it is the absence and presence of God that makes Heaven or Hell.

Many times hath Satan troubled me concerning the verity of the scriptures, many times by Atheisme how I could know whether there was a God; I never saw any miracles to confirm me, and those which I read of how did I know but they were feigned. That there is a God my Reason would soon tell me by the wondrous workes that I see, the vast frame of the Heaven and the Earth, the order of all things, night and day, Summer and Winter, Spring and Autumne, the dayly providing for this great houshold upon the Earth, the preserving and directing to All to its proper end. The consideration of these things would with amazement certainly resolve me that there is an Eternall Being.

But how should I know he is such a God as I worship in Trinity, and such a Saviour as I rely upon? tho: this hath thousands of Times been suggested to mee, yet God hath helped me over. I have argued thus with myself. That there is a God I see. If ever this God hath revealed himself, it must bee in his word, and this must bee it or none. Have I not found that operation by it that no humane Invention can work upon the Soul? hath not Judgments befallen Diverse who have scorned and contemd it? hath it not been preserved thro: All Ages maugre all the heathen Tyrants and all of the enemyes who have opposed it? Is there any story but that which showes the beginnings of Times, and how the world came to bee as wee see? Doe wee not know the prophecyes in it fullfilled which could not have been so long foretold by any but God himself?

When I have gott over this Block, then have I another putt in my way, That admitt this bee the true God whom wee worship, and that bee his word, yet why may not the Popish Religion bee the right? They have the same God, the same Christ, the same word: they only enterprett it one way, wee another.

This hath sometimes stuck with me, and more it would, but the vain fooleries that are in their Religion, together with their lying miracles and cruell persecutions of the Saints, which admitt were they as they terme them, yet not so to bee dealt withall.

The consideration of these things and many the like would soon turn me to my own Religion again.

But some new Troubles I have had since the world has been filled with Blasphemy, and Sectaries, and some who have been accounted sincere Christians have been carryed away with them, that somtimes I have said, Is there faith upon the earth? and I have not known what to think. But then I have remembred the words of Christ that so it must bee, and that, if it were possible, the very elect should bee deceived. Behold, faith our Saviour, I have told you before. That hath stayed my heart, and I can now say, Return, O my Soul, to thy Rest, upon this Rock Christ Jesus will I build my faith; and, if I perish, I perish. But I know all the Powers of Hell shall never prevail against it. I know whom I have trusted, and whom I have beleived, and that he is able to keep that I have committed to his charge.

Now to the King, Immortall, Eternall, and invisible, the only wife God, bee Honoure and Glory for ever and ever! Amen.

This was written in much sicknesse and weaknes, and is very weakly and imperfectly done; but, if you can pick any Benefitt out of it, it is the marke which I aimed at.

Selected Poems

To my Dear and loving Husband.

If ever two were one, then surely we.
If ever man were lov'd by wife, then thee;
If ever wife was happy in a man,
Compare with me ye women if you can.
I prize thy love more then whole Mines of gold,
Or all the riches that the East doth hold.
My love is such that Rivers cannot quench,
Nor ought but love from thee, give recompence.
Thy love is such I can no way repay,
The heavens reward thee manifold I pray.
Then while we live, in love lets so persever,
That when we live no more, we may live ever.

In reference to her Children, 23. June, 1656.[1]

I had eight birds hatcht in one nest,
Four Cocks there were, and Hens the rest,
I nurst them up with pain and care,
Nor cost, nor labour did I spare,
Till at the last they felt their wing.
Mounted the Trees, and learn'd to sing;
Chief of the Brood then took his flight,
To Regions far, and left me quite:

1. This date is clearly wrong, as events are referred to in the course of the poem which took place more than a year later. It is probably a misprint for 1658. [Date is now established as 1659. Ed.]

My mournful chirps I after send,
Till he return, or I do end,
Leave not thy nest, thy Dam and Sire,
Fly back and sing amidst this Quire.
My second bird did take her flight,
And with her mate flew out of sight;
Southward they both their course did bend,
And Seasons twain they there did spend.
Till after blown by *Southern* gales,
They Norward steer d with filled sayles.
A prettier bird was no where seen,
Along the Beach among the treen.
I have a third of colour white,
On whom I plac'd no small delight;
Coupled with mate loving and true,
Hath also bid her Dam adieu:
And where *Aurora* first appears,
She now hath percht, to spend her years;
One to the Academy flew
To chat among that learned crew:
Ambition moves still in his breast
That he might chant above the rest,
Striving for more then to do well,
That nightingales he might excell.
My fifth, whose down is yet scarce gone
Is 'mongst the shrubs and bushes flown,
And as his wings increase in strength,
On higher boughs he'l pearch at length.
My other three, still with me nest,
Untill they'r grown, then as the rest,
Or here or there, they'l take their flight,
As is ordain'd, so shall they light.
If birds could weep, then would my tears
Let others know what are my fears
Lest this my brood some harm should catch,
And be surpriz'd for want of watch,
Whilst pecking corn, and void of care
They fall un'wares in Fowlers snare:
Or whilst on trees they sit and sing,
Some untoward boy at them do sling:
Or whilst allur'd with bell and glass,

The net be spread, and caught, alas.
Or least by Lime-twigs they be foyl'd,
Or by some greedy hawks be spoyl'd.
O would my young, ye saw my breast,
And knew what thoughts there sadly rest,
Great was my pain when I you bred,
Great was my care, when I you fed,
Long did I keep you soft and warm,
And with my wings kept off all harm,
My cares are more, and fears then ever,
My throbs such now, as 'fore were never:
Alas my birds, you wisdome want,
Of perils you are ignorant,
Oft times in grass, on trees, in flight,
Sore accidents on you may light.
O to your safety have an eye,
So happy may you live and die:
Mean while my dayes in tunes Ile spend,
Till my weak layes with me shall end.
In shady woods I'le sit and sing,
And things that past, to mind I'le bring.
Once young and pleasant, as are you,
But former toyes (no joyes) adieu.
My age I will not once lament,
But sing, my time so near is spent.
And from the top bough take my flight,
Into a country beyond sight,
Where old ones, instantly grow young,
And there with Seraphims set song:
No seasons cold, nor storms they see;
But spring lasts to eternity,
When each of you shall in your nest
Among your young ones take your rest,
In chirping language, oft them tell,
You had a Dam that lov'd you well,
That did what could be done for young,
And nurst you up till you were strong,
And 'fore she once would let you fly,
She shew'd you joy and misery;
Taught what was good, and what was ill,
What would save life, and what would kill?

Thus gone, amonst you I may live,
And dead, yet speak, and counsel give:
Farewel my birds, farewel adieu,
I happy am, if well with you.

Margaret Dutchess of Newcastle.

Margaret Cavendish, Duchess of Newcastle *(Courtesy of the Houghton Library, Harvard University, from* Philosophical and Physical Opinions, *by Abraham van Diepenbeke, 1655)*

Margaret Cavendish, Duchess of Newcastle, 1623–1673

The True Relation of my Birth, Breeding, and Life (1656). The life of William, Duke of Newcastle (1667). The Description of a New World Called the Blazing World (1666).

Margaret Cavendish, the Duchess of Newcastle, was the daughter of a wealthy landowner, Sir Thomas Lucas, who died when she was an infant, leaving her and her four sisters and three brothers to be brought up by their mother in the difficult period of the Civil War in England. Margaret was given a permissive but elitist upbringing, which developed a bond of exclusiveness and affection between her and her family. According to the custom of her class and sex, she was not well educated–a practice that she once deplored as "the barbarous custom to breed women low"–but she was determined to make a mark even as a shy, unsophisticated young woman and, on her own initiative, she became a lady-in-waiting at twenty-one to Queen Henrietta Maria, following the Queen into exile in Paris while Charles I fought and lost battles. In Paris she met William Cavendish, then Marquis of Newcastle, who had led the king's armies to "glorious defeat," and they married, not without some disapproval from the court which considered the match not a brilliant one for the Marquis.

During exile in Paris and later in Antwerp, Margaret Cavendish began her career as a writer. She wrote her brief autobiography in 1649 and the early 1650's and followed it with poetry, fiction, philosophical essays, orations, and plays. Four of her books were published before she and her husband returned to England in 1659 and several more were composed in exile and published later. She became one of the few literary women in England, joining for a brief time on her return "The Society of Friendship" of Mrs. Katherine Phillips.

Her autobiography, *The True Relation of my Birth, Breeding, and Life* (published in 1656 as part of a larger collection of fictional and poetic pieces), is in the tradition of the seventeenth-century memoir and is indebted to literary portraiture of the day–the "character" inherited from classical models and the increasingly popular form of the biography. When she wrote her *Life,* few English women had written about themselves except in the religious tradition of autobiography. Some exceptions were Anne Clifford, Countess of Pembroke, Lady Anne Fanshawe, Lady Anne Halkett, and Lucie Hutchinson, wife of the Puritan Colonel Hutchinson; but their memoirs, which are often appended to their husbands' biographies, were their only literary productions. The Duchess, as her *Life* tells us, began her writing at the age of twelve and continued to practice her vocation all of her life. Working within the conventions of her time, she at first accepts herself as a shadow of the Duke and acknowledges his superiority as a writer. His writing, she says in her *Life,* is "what wit dictates to him" and hers mere "scribbling"; but then she goes on to analyze her method of writing and we see that she takes herself very seriously as an author and, with stoic resolve at the blind workings of fortune, she intends to control her destiny "with her own hand" and to seek immortality in "remembrances in after-ages."

On their return to England the Duke and Duchess (he was made a Duke in 1664) retired to the country at Welbeck, where they restored the Duke's estates and entertained each other and a select group of family and literary friends with their literary productions. The Duke was a generous patron of leading writers, including Dryden and Ben Jonson. He was also an occasional author but, above all, he was an enthusiastic supporter of his wife's work. The Duchess' most popular publication was the biography of her husband, written to assure his place in history as a loyal courtier and a heroic warrior, and also, as we learn from the excerpt quoted in the preface to this book, written to assure her fame and partnership with her husband as his bard and scribe. Somewhat undaunted or unaware of any adverse reactions to her work, she sent her philosophical and scientific treatises to Cambridge and Oxford scholars and spent her later years revising and reprinting many of her earlier writings.

In 1666 she published with one of her treatises on Experimental Philosophy her utopian fantasy, *The Description of a New World Called the Blazing World,* from which excerpts are included here. The story is indebted to her earlier tale "Assaulted and Pursued Chastity" and to voyage and utopian literature, but it is also a fantasy self-portrait, completing our picture of the Duchess' self-disclosure. Her heroine, who escapes abduction and rape by pirates, discovers a hidden kingdom where she becomes the Empress, the intellectual and spiritual leader, and the successful military commander. In her role as warrior-goddess, she appears "in her garments of light, like an angel or some Deity." The Duchess appears in the tale as the Empress' scribe and she is so impressed with the order and peace and harmony of the kingdom that she wants one herself, and thus she creates a new world "from within." In the Prologue to this work, Margaret Cavendish shows that she has come to terms with the ambition which had at times frustrated her as a woman but which had given her a vocation as a writer: "Though I have neither power, time nor occasion to conquer the world as Alexander and Caesar did; yet rather than not to be Mistress of one, since Fortune and the Fates would give me none, I have made a World of my own."

When the Duchess died suddenly in her fiftieth year in 1673, her husband had already received permission for their eventual interment in Westminster Abbey so she was taken to London and buried there with pomp and ceremony. In the epitaph he composed for her the Duke granted her the fame she wished to have: "The Dutches was a wise, wittie and learned lady, which her many Books do well testifie." Others have not been as generous to the Duchess. One of her own sex a century later, Louisa Costello, in a brief biography found her "of small talent and no genius." But Charles Lamb, Virginia Woolf, and others disagree with this verdict. In recent revaluations her considerable talent in poetry and innovative fictional forms has assured her a place in literary history. In her *Life* we see her as a pioneer autobiographer and a woman who was determined to participate in the intellectual and cultural life of her time.

EDITIONS USED:

The Life of William Cavendish, Duke of Newcastle, to which is added the True Relation of my Birth, Breeding, and Life by Margaret Duchess of Newcastle. Edited by C. H. Firth. London: George Routledge and Sons,1906.

The Description of a New World called the Blazing World written by the Thrice Noble, Illustrious, and Excellent Princesse the Duchess of New-Castle. London: Printed by A. Maxwell, 1666.

SUGGESTED READINGS:

Ballard, George. *Memoirs of Several Ladies of Great Britain.* Oxford: Printed for the author by W. Jackson, 1752.

Costello, Louisa. *Memoirs of Eminent Englishwomen.* 4 vols. London: R. Bentley, 1844.

Grant, Douglas. *Margaret the First: A Biography of Margaret Cavendish, Duchess of Newcastle, 1623-1673.* London: Rupert Hart-Davis, 1957.

Perry, Henry Ten Eyck. *The First Duchess of Newcastle and her Husband as Figures in Literary History.* Boston: Ginn and Co., 1918.

Woolf, Virginia. "The Duchess of Newcastle," in *The Common Reader: First Series.* New York: Harcourt Brace and World, Inc., 1953, pp. 70-80.

A True Relation of my Birth, Breeding, and Life

But, howsoever our fortunes are, we are both content, spending our time harmlessly, for my Lord pleaseth himself with the management of some few horses, and exercises himself with the use of the sword; which two arts he hath brought by his studious thoughts, rational experience, and industrious practice, to an absolute perfection. And though he hath taken as much pains in those arts, both by study and practice, as chymists for the philosopher's-stone, yet he hath his advantage of them, that he hath found the right and the truth thereof and therein, which chymists never found in their art, and I believe never will. Also here creates himself with his pen, writing what his wit dictates to him, but I pass my time rather with scribbling than writing, with words than wit. Not that I speak much, because I am addicted to contemplation, unless I am with my Lord, yet then I rather attentively listen to what he says, than impertinently speak. Yet when I am writing any sad feigned stories, or serious humours, or melancholy passions, I am forced many times to express them with the tongue before I can write them with the pen, by reason those thoughts that are sad, serious, and melancholy are apt to contract, and to draw too much back, which oppression doth as it were overpower or smother the conception in the brain. But when some of those thoughts are sent out in words, they give the rest more liberty to place themselves in a more methodical order, marching more regularly with my pen on the ground of white paper; but my letters seem rather as a ragged rout than a well-armed body, for the brain being quicker in creating than the hand in writing or the memory in retaining, many fancies are lost, by reason they ofttimes outrun the pen, where I, to keep speed in the race, write so fast as I stay not so long as to write my letters plain, insomuch as some have taken my handwriting for some strange character, and being accustomed so to do, I cannot now write very plain, when I strive to write my best; indeed, my ordinary handwriting is so bad as few can read it, so as to write it fair for the press; but however, that little wit I have, it delights me to scribble it out, and disperse it about. For I being addicted from my childhood to contemplation rather than conversation, to solitariness rather than society, to melancholy rather than mirth, to write with the pen than to work with a needle, passing my time with harmless fancies, their company being pleasing, their conversation innocent (in which I take such pleasure as I neglect my health, for it is as great a grief to leave their society as a joy to be in their company), my only trouble is, lest my brain should grow barren, or that the root of my fancies should become insipid, withering into a dull stupidity for want of maturing subjects to write on. For I being of a lazy nature, and not of an active disposition, as some are that love to journey from town to town, from place to place, from house to house, delighting in variety of company, making still one where the greatest number is—likewise in playing at cards, or any other games, in which I neither have practised, nor have I any skill therein:—as for dancing, although it be a graceful art, and becometh unmarried persons well, yet for those that are married, it is too light an action, disagreeing with the gravity thereof—and for revelling, I am of too dull a nature to make one in a merry society—as for feasting, it would neither agree with my humour or constitution, for my diet is for the most part sparing, as a little boiled chicken, or the like, my drink most commonly water; for though I have an indifferent good appetite, yet I do often fast, out of an opinion that if I should eat much, and exercise little, which I do, only walking a slow pace in my chamber, whilst my thougts run apace in my brain, so that the motions of my mind hinders the active exercises of my body; for should I dance or run, or walk apace, I should dance my thoughts out of measure, run my fancies out of breath, and tread out the feet of my numbers. But because I would not bury myself quite from the sight of the world, I go sometimes abroad, seldom to visit, but only in my coach about the town, or about some of the streets, which we call here a tour, where all the chief of the town go to see and to be seen, likewise all strangers of what quality soever, as all great princes or queens that make any short stay. For this town being a passage or thoroughfare to most parts, causeth many times persons of great quality to be here, though not as inhabitants, yet to lodge for some short time; and all such, as I said, take a delight, or at least go to see the customs thereof, which most cities of note in Europe, for all I can hear, hath such like recreations for the effeminate sex, although for my part I had rather sit at home and write, or walk, as I said, in my chamber and contemplate: but I hold necessary sometimes to appear abroad, besides I do find, that several objects do bring new materials for my thoughts and fancies to build upon. Yet I must say this in the behalf of my thoughts, that I never found them idle; for if the senses bring no work in, they will work of themselves, like silk-worms that spins out of their own bowels. Neither can I say I think the time tedious, when I am alone, so I be near my Lord, and know he is well.

But now I have declared to my readers my birth, breeding, and actions, to this part of my life (I mean the material parts, for should I write every particular, as my childish sports and the like, it would be ridiculous and tedious); but I have been honourably born and nobly matched; I have been bred to elevated thoughts, not to a dejected spirit, my life hath been ruled with honesty, attended by modesty, and directed by truth. But since I have writ in general thus far of my life, I think it fit I should speak something of my humour, particular practice and disposition. As for my humour, I was from my childhood given to contemplation, being more taken or delighted with thoughts than in conversation with a society, insomuch as I would walk two or three hours, and never rest, in a musing, considering, contemplating manner, reasoning with myself of everything my senses did present. But when I was in the company of my natural friends, I was very attentive of what they said or did; but for strangers I regarded not much what they said, but many times I did observe their actions, whereupon my reason as judge, and my thoughts as accusers, or excusers, or approvers and commenders, did plead, or appeal to accuse, or complain thereto. Also I never took delight in closets, or cabinets of toys, but in the variety of fine clothes, and such toys as only were to adorn my person. Likewise I had a natural stupidity towards the learning of any other language than my native tongue, for I could sooner and with more facility understand the sense, than remember the words, and for want of such memory makes me so unlearned in foreign languages as I am. As for my practice, I was never very active, by reason I was given so much to contemplation; besides my brothers and sisters were for the most part serious and staid in their actions, not given to sport or play, nor dance about, whose company I keeping, made me so too. But I observed, that although their actions were staid, yet they would be very merry amongst themselves, delighting in each other's company: also they would in their discourse express the general actions of the world, judging, condemning, approving, commending, as they thought good, and with those that were innocently harmless, they would make themselves merry therewith. As for my study of books it was little, yet I chose rather to read, than to employ my time in any other work, or practice, and when I read what I understood not, I would ask my brother, the Lord Lucas, he being learned, the sense or meaning thereof. But my serious study could not be much, by reason I took great delight in attiring, fine dressing, and fashions especially such fasions as I did invent myself, not taking that pleasure in such fasions as was invented by others. Also I did dislike any should follow my fashions, for I always took delight in a singularity, even in accoutrements of habits. But whatsoever I was addicted to, either in fashion of clothes, contemplation of thoughts, actions of life, they were lawful, honest, honourable, and modest, of which I can avouch to the world with a great confidence, because it is a pure truth. As for my disposition, it is more inclining to be melancholy than merry, but not crabbed or peevishly melancholy, but soft, melting, solitary, and contemplating melancholy. And I am apt to weep rather than laugh, not that I do often either of them. Also I am tender natured, for it troubles my conscience to kill a fly, and the groans of a dying beast strike my soul. Also where I place a particular affection, I love extraordinarily and constantly, yet not fondly, but soberly and observingly, not to hang about them as a trouble, but to wait upon them as a servant; but this affection will take no root, but where I think or find merit, and have leave both from divine and moral laws. Yet I find this passion to troublesome, as it is the only torment of my life, for fear any evil misfortune or accident, or sickness, or death, should come unto them, insomuch as I am never freely at rest. Likewise I am grateful, for I never received a courtesy—but I am impatient and troubled until I can return it. Also I am chaste, both by nature, and education, insomuch as I do abhor an unchaste thought. Likewise, I am seldom angry, as my servants may witness for me, for I rather choose to suffer some inconveniences than disturb my thoughts, which makes me wink many times at their faults; but when I am angry, I am very angry, but yet it is soon over, and I am easily pacified, if it be not such an injury as may create a hate. Neither am I apt to be exceptious or jealous, but if I have the least symptom of this passion, I declare it to those it concerns, for I never let it lie smothering in my breast to breed a malignant disease in the mind, which might break out into extravagant passions, or railing speeches, or indiscreet actions; but I examine moderately, reason soberly, and plead gently in my own behalf, through a desire to keep those affections I had, or at least thought to have. And truly I am so vain, as to be so self-conceited, or so naturally partial, to think my friends have as much reason to love me as another, since none can love more sincerely than I, and it were an injustice to prefer a fainter affection, or to esteem the body more than the mind. Likewise I am neither spiteful, envious, nor malicious. I repine not at the gifts that Nature or Fortune bestows upon others, yet I am a great emulator; for, though I wish none worse than they are, yet it is lawful for me to wish myself the best, and to do my honest endeavour thereunto. For I think it no crime to wish myself the exactest of Nature's works, my thread of life the longest, my chain of destiny the strongest, my mind the peaceablest, my life the pleasantest, my death the easiest, and the greatest saint in heaven; also to do my endeavour, so far as honour and honesty doth allow of, to be the highest on Fortune's wheel and to hold the wheel from turning, if I can. And if it be commendable to wish another's good, it were a sin not to wish my own; for as envy is a vice, so emulation is a virtue, but emulation is in the way to ambition, or indeed it is a noble ambition. But I fear my ambition inclines to vain-glory, for I am very ambitious; yet 'tis neither for beauty, wit, titles, wealth, or power, but as they are steps to raise me to Fame's tower, which is to live by remembrance in after-ages. Likewise I am that the vulgar call proud, not out of self-conceit, or to slight or condemn any, but scorning to do a base or mean act, and disdaining rude or unworthy persons; insomuch, that if I should find any that were rude, or too bold, I should be apt to be so passionate, as to affront them, if I can, unless discretion should get betwixt my passion and their boldness, which sometimes perchance it might if discretion should crowd hard for place. For though I am naturally bashful, yet in such a cause my spirits would be all on fire. Otherwise I am so well bred, as to be civil to all persons, of all degrees, or qualities. Likewise I am so proud, or rather just to my Lord, as to abate nothing of the quality of his wife, for if honour be the mark of merit, and his master's royal favour, who will favour none but those that have merit to deserve, it were a baseness for me to neglect the ceremony thereof. Also in some cases I am naturally a coward, and in other cases very valiant. As for example, if any of my nearest friends were in danger I should never consider my life in striving to help them though I were sure to do them no good, and would willingly, nay cheerfully, resign my life for their sakes: likewise I should not spare my life, if honour bids me die. But in a danger where my friends, or my honour is not concerned, or engaged, but only my life to be unprofitably lost, I am the veriest coward in nature, as upon the sea, or any dangerous places, or of thieves, or fire, or the like. Nay the shooting of a gun, although but a pot-gun will make me start, and stop my hearing, much less have I courage to discharge one; or if a sword should be held against me, although but in jest, I am afraid. Also as I am not covetous, so I am not prodigal, but of the two I am inclining to be prodigal, yet I cannot say to a vain prodigality, because I imagine it is to a profitable end; for perceiving the world is given, or apt to honour the outside more than the inside, worshipping show more than substance; and I am so vain (if it be a vanity) as to endeavour to be worshipped, rather than not to be regarded. Yet I shall never be so prodigal as to impoverish my friends, or go beyond the limits or facility of our estate. And though I desire to appear to the best advantage, whilst I live in the view of the public world, yet I could most willingly exclude myself, so as never to see the face of any creature but my Lord as long as I live, inclosing myself like an anchorite, wearing a frieze gown, tied with a cord about my waist. But I hope my readers will not think me vain for writing my life, since there have been many that have done the like, as Caesar, Ovid, and many more, both men and women, and I know no reason I may not do it as well as they: but I verily believe some censuring readers will scornfully say, why hath this Lady writ her own life? since none cares to know whose daughter she was or whose wife she is, or how she was bred, or what fortunes she had, or how she lived, or what humour or disposition she was of. I answer that it is true, that 'tis to no purpose to the readers, but it is to the authoress, because I write it for my own sake, not theirs. Neither did I intend this piece for to delight, but to divulge; not to please the fancy, but to tell the truth, lest after-ages should mistake, in not knowing I was daughter to one Master Lucas of St. Johns, near Colchester, in Essex, second wife to the Lord Marquis of Newcastle; for my Lord having had two wives; I might easily have been mistaken, especially if I should die and my Lord marry again.

The Life of William Cavendish, Duke of Newcastle

To His Grace the Duke of Newcastle

I have been a student even from my childhood; and since I have been your Lordship's wife, I have lived for the most part a strict and retired life, as is best known to your Lordship, and therefore my censurers cannot know much of me, since they have little or no acquaintance with me. 'Tis true, I have been a traveller both before and after I was married to your Lordship, and sometimes show myself at your Lordship's command in public places or assemblies; but yet I converse with few. Indeed, my Lord, I matter not the censures of this age, but am rather proud of them; for it shows that my actions are more than ordinary, and according to the old proverb, it is better to be envied than pitied: for I know well, that it is merely out of spite and malice, whereof this present age is so full, that none can escape them, and they'll make no doubt to stain even your Lordship's loyal, noble, and heroic actions, as well as they do mine, though yours have been of war and fighting, mine of contemplating and writing: yours were performed publicly in the field, mine privately in my closet: yours had many thousand eye-witnesses, mine none but my waiting-maids. But the great God, that hath hitherto blessed both your Grace and me, will, I question not, preserve both our fames to after ages, for which we shall be bound most humbly to acknowledge His great mercy; and I myself, as long as I live, be your grace's honest wife, and humble servant,

M. NEWCASTLE.

The Description of a New World Called The Blazing World

[The Duchess of Newcastle, visiting the Empress of the Blazing World as her scribe, expresses her ambition to be the Empress of the Blazing World.] Well, said the Duchess, setting aside this dispute, my ambition is, that I would fain be as you are, that is, an Emperess of a World, and I shall never be at quiet until I be one. I love you so well, replied the Emperess, that I wish with all my soul, you had the fruition of your ambitious desire, and I shall not fail to give you my best advice how to accomplish it; the best informers are the Immaterial Spirits, and they'l soon tell you, whether it be possible to obtain your wish. But, said the Duchess, I have little acquaintance with them, for I never knew any before the time you sent for me. They know you, replied the Emperess; for they told me of you, and were the means and instrument of your coming hither: Wherefore I'le confer with them, and enquire whether there be not another World, whereof you may be Emperess as well as I am of this? No sooner had the Emperess said this, but some Immaterial Spirits came to visit her, of whom she inquired, whether there were but three Worlds in all, to wit, the Blazing-world where she was in, the World which she came from, and the World where the Duchess lived? The Spirits answered, That there were more numerous Worlds then the Stars which appeared in these three mentioned Worlds. Then the Emperess asked, whether it was not possible, that her dearest friend the Duchess of *Newcastle,* might be Emperess of one of them. Although there be numerous, nay, infinite Worlds, answered the Spirits, yet none is without Government. But is none of these Worlds so weak, said she, that it may be surprised or conquered. The Spirits answered, *That Lucian's* World of Lights, had been for some time in a snuff, but of late years one *Helmont* had got it, who since he was Emperour of it, had so strengthened the Immortal parts thereof with mortal out-works, as it was for the present impregnable. Said the Emperess, If there be such an Infinite number of Worlds, I am sure, not onely my friend, the Duchess, but any other might obtain one. Yes, answered the Spirits, if those Worlds were uninhabited; but they are as populous as this, your Majesty governs. Why, said the Emperess, it is not impossible to conquer a World. No, answered the Spirits, but, for the most part, Conquerers seldom enjoy their conquest, for they being more feared then loved, most commonly come to an untimely end. If you will but direct me, said the Duchess to the Spirits, which World is easiest to be conquered, her Majesty will assist me with means, and I will trust to Fate and Fortune; for I had rather die in the adventure of noble atchievements, then live in obscure and sluggish security; since by the one, I may live in a glorious Fame, and by the other I am buried in oblivion. The Spirits answered, That the lives of Fame were like other lives; for some lasted long, and some died soon. 'Tis true, said the Duchess; but yet the shortest-lived Fame lasts longer then the longest life of Man. But, replied the Spirits, if occasion does not serve you, you must content your self to live without such atchievements that may gain you a Fame: But we wonder, proceeded the Spirits, that you desire to be Emperess of a Terrestrial World, when as you can create your self a Celestial World if you please. What, said the Emperess, can any Mortal be a Creator? Yes, answered the Spirits; for every humane Creature can create an Immaterial World fully inhabited by immaterial Creatures, and populous of immaterial subjects, such as we are, and all this within the compass of the head or scull; nay, not onely so, but he may create a World of what fashion and Government he will, and give the Creatures thereof such motions, figures, forms, colours, perceptions, etc. as he pleases, and make Whirl-pools, Lights, Pressures and Reactions, etc. as he thinks best; nay, he may make a World full of Veins, Muscles, and Nerves, and all these to move by one jolt or stroke: also he may alter that world as often as he pleases, or change it from a natural world, to an artificial; he may make a world of Ideas, a world of Atomes, a world of Lights, or whatsoever his fancy leads him to. And since it is in your power to create such a world, What need you to venture life, reputation and tranquility, to conquer a gross material world? For you can enjoy no more of a material world then a particular Creature is able to enjoy, which is but a small part, considering the compass of such a world; and you may plainly observe it by your friend the Emperess here, which although she possesses a whole world, yet enjoys she but a part thereof; neither is she so much acquainted with it, that she knows all the places, Countries and Dominions she Governs. The truth is, a Soveraign Monarch has the general trouble; but the Subjects enjoy all the delights and pleasures in parts; for it is impossible, that a Kingdom, nay, a County should be injoyed by one person at once, except he take the pains to travel into every part, and endure the inconveniencies of going from one place to another; wherefore, since glory, delight and pleasure lives but in other mens opinions, and can neither add tranquility to your mind, nor give ease to your body, why should you desire to be Emperess of a material world, and be troubled with the cares that attend Government? when as by creating a world within your self, you may enjoy all both in whole and in parts, without controle or opposition, and may make what world you please, and alter it when you please, and enjoy as much pleasure and delight as a world can afford you? You have converted me, said the Duchess to the Spirits, from my ambitious desire; wherefore I'le take your advice, reject and despise all the worlds without me, and create a world of my own. The Emperess said, If I do make such a world, then I shall be Mistress of two world, one within, and the other without me. That your Majesty may, said the Spirits; and so left these two Ladies to create two worlds within themselves: who did also part from each other, until such time as they had brought their worlds to perfection.

.   .   .   .

And now to return to my former Story; when the Emperess's and Duchess's Soul were travelling into *Nottingham*-shire, for that was the place where the Duke did reside; passing through the forrest of *Sherewood,* the Emperess's soul was very much delighted with it, as being a dry, plain and woody place, very pleasant to travel in both in Winter and Summer; for it is neither much dirty, not dusty at no time: at last they arrived at *Welbeck,* a House where the Duke dwell'd, surrounded all with Wood, so close and full, that the Emperess took great pleasure and delight therein, and told the Duchess she never had observed more wood in so little a compass in any part of the Kingdom she had passed through; The truth is, said she, there seems to be more wood on the Seas, she meaning the Ships, then on the Land. The Duchess told her, the reason was, that there had been a long Civil War in that Kingdom, in which most of the best Timber-trees and Principal Palaces were ruined and destroyed; and my dear Lord and Husband, said she, has lost by it half his Woods, besides many Houses, Land, and moveable Goods; so that all the loss out of his particular Estate, did amount to above half a Million of Pounds. I wish, said the Emperess, he had some of the Gold that is in the Blazing world, to repair his losses. The Duchess most humbly thank'd her Imperial Majesty for her kind wishes; but, said she, wishes will not repair his ruines: however, God has given my Noble Lord and Husband great Patience, by which he bears all his losses and misfortunes. At last, they enter'd into the Dukes House, an habitation not so magnificent, as useful; and when the Emperess saw it, Has the Duke, said she, no other house but this? Yes, answered the Duchess, some five miles from this place, he has a very fine Castle, called *Bolesover.* That place then, said the Emperess, I desire to see. Alas! replied the Duchess, it is but a naked house, and uncloath'd of all Furniture. However, said the Emperess, I may see the manner of its structure and building. That you may, replied the Duchess: and as they were thus discoursing, the Duke came out of the House into the Court, to see his Horses of mannage; whom when the Duchess's soul perceived, she was so overjoyed, that her aereal Vehicle became so splendorous, as if it had been enlightned by the Sun; by which we may perceive, that the passions of Souls or Spirits can alter their bodily Vehicles. Then these two Ladies Spirits went close to him, but he could not perceive them; and after the Emperess had observed the Art of Mannage, she was much pleased with it, and commended it as a noble pastime, and an exercise fit and proper for noble and heroick Persons: But when the Duke was gone into the house again, those two Souls followed him; where the Emperess observing, that he went to the exercise of the Sword, and was such an excellent and unparallell'd Master thereof, she was as much pleased with that exercise, as she was with the former: But the Duchess's soul being troubled, that her dear Lord and Husband used such a violent exercise before meat, for fear of overheating himself, without any consideration of the Emperess's soul, left her aereal Vehicle, and entred into her Lord. The Emperess's soul perceiving this, did the like: And then the Duke had three Souls in one Body; and had there been but some such Souls more, the Duke would have been like the Grand-Signior in his Seraglio, onely it would have been a Platonick Seraglio. But the Dukes soul being wife, honest, witty, complaisant and noble, afforded such delight and pleasure to the Emperess's soul by her conversation, that these two souls became enamoured of each other; which the Duchess's soul perceiving, grew jealous at first, but then considering that no Adultery could be committed amongst Platonick Lovers, and that Platonism was Divine, as being derived from Divine *Plato,* cast forth of her mind that Idea of Jealousie. Then the Conversation of these three souls was so pleasant, that it cannot be expressed; for the Dukes soul entertained the Emperesses soul with Scenes, Songs, Musick, witty Discourses, pleasant Recreations, and all kinds of harmless sports; so that the time passed away faster then they expected.

.   .   .   .

The Epilogue to the Reader

By this Poetical Description, you may perceive, that my ambition is not onely to be Emperess, but Authoress of a whole World; and that the Worlds I have made, both the Blazing *and the other* Philosophical *World, mentioned in the first part of this Description, are framed and composed of the most pure, that is, the rational parts of Matter, which are the parts of my Mind; which Creation was more easily and suddenly effected, then the Conquests of the two famous Monarchs of the World,* Alexander *and* Caesar: *Neither have I made such disturbances, and caused so many dissolutions of particulars, otherwise named deaths, as they did; for I have destroyed but some few men in a little Boat, which died through the extremity of cold, and that by the hand of Justice, which was necessitated to punish their crime of stealing away a young and beauteous Lady. And in the formation of those Worlds, I take more delight and glory, then ever* Alexander *or* Caesar *did in conquering this terrestrial world; and though I have made my* Blazing-world, *a Peaceable World, allowing it but one Religion, one Language, and one Government; yet could I make another World, as full of Factions, Divisions, and Wars, as this is of Peace and Tranquility; and the rational figures of my Mind might express as much courage to fight, as* Hector *and* Achilles *had; and be as wise as* Nestor, *as Eloquent as* Ulysses, *and as beautiful as* Helen. *But I esteeming Peace before War, Wit before Policy, Honesty before Beauty; instead of the figures of* Alexander, Caesar, Hector, Achilles, Nestor, Ulysses, Helen, *etc. chose rather the figure of Honest* Margaret Newcastle, *which now I would not change for all this terrestrial World; and if any should like the World I have made, and be willing to be my Subjects, they may imagine themselves such, and they are such; I mean, in their Minds, Fancies or Imaginations; but if they cannot endure to be subjects, they may create Worlds of their own, and Govern themselves as they please: But yet let them have a care, not to prove unjust Usurpers, and to rob me of mine; for concerning the* Philosophical *World, I am Empress of it my self; and as for the* Blazing-*world, it having an Empress already, who rules it with great wisdom and conduct, which Empress is my dear Platonick Friend; I shall never prove so unjust, treacherous and unworthy to her, as to disturb her Government; much less to depose her from her Imperial Throne, for the sake of any other; but rather chuse to create another World for another Friend.*

Lady Mary Wortley Montagu (*Courtesy of the Houghton Library, Harvard University, from* The Letters and Works of Lady Mary Wortley Montagu, *1861*)

Lady Mary Wortley Montagu, 1689–1762

Selections from the Letters; including "Turkish Embassy Letters" (1766)

Mary Pierrepont was born in 1689 to Evelyn Pierrepont, who became Lord Kingston, and his wife Mary, a cousin of the novelist Henry Fielding. Although from the aristocracy, Lady Mary, unlike her literary predecessor Margaret Cavendish, did not feel free to publish her works in the Georgian society in which she lived. Very little of what she wrote was made public in her lifetime except through private circulation in her own court circles and through some anonymous publications. *Court Poems,* published in 1716, was printed without her permission. Her "Turkish Embassy Letters" did not appear until a year after her death. Nevertheless, Lady Mary thought of herself as a writer. Her famous friendship and quarrel with Alexander Pope, who gave her notoriety as Sappho in his *Dunciad,* her considerable production of poems, essays, and plays, and above all, her extensive correspondence, which further developed the eighteenth-century epistolatory genre, bear witness to her literary vocation.

Unlike other aristocratic women of her day, Lady Mary was favored in her youth with an education, at first at the hand of governesses and later with tutoring from the distinguished scholar, Gilbert Burnet, Bishop of Salisbury. In addition, she gathered much learning on her own. At nineteen, she was taken to London where she met many of her father's literary friends, including Joseph Addison, Richard Steele, and William Congreve. She was aware that most "women of quality" were not as lucky as she was, and in 1710 she wrote to Bishop Burnet that because of their lack of education women were "the most uselesse and most worthlesse part of creation." This assessment of the condition of her sex is characteristic of the social commentary in her correspondence. Her friend Mary Astell (1688-1731), writing a Preface (1724) to Lady Mary's "Embassy Letters" praises her for similar astute observations about other cultures. Astell maintains that Lady Montagu gives "a more true and accurate account of the customs and manners of the several nations" than her male predecessors and she congratulates her on having "the skill to strike out a new path." The "Embassy

Letters", which Lady Mary composed from summaries, copies, and extracts of real letters, represent a unique literary genre developed by her into a travel memoir.

While the "Turkish Embassy Letters" show Lady Mary's genius as an informed and objective commentator, her letters to Algarotti and much of her correspondence with her daughter, Lady Bute, reveal another aspect of her portrait. Lady Mary was also a Romantic and liked to create a world of romance. Among her early literary fragments is a work entitled "Auto-biography" dated 1711 when she was twenty-two years old. It is an account of her meeting and courtship with Edward Wortley Montagu, written "after the fashion of a French romance," as her biographer Halsband has noted. In it Lady Mary tells us there is not a "sillable feigned" except the names. A comparison with her actual correspondence with Montagu during their courtship and elopement (in the face of her father's opposition to the match) suggests that while she was writing to him of the practical details of their elopement, she was creating in her own mind a chapter of a romance with herself as heroine. Although she was an active and important partner in her husband's public career, she was clearly a person whose temperament was incompatible with his. The romantic choice of her middle-aged years, Francesco Algarotti (1712-1764) a young Venetian scholar and poet and a favorite in the court of Frederick the Great, also seems to have been an inappropriate choice. Her uncharacteristically passionate and reckless cor-respondence with him—made available in its entirety only as recently as 1938—shows that, despite her pursuit of Algarotti to Italy in 1739 where she waited two years for a rendezvous with him, the romance was never more than her fantasy.

During the next twenty-three years in Italy and Europe, Lady Mary spent ten years in retirement in Brescia after a brief period in Avignon. Her last six years were spent in Venice and Padua. Her extensive correspondence with her daughter, as well as her diligent exchange of letters with her husband, give us a portrait of a woman who had chosen self-exile. She developed, through her correspondence, affectionate bonds with her daughter that had never been possible when they were together. Although her life was by no means entirely serene—the scandalous entrepreneur Palazzi swindled her of much of her property and goods—she painted for her family in these letters a picture of idyllic retreat in her garden, dairy farm, woods, and vineyards at Brescia. The letters that follow give an account of more sociable periods in Venice and Padua. She returned to London in late 1761 and died there in August 1762.

Lady Mary was a controversial woman in her own day and she still causes disagreement when her character is assessed. She was neither the promiscuous slattern that Pope accused her of being after their quarrel, nor even the misunderstood feminist that some recent critics make her, rather she was a talented, complex, and original woman whose literary talents gave a focus to her life and enabled her to escape the confinement of a decadent and frivolous society.

EDITIONS USED:

The Complete Letters of Lady Mary Wortley Montagu. Edited by Robert
    Halsband. Vol. II: 1721-51. Oxford: Clarendon Press, 1966-67.
The Letters and Works of Lady Mary Wortley Montagu. Edited by Lord
    Wharncliffe. Third edition with a new memoir by W. Moy Thomas. 2 vols.
    London: Bickers and Son, 1861.

SUGGESTED READINGS:

*Letters of the Right Honourable Lady Mary Wortley Montagu. Written During
    her Travels in Europe, Asia, and Africa* [1766]. With a Preface by Mary
    Astell [1724]. Fourth edition. New York, n.d.
Halsband, Robert. *The Life of Lady Mary Worltey Montagu.* Oxford:
    Clarendon Press, 1956.
Hufstader, Alice Anderson. "Lady Mary Wortley Montagu," in *Sisters of the
    Quill* New York: Dodd, Mead and Co., 1978.
Paston, George [Emily Morse Symonds]. *Lady Mary Wortley Montagu and
    her Times.* London and New York: G. P. Putnam's Sons, 1907.
Stuart, Lady Louisa. "Introductory Anecdotes" in *The Letters and Works of
Lady Mary Wortley Montagu,* Edited by Lord Wharncliffe. Third edition,
vol I. London: Bickers and Son, 1861.

Turkish Embassy Letters

To the Countess of Mar

Leipzig, Nov. 21, O.S. 1716.

I believe, dear sister, you will easily forgive my not writing to you from Dresden, as I promised, when I tell you, that I never went out of my chaise from Prague to this place.

You may imagine how heartily I was tired with twenty-four hours' post-travelling, without sleep or refreshment (for I can never sleep in a coach, however fatigued). We passed, by moonshine, the frightful precipices that divide Bohemia from Saxony, at the bottom of which runs the river Elbe; but I cannot say, that I had reason to fear drowning in it, being perfectly convinced, that, in case of a tumble, it was utterly impossible to come alive to the bottom. In many places, the road is so narrow, that I could not discern an inch of space between the wheels and the precipice. Yet I was so good a wife, as not to wake Mr. Wortley, who was fast asleep by my side, to make him share in my fears, since the danger was unavoidable, till I perceived, by the bright light of the moon, our postilions nodding on horseback, while the horses were on a full gallop. Then indeed I thought it very convenient to call out to desire them to look where they were going. My calling waked Mr. Wortley, and he was much more surprised than myself at the situation we were in, and assured me, that he passed the Alps five times in different places, without ever having gone a road so dangerous. I have been told since, that it is common to find the bodies of travellers in the Elbe; but, thank God, that was not our destiny; and we came safe to Dresden, so much tired with fear and fatigue, it was not possible for me to compose myself to write.

After passing these dreadful rocks, Dresden appeared to me a wonderfully agreeable situation, in a fine large plain on the banks of the Elbe. I was very glad to stay there a day to rest myself. The town is the neatest I have seen in Germany; most of the houses are new built; the Elector's palace is very handsome, and his repository full of curiosities of different kinds, with a collection of medals very much esteemed. Sir Robert Sutton, our King's envoy, came to see me here, and Madame de L———, whom I knew in London, when her husband was minister to the King of Poland there. She offered me all things in her power to entertain me, and brought some ladies with her, whom she presented to me. The Saxon ladies resemble the Austrian no more than the Chinese do those of London; they are very genteelly dressed, after the English and French modes, and have generally pretty faces, but they are the most determined *minaudières* in the whole world. They would think it a mortal sin against good-breeding, if they either spoke or moved in a natural manner. They all affect a little soft lisp, and a pretty pitty-pat step; which female frailties ought, however, to be forgiven them, in favour of their civility and good-nature to strangers, which I have a great deal of reason to praise.

The Countess of Cozelle is kept prisoner in a melancholy castle, some leagues from hence; and I cannot forbear telling you what I have heard of her, because it seems to me very extraordinary, though I foresee I shall swell my letter to the size of a pacquet.———She was mistress to the King of Poland (Elector of Saxony), with so absolute a dominion over him, that never any lady had so much power in that court. They tell a pleasant story of his Majesty's first declaration of love, which he made in a visit to her, bringing in one hand a bag of a hundred thousand crowns, and in the other a horse-shoe, which he snapped asunder before her face, leaving her to draw the consequences of such remarkable proofs of strength and liberality. I know not which charmed her most; but she consented to leave her husband, and to give herself up to him entirely, being divorced publicly, in such a manner as, by their laws, permits either party to marry again. God knows whether it was at this time, or in some other fond fit, but it is certain, the King had the weakness to make her a formal contract of marriage; which, though it could signify nothing during the life of the Queen, pleased her so well, that she could not be contented, without telling it to all the people she saw, and giving herself the airs of a queen. Men endure every thing while they are in love; but when the excess of passion was cooled by long possession, his Majesty began to reflect on the ill consequences of leaving such a paper in her hands, and desired to have it restored to him. But she rather chose to endure all the most violent effects of his anger, than give it up; and though she is one of the richest and most avaricious ladies of her country, she has refused the offer of the continuation of a large pension, and the security of a vast sum of money she has amassed; and has, at last, provoked the King to confine her person to a castle, where she endures all the terrors of a strait imprisonment, and remains still inflexible, either to threats or promises. Her violent passions have brought her indeed into fits, which it is supposed will soon put an end to her life. I cannot forbear having some compassion for a woman that suffers for a point of honour, however mistaken, especially in a country where points of honour are not over-scrupulously observed among ladies.

I could have wished Mr. Wortley's business had permitted him a longer stay at Dresden.

Perhaps I am partial to a town where they profess the protestant religion; but every thing seemed to me with quite another air of politeness than I have found in other places. Leipzig, where I am at present, is a town very considerable for its trade; and I take this opportunity of buying pages' liveries, gold stuffs for myself, &c. all things of that kind being at least double the price at Vienna; partly because of the excessive customs, and partly through want of genius and industry in the people, who make no one sort of thing there; so that the ladies are obliged to send, even for their shoes, out of Saxony. The fair here is one of the most considerable in Germany, and the resort of all the people of quality, as well as of the merchants. This is also a fortified town, but I avoid ever mentioning fortifications, being sensible that I know not how to speak of them. I am the more easy under my ignorance, when I reflect that I am sure you will willingly forgive the omission; for if I made you the most exact description of all the ravelins and bastions I see in my travels, I dare swear you would ask me, What is ravelin? and, What is a bastion?

Adieu, my dear sister!

To the Countess of Bristol

I am now preparing to leave Constantinople, and perhaps you will accuse me of hypocrisy when I tell you 'tis with regret; but as I am used to the air, and have learnt the language, I am easy here; and as much as I love travelling, I tremble at the inconveniences attending so great a journey with a numerous family, and a little infant hanging at the breast. However I endeavour upon this occasion to do as I have hitherto done in all the odd turns of my life; turn them, if I can, to my diversion. In order to this, I ramble every day, wrapped up in my *ferigée* and *asmáck,* about Constantinople, and amuse myself with seeing all that is curious in it.

I know you will expect that this declaration should be followed with some account of what I have seen. But I am in no humour to copy what has been writ so often over. To what purpose should I tell you that Constantinople is the ancient Byzantium? that 'tis at present the conquest of a race of people, supposed Scythians? that there are five or six thousand mosques in it? that Sancta Sophia was founded by Justinian? &c. I'll assure you 'tis not for want of learning that I forbear writing all these bright things. I could also, with very little trouble, turn over Knolles and Sir Paul Rycaut, to give you a list of Turkish emperors; but I will not tell you what you may find in every author that has writ of this country. I am more inclined, out of a true female spirit of contradiction, to tell you the falsehood of a great part of what you find in authors; as, for instance, in the admirable Mr. Hill, who so gravely asserts, that he saw in Sancta Sophia a sweating pillar, very balsamic for disordered heads. There is not the least tradition of any such matter; and I suppose it was revealed to him in vision during his wonderful stay in the Egyptian catacombs; for I am sure he never heard of any such miracle here.

'Tis also very pleasant to observe how tenderly he and all his brethren voyage-writers lament the miserable confinement of the Turkish ladies, who are perhaps more free than any ladies in the universe, and are the only women in the world that lead a life of uninterrupted pleasure exempt from cares; their whole time being spent in visiting, bathing, or the agreeable amusement of spending money, and inventing new fashions. A husband would be thought mad that exacted any degree of economy from his wife, whose expences are no way limited but by her own fancy. 'Tis his business to get money, and hers to spend it: and this noble prerogative extends itself to the very meanest of the sex. Here is a fellow that carries embroidered handkerchiefs upon his back to sell. And, as miserable a figure as you may suppose such a mean dealer, yet I'll assure you his wife scorns to wear any thing less than cloth of gold; has her ermine furs, and a very handsome set of jewels for her head. 'Tis true they have no places but the bagnios, and these can only be seen by their own sex; however, that is a diversion they take great pleasure in.

I was three days ago at one of the finest in the town, and had the opportunity of seeing a Turkish bride received there, and all the ceremony used on that occasion, which made me recollect the epithalamium of Helen, by Theocritus; and it seems to me, that the same customs have continued ever since. All the she-friends, relations, and acquaintance of the two families, newly allied, meet at the bagnio; several others go out of curiosity, and I believe there were that day two hundred women. Those that were or had been married placed themselves round the rooms on the marble sofas; but the virgins very hastily threw off their clothes, and appeared without other ornament or covering than their own long hair braided with pearl or ribbon. Two of them met the bride at the door, conducted by her mother and another grave relation. She was a beautiful maid of about seventeen, very richly dressed, and shining with jewels, but was presently reduced to the state of nature. Two others filled silver gilt pots with perfume, and began the procession, the rest following in pairs, to the number of thirty. The leaders sung an epithalamium, answered by the others in chorus, and the two last led the fair bride, her eyes fixed on the ground, with a charming affectation of modesty. In this order they marched round the three largest rooms of the bagnio. 'Tis not easy to represent to you the beauty of this sight, most of them being well proportioned and white skinned; all of them perfectly smooth and polished by the frequent use of bathing. After having made their tour, the bride was again led to every matron round the rooms, who saluted her with a compliment and a present, some of jewels, others of pieces of stuff, handkerchiefs, or little gallantries of that nature, which she thanked them for, by kissing their hands.

I was very well pleased with having seen this ceremony; and, you may believe me, the Turkish ladies have at least as much wit and civility, nay liberty, as among us. 'Tis true, the same customs that give them so many opportunities of gratifying their evil inclinations (if they have any), also put it very fully in the power of their husbands to revenge themselves if they are discovered; and I do not doubt but they suffer sometimes for their indiscretions in a very severe manner. About two months ago, there was found at day break, not very far from my house, the bleeding body of a young woman, naked, only wrapped in a coarse sheet, with two wounds of a knife, one in her side and another in her breast. She was not quite cold, and was so surprisingly beautiful, that there were very few men in Pera that did not go to look upon her; but it was not possible for any body to know her, no woman's face being known. She was supposed to have been brought in the dead of the night from the Constantinople side and laid there. Very little enquiry was made about the murderer, and the corpse was privately buried without noise. Murder is never pursued by the king's officers as with us. 'Tis the business of the next relations to revenge the dead person; and if they like better to compound the matter for money (as they generally do), there is no more said of it. One would imagine this defect in their government should make such tragedies very frequent, yet they are extremely rare; which is enough to prove the people are not naturally cruel. Neither do I think in many other particulars they deserve the barbarous character we give them. I am well acquainted with a Christian woman of quality who made it her choice to live with a Turkish husband, and is a very agreeable sensible lady. Her story is so extraordinary, I cannot forbear relating it; but I promise you it shall be in as few words as I can possibly express it.

She is a Spaniard, and was at Naples with her family when that kingdom was part of the Spanish dominion. Coming from thence in a felucca, accompanied by her brother, they were attacked by the Turkish admiral, boarded, and taken.—And now, how shall I modestly tell you the rest of her adventure? The same accident happened to her that happened to the fair Lucretia so many years before her. But she was too good a Christian to kill herself, as that heathenish Roman did. The admiral was so much charmed with the beauty and long-suffering of the fair captive, that, as his first compliment, he gave immediate liberty to her brother and attendants, who made haste to Spain, and in a few months sent the sum of four thousand pounds sterling as a ransom for his sister. The Turk took the money, which he presented to her, and told her she was at liberty. But the lady very discreetly weighed the different treatment she was likely to find in her native country. Her relations (as the kindest thing they could do for her in her present circumstances) would certainly confine her to a nunnery for the rest of her days. Her infidel lover was very handsome, very tender, very fond of her, and lavished at her feet all the Turkish magnificence. She answered him very resolutely, that her liberty was not so precious to her as her honour; that he could no way restore that but by marrying her; and she therefore desired him to accept the ransom as her portion, and give her the satisfaction of knowing, that no man could boast of her favours without being her husband. The admiral was transported at this kind offer, and sent back the money to her relations, saying, he was too happy in her possession. He married her, and never took any other wife, and (as she says herself) she never had reason to repent the choice she made. He left her some years after one of the richest widows in Constantinople. But there is no remaining honourably a single woman, and that consideration has obliged her to marry the present captain pashá (i.e. admiral), his successor.—I am afraid that you will think my friend fell in love with her ravisher; but I am willing to take her word for it, that she acted wholly on principles of honour, though I think she might be reasonably touched at his generosity, which is often found among the Turks of rank. . . .

Selections from the Letters*

To Francesco Algarotti [10 Sept. 1736]

Friday, past midnight

... I am a thousand times more to be pitied than the sad Dido, and I have a thousand more reasons to kill myself. But since until now I have not imitated her conduct, I believe that I shall live either by cowardice or by strength of character. I have thrown myself at the head of a foreigner just as she did, but instead of crying perjurer and villain when my little AEneas shows that he wants to leave me, I consent to it through a feeling of Generosity which Virgil did not think women capable of. In truth I admire myself for such extraordinary disinterestedness, and you should be happy to be loved in so singular a manner. The pure love which M[onsieu]r de Cambrai speaks of so eloquently is not so perfect as mine, and I have a devotion for you more zealous than any of the adorers of the Virgin has ever had for her. I believe that all these men have had a little vanity in their devotion, or they hoped for great rewards for their prayers. Here am I praying to you without hope that you will give me any credit at all for it, and I spend whole hours in my Study absorbed in the contemplation of your perfections. I remember the least of your words, your puerilities, your follies, even your very impertinences; I like everything in you, and I find you so different from the rest of mankind (who yet have the insolence to think themselves of the same species) that it does not surprise me that you have inspired sentiments which until now have not been inspired in anybody.—

Perhaps it is bad French that I write, but as my letters are in your hands to burn the moment that they bore you, I write whatever comes into my head. I haven't the vanity to dare hope I please you; I have no purpose except to satisfy myself by telling you that I love you,—and who will not love you? I invited Mademoiselle———to supper last night. We drank to your health, and she said naively that she had never seen anybody so attractive as you. I did

*Translated from French.

not answer, but these few words made her conversation so charming to me that I kept the poor girl until two o'clock in the morning, without speaking further of you, but happy to be with somebody who had seen you—what a bizarre pleasure! One must have a Heart filled with a strong passion, to be touched by trifles which seem of such little importance to others. My reason makes me see all its absurdity, and my Heart makes me feel all its importance. Feeble Reason! which battles with my passion and does not destroy it, and which vainly makes me see all the folly of loving to the degree that I love without hope of return. Yet you were sorry to leave; I saw it in your eyes, and there was no pretence at all in the chagrin which showed in your manner. I do not delude myself about the impossible; it was not me that you were sorry to leave, but surely you were sorry to leave London. So I could have held on to you, and it was a false delicacy which prevented me from making the proposal to you, and so I lost, through false shame, fear, and misplaced nobility, all the pleasure of my life.—

I don't know whether you understand anything of this Gibberish, but you must believe that you possess in me the most perfect friend and the most passionate lover. I should have been delighted if nature permitted me to limit myself to the first title; I am enraged at having been formed to wear skirts. . . .

This is the 2nd letter that I write. It is the only pleasure which is left to me. How mixed with bitterness that sad pleasure is!

To Francesco Algarotti [24 July 1739]

At last I depart tomorrow with the Resolution of a man well persuaded of his Religion and happy in his conscience, filled with faith and hope. I leave my friends weeping for my loss and bravely take the leap for another world. If I find you such as you have sworn to me, I find the Elysian Fields, and Happiness beyond imagining; if—But I wish to doubt no more, and at least I wish to enjoy my hopes. If you want to repay me for all that I am sacrificing, hurry to me in Venice, where I shall hasten my arrival as much as possible.

To Francesco Algarotti [c. 6 Sept. 1739]

Here I am at the feet of the Alps, and tomorrow I take the step which is to lead me into Italy. I commend myself to you in all perils like Don Quixote to his Dulcinea, and I have an imagination no less inflamed than his. Nothing frightens me, nothing diverts me a moment; absorbed in my own thoughts, neither the fatigues of the road nor the pleasures offered me in the towns have distracted me for an instant from the sweet contemplation in which I am immersed. . . .

To Francesco Algarotti 12 March [1740]

Why so little Sincerity? Is it possible that you could say that you remonstrated with me against Italy? On the contrary, I still have one of your letters, in which you assure me that whatever town I establish myself in you will not fail to go there yourself, and I chose Venice as that which suited you the most. You know that the least of your desires would have led me to decide even on Japan. Provence or Languedoc would have pleased me perfectly, and saved me much Fatigue and Expense. Recall, if you please, the Conversations which we had together, and you will confess that I should naturally have believed that the journey I have made was the one to bring me closest to you. Geneva is always full of English people, consequently hardly suitable for my Sojourn, Holland even less because of its proximity.

I am settled here where I have found pleasures which I had not at all expected. The Procurator Grimani (whose merit and importance you doubtless know) is so very much a Friend of mine that he has made it a point of pride to render Venice agreeable to me. I am sought out by all the most considerable Ladies and Gentlemen here. In brief, I am miraculously much better off than in London. I should certainly leave all the conveniences of my life a second time to make the happiness of yours if I were persuaded I was necessary to it. Be honourable enough to think about this seriously. Consult your Heart; if it tells you that you would be happy near me, I sacrifice all for that. It is no longer a sacrifice; your Friendship and your conversation will make the delights of my life. It is not possible for us to live in the same house, but you could lodge close to mine, and see me every day if you should want to. Tell me your thoughts frankly. If it is true that your inclination persuades you to choose this plan, I would return to France and settle in some provincial town where we could live in Tranquility.
March 12. N.S.

To Lady Bute [10 July 1748]

Dear Child,

I receiv'd yours of May the 12th but yesterday, July the 9th. I am surpriz'd you complain of my silence. I have never fail'd answering yours the post after I receiv'd them, but I fear, being directed to Twictnam (having no other direction from you), your servants there may have neglected them.

I have been this six weeks, and still am, at my Dairy house, which joins to my Garden. I believe I have allready told you it is a long mile from the Castle, which is situate in the midst of a very large village (once a considerable Town, part of the walls still remaining) and has not vacant ground enough about it to make a Garden, which is my greatest amusement; and it being now troublesome to walk or even go in the chaise till the Evening, I have fitted up in this farm house a room for my selfe, that is to say, strewd the floor with Rushes, cover'd the chimney with moss and branches, and adorn'd the Room with Basons of earthern ware (which is made here to great perfection) fill'd with Flowers, and put in some straw chairs and a Couch Bed, which is my whole Furniture.

This Spot of Ground is so Beautifull I am afraid you will scarce credit the Description, which, however, I can assure you shall be very litteral, without any embellishment from Imagination. It is on a Bank forming a kind of Peninsula rais'd from the River Oglio 50 foot, to which you may descend by easy staris cut in the Turf, and either take the air on the River, which is as large as the Thames at Richmond, or by walking an avenu two hundred yards on the side of it you find a Wood of a hundred acres, which was allready cut into walks and rideings when I took it. I have only added 15 Bowers in different views, with seats of Turf. They were easily made, here being a large quantity of under Wood, and a great number of wild Vines which twist to the Top of the highest Trees, and from which they make a very good sort of Wine they call Brusco. I am now writeing to you in one of these arbours, which is so thick shaded the Sun is not troublesome even at Noon. Another is on the side of the River, where I have made a camp Kitchin, that I may take the Fish, dress and eat it immediately, and at the same time see the Barks which ascend or Descend every day, to or from Mautua, Guastalla or Pont de vic, all considerable Towns. This little Wood is carpetted (in their succeeding seasons) with violets and strawberry, inhabited by a nation of Nightingales, and fill'd with Game of all kinds excepting Deer and wild Boar, the first being unknown here, and not being large enough for the other.

My Garden was a plain Vineyard when it came into my hands not two year ago, and it is with a small expence turn'd into a Garden that (apart from the advantage of the climate) I like better than that of Kensington. The Italian Vineyards are not planted like those in France, but in clumps fasten'd to Trees planted in equal Ranks (commonly fruit Trees) and continu'd in festoons from one to another, which I have turn'd into cover'd Gallerys of shade, that I can walk in the heat without being incommoded by it. I have made a dineing room of Verdure, capable of holding a Table of 20 Covers. The whole ground is 317 feet in length and 200 in Breadth. You see it is far from large, but so prettily dispos'd (thô I say it) that I never saw a more agreable rustic Garden, abounding with all sort of Fruit, and produces a variety of Wines. I would send you a piece if I did not fear the custom would make you pay too dear for it. I believe my Description gives you but an imperfect Idea of my Garden.

Perhaps I shall succeed better in describing my manner of life which is as regular as that of any Monastery. I generally rise at six, and as soon as I have breakfasted put my selfe at the head of my Weeder Women, and work with them till nine. I then inspect my Dairy and take a Turn amongst my Poultry, which is a very large enquiry. I have at present 200 chicken, besides Turkys, Geese, Ducks, and Peacocks. All things have hitherto prosper'd under my Care. My Bees and silk worms are double'd, and I am told that, without accidents, my Capital will be so in two years time. At 11 o'clock I retire to my Books. I dare not indulge my selfe in that pleasure above an hour. At 12 I constantly dine, and sleep after dinner till about 3. I then send for some of my old Priests and either play at picquet or Whist till tis cool enough to go out. One Evening I walk in my Wood where I often Sup, take the air on Horseback the next, and go on the Water the third. The Fishery of this part of the River belongs to me, and my Fisherman's little boat (where I have a green Lutestring Awning) serves me for a Barge. He and his Son are my Rowers, without any expence, he being very well paid by the profit of the Fish, which I give him on condition of having every day one dish for my Table. Here is plenty of every sort of Fresh Water Fish, excepting Salmon, but we have a large Trout so like it that I, that have allmost forgot the taste, do not distinguish it.

We are both plac'd properly in regard to our Different times of Life: you amidst the Fair, the Galant and the Gay, I in a retreat where I enjoy every amusement that Solitude can afford. I confess I sometimes wish for a little conversation, but I refflect that the commerce of the World gives more uneasyness than pleasure, and Quiet is all the Hope that can reasonably be indulg'd at my Age.

My letter is of an unconscionable length. I should ask your pardon for it, but I had a mind to give you an Idea of my passing my time. Take it as an instance of the affection of, Dear Child, your most affectionate Mother,

M. Wortley.

My Compliments to Lord Bute and blessing to my Grand children.

MRS JARENA LEE

Preacher of the A.M.E. Church.

Aged 60 years on the 11th day of the 2d month 1844.

Phila. 1844.

Jarena Lee (*Courtesy of the Houghton Library, Harvard University, from* Religious Experience and Journal of Mrs. Jarena Lee . . . , *1849*)

Jarena Lee, 1783–18?

Religious Experience and Journal of Mrs. Jarena Lee (1849)

In November 1787, Richard Allen and a friend, Absolom Jones, were in attendance at a Methodist church service in Philadelphia. Told to sit in the gallery, the place assigned to blacks, they refused and continued to pray as the white sexton attacked them. This early act of nonviolent resistance marked a significant point in the growing attempts on the part of whites in the post-Revolutionary years to segregate the churches. The experience determined both Allen and Jones to join the movement for separatist churches in which blacks could worship freely, one indication of black realization that the Revolution's rhetoric of freedom and independence had not been intended for them.

Richard Allen founded the African Methodist Episcopal Church and became a major figure in the history of black evangelical Protestantism. He came to symbolize, as Lerone Bennett has pointed out in *Pioneers in Protest,* "the importance of collective action on the part of Afro-Americans and the defiant assertion, backed by action, that Afro-Americans would not accept a subordinate role in any American organization."

Famous for his preaching as well as for his organizational skills, Allen was already a well-known figure in Philadelphia—the home of large numbers of free blacks—by the time Jarena Lee first came there in 1804 or 1805. Born in Cape May, New Jersey, on February 11, 1783, apparently of free parents, Jarena was sent to work as a serving maid at the age of seven. Her parents had been "wholly ignorant of the knowledge of God" and so she first learned of the power of religion through her employers. (After her conversion and during her preaching career she returned when she could to her family, as the following selection shows.) From a local preacher she received the conviction of sin and was so moved by it that she considered suicide. Four years later she was converted by the preaching of Richard Allen, and some time later experienced sanctification. "Four or five years after" she became convinced of her call to preach and again approached Allen, who suggested that she conduct prayer meetings instead. Their discipline, he said, "did not call for women preachers." Looking back as she writes her journal, she defends her request: "If the man may preach, because the Saviour died for him, why not the woman? seeing he died for her also. Is he not a whole Saviour instead of a half one? as those who hold it wrong for the woman to preach, would seem to make it appear. Did not Mary *first* preach the risen Saviour, and is not the doctrine of the resurrection the very climax of Christianity—hangs not all our hope on this, as argued by St. Paul? Then did not Mary, a woman, preach the gospel: for she preached the resurrection of the crucified Son of God." At the time, she accepted Allen's rejection of her request, feeling that "the holy energy which burned within me, as a fire, began to be smothered."

In 1811, Jarena married Joseph Lee, pastor to a congregation at Snow Hill, about six miles from Philadelphia. Between their move to Snow Hill and 1817, five members of her family died, including her husband. A widow with two very small children, she felt again the call to preach, and once again turned to Allen, by then Bishop of the African Methodist Episcopal Church. Hearing her preach, he rose in the congregation and announced her right to be a preacher. From that day began her remarkable career as a circuit-riding, Methodist preacher—going up and down the east coast, even into the slave-holding state of Maryland, and as far west as Ohio and Illinois, speaking to whites as well as to blacks, leading prayer meetings and "shoutings," encountering and resisting prejudices against women preachers.

She wrote her journal as she travelled, publishing it herself as she had earlier tracts. It blends the narrative of her pilgrimage with exhortations to the faithful and to those who might be falling away, designed, it appears, to make the story of her life an extension of her preaching. It is not certain that she was, as she claimed to be, the "first female preacher of the First African Methodist Episcopal Church." What does seem certain, however, is that she combines those qualities which W. E. B. DuBois was later to see as the source of the uniqueness of the black preacher, "the most unique personality developed by the Negro on American soil, . . . the combination of a certain adroitness with deep-seated earnestness, and of tact with consummate ability."

EDITION USED:

*Religious Experience and Journal of Mrs. Jarena Lee, Giving an Account of
Her Call to Preach the Gospel.* Philadelphia: Printed and Published for
the author, 1849.

SUGGESTED READING:

Bogin, Ruth, and Bert Loewenberg, eds., *Black Women in Nineteenth-
Century American Life.* University Park: Pennsylvania State University
Press, 1976.

Religious Experience and Journal of Mrs. Jarena Lee

The man who was to speak in the afternoon of that day, was the Rev. Richard Allen, since bishop of the African Episcopal Methodists in America. During the labors of this man that afternoon, I had come to the conclusion, that this is the people to which my heart unites, and it so happened, that as soon as the service closed he invited such as felt a desire to flee the wrath to come, to unite on trial with them—I embraced the opportunity. Three weeks from that day, my soul was gloriously converted to God, under preaching, at the very outset of the sermon. The text was barely pronounced, which was "I perceive thy heart is not right in the sight of God," when there appeared to *my* view, in the centre of the heart, *one* sin; and this was *malice* against one particular individual, who had strove deeply to injure me, which I resented. At this discovery I said, *Lord* I forgive *every* creature. That instant, it appeared to me as if a garment, which had entirely enveloped my whole person, even to my fingers' ends, split at the crown of my head, and was stripped away from me, passing like a shadow from my sight—when the glory of God seemed to cover me in its stead.

That moment, though hundreds were present, I did leap to my feet and declare that God, for Christ's sake, had pardoned the sins of my soul. Great was the ecstacy of my mind, for I felt that not only the sin of *malice* was pardoned, but all other sins were swept away together. That day was the first when my heart had believed, and my tongue had made confession unto salvation—the first words uttered, a part of that song, which shall fill eternity with its sound, was *glory to God*. For a few moments I had power to exhort sinners, and to tell of the wonders and of the goodness of Him who had clothed me with *His* salvation. During this the minister was silent, until my soul felt its duty had been performed, when he declared another witness of the power of Christ to forgive sins on earth, was manifest in my conversion.

From the day on which I first went to the Methodist Church, until the hour of my deliverance, I was strangely buffeted by that enemy of all righteousness—the devil.

I was naturally of a lively turn of disposition; and during the space of time from my first awakening until I knew my peace was made with God, I rejoiced in the vanities of this life, and then again sunk back into sorrow.

For four years I had continued in this way, frequently laboring under the awful apprehension, that I could never be happy in this life. This persuasion was greatly strengthened during the three weeks, which was the last of Satan's power over me, in this peculiar manner, on which account I had come to the conclusion that I had better be dead than alive. Here I was again tempted to destroy my life by drowning; but suddenly this mode was changed—and while in the dusk of the evening, as I was walking to and fro in the yard of the house, I was beset to hang myself with a cord suspended from the wall enclosing the secluded spot.

But no sooner was the intention resolved on in my mind, than an awful dread came over me, when I ran into the house; still the tempter pursued me. There was standing a vessel of water—into this I was strangly impressed to plunge my head, so as to extinguish the life which God had given me. Had I done this, I have been always of the opinion, that I should have been unable to have released myself; although the vessel was scarcely large enough to hold a gallon of water. Of me may it not be said, as written by Isaiah, (chap. 65, verses 1, 2.) "I am sought of them that asked not for me; I am found of them that sought me not." Glory be to God for his redeeming power, which saved me from the violence of my own hands, from the malice of Satan, and from eternal death; for had I have killed myself, a great ransom could not have delivered me; for it is written—"No murderer hath eternal life abiding in him." How appropriately can I sing—

> "Jesus sought me when a stranger,
>   Wandering from the fold of God;
> He to rescue me from danger,
>   Interposed his precious blood"

But notwithstanding the terror which seized upon me, when about to end my life, I had no view of the precipice on the edge of which I was tottering, until it was over, and my eyes were opened. Then the awful gulf of hell seemed to be open beneath me, covered only, as it were, by a spider's web, on which I stood. I seemed to hear the howling of the damned, to see the smoke of the bottomless pit, and to hear the rattling of those chains, which hold the impenitent under clouds of darkness to the judgment of the great day.

I trembled like Belshazzar, and cried out in the horror of my spirit, "God be merciful to me a sinner." That night I formed a resolution to pray; which, when resolved upon, there appeared, sitting in one corner of the room, Satan, in the form of a monstrous dog, and in a rage, as if in pursuit, his tongue protruding from his mouth to a great length, and his eyes looked like two balls of fire; it soon, however, vanished out of my sight. From this state of terror and dismay, I was happily delivered under the preaching of the Gospel as before related. . . .

The Subject of my Call to Preach Renewed

It was now eight years since I had made application to be permitted to preach the gospel, during which time I had only been allowed to exhort, and even this privilege but seldom. This subject now was renewed afresh in my mind; it was as a fire shut up in my bones. About thirteen months passed on, while under this renewed impression. During this time, I had solicited of the Rev. Bishop Richard Allen, who at this time had become bishop of the African Episcopal Methodists in America, to be permitted the liberty of holding prayer meetings in my own hired house, and of exhorting as I found liberty, which was granted me. By this means, my mind was relieved, as the house soon filled when the hour appointed for prayer had arrived.

I cannot but relate in this place, before I proceed further with the above subject, the singular conversion of a very wicked young man. He was a colored man, who had generally attended our meetings, but not for any good purpose; but rather to disturb and to ridicule our denomination. He openly and uniformly declared that he neither believed in religion, nor wanted any thing to do with it. He was of a Gallio disposition, and took the lead among the young people of color. But after a while he fell sick, and lay about three months in a state of ill health; his disease was a consumption. Toward the close of his days, his sister who was a member of the society, came and desired me to go and see her brother, as she had no hopes of his recovery, perhaps the Lord might break into his mind. I went alone, and found him very low. I soon commenced to inquire respecting his state of feeling, and how he found his mind. His answer was, "O tolerable well," with an air of great indifference. I asked him if I should pray for him. He answered in a sluggish and careless manner. "O yes, if you have time." I then sung a hymn, kneeled down and prayed for him, and then went my way.

Three days after this, I went again to visit the young man. At this time there went with me two of the sisters in Christ. We found the Rev. Mr. Cornish, of our denomination, laboring with him. But he said he received but little satisfaction from him. Pretty soon, however, brother Cornish took his leave; when myself, with the other two sisters, one of which was an elderly woman named Jane Hutt, the other was younger, both colored, commenced conversing with him, respecting his eternal interest, and of his hopes of a happy eternity, if any he had. He said but little, we then kneeled down together and besought the Lord in his behalf, praying that if mercy were not clear gone for ever, to shed a ray of softening grace upon the hardness of his heart. He appeared now to be somewhat more tender, and we thought we could perceive some tokens of conviction, as he wished us to visit him again, in a tone of voice not quite as indifferent as he had hitherto manifested.

But two days had elapsed after this visit, when his sister came to me in haste, saying, that she believed her brother was then dying, and that he had *sent* for me. I immediately called on Jane Hutt, who was still among us as a mother in Israel, to go with me. When we arrived there, we found him sitting up in bed, very restless and uneasy, but he soon laid down again. He now wished me to come to him, by the side of his bed. I asked him how he was. He said, Very ill; and added, "Pray for me, quick." We now perceived his time in this world to be short. I took up the hymn-book, and opened to a hymn suitable to his case, and commenced to sing, but there seemed to be a *horror* in the room—a darkness of a mental kind, which was felt by us all; there being five persons, except the sick young man and his nurse. We had sung but one verse, when they all gave over singing, on account of this unearthly sensation, but myself. I continued to sing on alone, but in a dull and heavy manner, though looking up to God all the while for help. Suddenly I felt a spring of energy awake in my heart, when darkness gave way in some degree. It was but a glimmer from above. When the hymn was finished, we all kneeled down to pray for him. While calling on the name of the Lord, to have mercy on his soul, and to grant him repentance unto life, it came suddenly into my mind never to rise from my knees until God should hear prayer in his behalf, until he should convert and save his soul.

Now, while I thus continued importuning heaven, as I felt I was led, a ray of light, more abundant, broke forth among us. There appeared to my view, though my eyes were closed, the Saviour in full stature, nailed to the cross, just over the head of the young man, against the ceiling of the room. I cried out, brother look up, the Saviour is come, he will pardon you, your sins he will forgive. My sorrow for the soul of the young man was gone; I could no longer pray—joy and rapture made it impossible. We rose up from our knees, when lo, his eyes were gazing with ecstacy upwards; over his face there was an expression of joy; his lips were clothed in a sweet and holy smile; but no sound came from his tongue; it was heard in its stillness of bliss; full of hope and immortality. Thus, as I held him by the hand, his happy and purified soul soared away, without a sigh or a groan, to its eternal rest.

I now closed his eyes, straightened out his limbs, and left him to be dressed for the grave. But as for me, I was filled with the power of the Holy Ghost—the very room seemed filled with glory. His sister and all that were in the room rejoiced, nothing doubting but he had entered into Paradise; and I believe I shall see him at the last and great day, safe on the shores of salvation.

But to return to the subject of my call to preach, soon after this, as above related, the Rev. Richard Williams was to preach at Bethel Church, where I with others were assembled. He entered the pulpit, gave out the hymn, which was sung, and then addressed the throne of grace; took his text, passed through the exordium, and commenced to expound it. The text he took is in Jonah, 2d chap. 9th verse,—"Salvation is of the Lord." But as he proceeded to explain, he seemed to have lost the spirit; when in the same instant, I sprang, as by altogether supernatural impulse, to my feet, when I was aided from above to give an exhortation on the very text which my brother Williams had taken.

I told them I was like Jonah; for it had been then nearly eight years since the Lord had called me to preach his gospel to the fallen sons and daughters of Adam's race, but that I had lingered like him, and delayed to go at the bidding of the Lord, and warn those who are as deeply guilty as were the people of Ninevah.

During the exhortation, God made manifest his power in a manner sufficient to show the world that I was called to labor according to my ability, and the grace given unto me, in the vineyard of the good husband-man.

I now sat down, scarcely knowing what I had done, being frightened. I imagined, that for this indecorum, as I feared it might be called, I should be expelled from the church. But instead of this, the Bishop rose up in the assembly, and related that I had called upon him eight years before, asking to be permitted to preach, and that he had put me off; but that he now as much believed that I was called to that work, as any of the preachers present. These remarks greatly strengthened me, so that my fears of having given an offence, and made myself liable as an offender, subsided, giving place to a sweet serenity, a holy joy of a peculiar kind, untasted in my bosom until then.

The next Sabbath day, while sitting under the word of the gospel, I felt moved to attempt to speak to the people in a public manner, but I could not bring my mind to attempt it in the church. I said, Lord, anywhere but here. Accordingly, there was a house not far off which was pointed out to me; to this I went. It was the house of a sister belonging to the same society with myself. Her name was Anderson. I told her I had come to hold a meeting in her house, if she would call in her neighbors. With this request she immediately complied. My congregation consisted of but five persons. I commenced by reading and singing a hymn; when I arose I found my hand resting on the Bible, which I had not noticed till that moment. It now occurred to me to take a text. I opened the Scripture, as it happened, at the 141st Psalm, fixing my eye on the third verse, which reads: "Set a watch, O Lord, before my mouth, keep the door of my lips." My sermon, such as it was, applied wholly to myself, and added an exhortation. Two of my congregation wept much, as the fruit of my labor this time. In closing, I said to the few, that if any one would open a door, I would hold a meeting the next sixth-day evening: when one answered that her house was at my service.

Accordingly I went, and God made manifest his power among the people. Some wept, while others shouted for joy. One whole seat of females, by the power of God, as the rushing of the wind, were all bowed to the floor, at once, and screamed out. Also a sick man and woman in one house, the Lord convicted them both; one lived, and the other died. God wrought a judgment—some were well at night, and died in the morning. At this place I continued to hold meetings about six months. During that time I kept house with my little son, who was very sickly. About this time I had to call to preach at a place about thirty miles distant, among the Methodists, with whom I remained one week, and during the whole time, not a thought of my little son came into my mind; it was hid from me, lest I should have been diverted from the work I had to do, to look after my son. Here by the instrumentality of a poor coloured woman, the Lord poured forth his spirit among the people. Though, as I was told, there were lawyers, doctors, and magistrates present, to hear me speak, yet there was mourning and crying among sinners, for the Lord scattered fire among them of his own kindling. The Lord gave his hand-maiden power to speak for his great name, for he arrested the hearts of the people, and caused a shaking amongst the multitude, for God was in the midst.

I now returned home, found all well; no harm had come to my child, although I left it very sick. Friends had taken care of it which was of the Lord. I now began to think seriously of breaking up housekeeping, and forsaking all to preach the everlasting Gospel. I felt a strong desire to return to the place of my nativity, at Cape May, after an absence of about fourteen years. To this place, where the heaviest cross was to be met with, the Lord sent me, as Saul of Tarsus was sent to Jerusalem, to preach the same gospel which he had neglected and despised before his conversion. I went by water, and on my passage was much distressed by sea sickness, so much so that I expected to have died, but such was not the will of the Lord respecting me. After I had disembarked, I proceeded on as opportunities offered, toward where my mother lived. When within ten miles of that place, I appointed an evening meeting. There were a goodly number came out to hear. The Lord was pleased to give me light and liberty among the people. After meeting, there came an elderly lady to me and said, she believed the Lord had sent me among them; she then appointed me another meeting there two weeks from that night. The next day I hastened forward to the place of my mother, who was happy to see me, and the happiness was mutual between us. With her I left my poor sickly boy, while I departed to do my Master's will. In this neighborhood I had an uncle, who was a Methodist, and who gladly threw open his door for meetings to be held there. At the first meeting which I held at my uncle's house, there was, with others who had come from curiosity to hear the woman preacher, an old man, who was a Deist, and who said he did not believe the coloured people had any souls—he was sure they had none. He took a seat very near where I was standing, and boldly tried to look me out of countenance. But as I labored on in the best manner I was able, looking to God all the while, though it seemed to me I had but little liberty, yet there went an arrow from the bent bow of the gospel, and fastened in his till then obdurate heart. After I had done speaking, he went out, and called the people around him, said that my preaching might seem a small thing, yet he believed I had the worth of souls at heart. This language was different from what it was a little time before, as he now seemed to admit that coloured people had souls, as it was to these I was chiefly speaking; and unless they had souls, whose good I had in view, his remark must have been without meaning. He now came into the house, and in the most friendly manner shook hands with me, saying, he hoped God had spared him to some good purpose. This man was a great slave holder, and had been very cruel; thinking nothing of knocking down a slave with a fence stake, or whatever might come to hand. From this time it was said of him that he became greatly altered in his ways for the better. At that time he was about seventy years old, his head as white as snow; but whether he became a converted man or not, I never heard. . . .

I travelled seven miles from the above place to Snow Hill on Sabbath morning, where I was to preach in the Church of which I was a member; and although much afflicted in body, I strove, by the grace of God, to perform the duty. This was once the charge of JOSEPH LEE. In this desk my lamented husband had often stood up before me, proclaiming the "acceptable year of the Lord"—here he labored with zeal and spent his strength to induce sinners to be "reconciled to God"—here his toils ended. And could it be, that a poor unworthy being like myself should be called to address his former congregation, and should stand in the same pulpit! The thought made me tremble. My heart sighed when memory brought back the image, and the reminiscences of other days crowded upon me. But why, my heart, dost though sigh? He has ceased from his labor, and I here see his works do follow. It will be enough, if these, the people of his care, press on and gain the kingdom. It will be enough, if, on the final day, "for which all other days were made," we pass through the gates into the city, and live again together where death cannot enter, and separations are unknown. Cease then, my tears—a little while, my fluttering heart! and the turf that covers my companion, perchance, may cover thee—a little while, my soul! if faithful, and the widow's God will call thee from this valley of tears and sorrows to rest in the mansions the Saviour has gone to prepare for his people. "Good what God gives—just what he takes away."

My mind was next exercised to visited Trenton, N.J. I spoke for the people there, but soon had felt the cross so heavy. Perhaps it was occasioned through grieving over the past, and my feelings of loneliness in the world. A sister wished me to go with her to Bridgeport—where I found brother Orwin, then elder over that church. He gave me an appointment. We had a full house, and

God's power was manifest among the people, and I returned to the elder's house rejoicing. The following day I walked fourteen miles to a meeting, where also we were greatly favored with the presence of God. Soon after this, I thought of going home to Philadelphia. I got about three miles on foot, when an apparent voice said, "If thou goest home thou wilt die." I paused for a moment, and not comprehending what it meant, pursued my journey. Again I was startled by something like a tapping on my shoulder, but, on turning round, I found myself alone, which two circumstances created a singular feeling I could not understand. I thought of Balaam when met by the angel in the way. I was taken sick and it seemed I should die in the road. I said I will go back, and walked about four miles to Bridgeport. Told a good sister my exercise, who was moved with sympathy, and got brandy and bathed me. On Wednesday night I spoke to the people at Trenton Bridge, and notwithstanding the opposition I had met with from brother Samuel R———, then on the circuit, the Lord supported the "woman preacher" and my soul was cheered. On Thursday I walked fourteen miles, when the friends applied to the elder to let me talk for them, but his prejudices also, against women preaching were very strong, and tried hard to disaffect the minds of the people. The dear man has since gone to stand before that God who knows the secrets of all hearts—and where, I earnestly pray, he may find some who have been saved by grace through the instrumentality of female preaching. . . .

I have travelled, in four years, sixteen hundred miles and of that I walked two hundred and eleven miles, and preached the kingdom of God to the falling sons and daughters of Adam, counting it all joy for the sake of Jesus. Many times cast down but not forsaken; willing to suffer as well as love. I spoke at Harris's Mills, in a dwelling house, to a large concourse of people, from Paul's Epistle to the Ephesians, xviii. 19-20. I felt much drawn out, in the Spirit of God, meanwhile from my feelings. I observed there were some present that never would meet me again. Mr. J. B., the elder, then requested me to lead the class. Much mourning, weeping and rejoicing. Four days afterwards, a man that sat under this sermon, (a shoemaker by occupation) fell dead from his bench without having any testimony of a hope in Christ. How dreadful to relate the wicked shall not live out half their days. In Easton I spoke from the Evan. John, 1 chap. 45 ver., the Lord's time. Then proceeded to Dagsberry, 25 miles, preached in Bethel Church to a multitude of people, it being to them a new thing, but only the old made more manifest. Bless God for what my heart feels, for a good conscience is better than a sacrifice. Two sermons preached in said Church, I spoke from Acts 13 chap., 41 ver.,—the power of God filled the place—some shouted, others mourned, some testified God for Christ's sake had forgiven sin, whilst others were felled to the floor. From thence we went to Sinapuxom, spoke on Sabbath day to a large congregation from Num. 24 chap., 17 ver.—the Lord gave light, life and liberty on that portion of Scripture. Great time. The elder closed the meeting, the memory of which will be sweet in eternity. I intended to take an appointment, but being taken sick the elder filled the appointment, and while preaching, there were 10 or 11 white men came and said they wanted to see the preacher; he sent for them to come into the house, but they seemed afraid or refused; after he had finished, they came to the door to know by what authority he was preaching—but it was me they were after, but I was fortified, for their laws, by my credentials, having the United States seal upon them,—they tried to get him out of the house, they said, on business. But he told them he would meet them at 9 o'clock in the morning before the magistrate, seven miles distant. Brother J. B. then took my credentials and also showed his own, and, upon examination, the magistrate said, she is highly recommended and I am bound to protect her. An under-officer, anxious to get hold of my papers, very much opposed to our being in the State, tried hard to frighten us out of it, and went to lay his hands on it, but was rebuked by the magistrate; and two days after the magistrate sent word to me to go on and preach, he did not care if I preached till I died. . . .

I was then sent for to return again to Owego, a distance of 38 miles, and they would pay my way on to Montrose, on my way to Philadelphia. I obeyed the request and found things very prosperous indeed. At night we had prayer meetings, and the Lord continued to pour out his spirit upon the people, and we had a meeting every night. Mr. J. H., formerly of Columbia, whose lot was cast as in a strange land, where there were only a few people that were members of the M. E. church; several husbands, strangers to God until now, and their wives, servants of the most High God, and two daughters of Mr. J. H., were justified through faith—three joined the church previously. I was selected to make a class book, and did so, as I wanted to see how many were for us. The Baptists had held an anxious meeting, after which five joined them. I made the trial by special invitation, and thirteen joined us. I had preached on Sabbath morning and night, and then held prayer meetings every night afterwards that week, except Saturday night; a man and his wife fell to the floor and cried for mercy, and both arose in the same hour soundly converted, giving God the glory. I preached on the next Sabbath morning and then led class, and at night again—text, Judges iv. 25, 26. They all marvelled at a woman taking such a deep subject, but the Lord assisted the organ of clay, and we had the victory, as there were twenty-one persons joined from that revival, and nearly all of them evinced justifying grace. On 3d day night we wound up, as I was to start on my journey on next day, which I did—brother paid my passage. I rode 28 miles in good company with a lady and gentleman who were going to New York. She said she was sorry to part; we had a heavy thunder storm with rain, and it was very dark, but we had a very careful driver, and we arrived safe at Montrose and took supper—between 12 and 1 o'clock at night I took stage for Wilkesbarre and arrived there at 8 next morning, and there I crossed the Susquehanna; I was very hungry, and having a little time I went to the house and asked the lady for breakfast and I would pay her. She said she had nothing, but would try and get me a good breakfast and take no pay, which she did. I truly feel thankful to God that he has proved himself a table in the wilderness. About 4 o'clock in the afternoon I arrived safe and was kindly received, and preached on Sabbath morning and night. Between the two appointments I rode two miles and preached in the afternoon. That day the Lord was in the house in power. Tuesday evening we had a glorious prayer meeting. I rode all night around the mountain, and some walked and appeared to be a quarter of a mile off. But the Lord preserved me in the mail stage alone. I adore his name now and I shall for evermore. The preacher in charge arrived the next day after I did, and spent his labors of love among the people. On the Wednesday following he went away and left me in charge of the class, (eight persons) to regulate them, and by the permission of the elder I addressed them. After I had relieved my mind and taken my seat the preacher formed them into a class and appointed a leader, who but three months before, was unconverted; but being so interested for the prosperity of Zion, seemed worthy of the appointment. After this I endeavored to hold prayer meetings through the week; preached twice on Sabbath day and helped to lead class, as the brother was young,—but they were all willing people, and truly it seemed to be the day of God's power among them, and "Peace abided at our House."

At the expiration of three weeks and four days I left them fifteen names on their class book. I then rode a distance of sixty miles over a hard road, hills and mountains, (there being no turn-pike or rail-road on that rout from Wilksbarre to Easton;)—some part of the way there was good sleighing. Through the help of Providence we arrived at Easton about 8'clock, P.M. I took supper and lodging in the Hotel, where I was well accommodated; after which I found a small number of colored friends. We had a meeting, and "it was good for us to be there." After this I called at New Hope, thirty-two miles I think from Philadelphia; visited the family I was brought up in, stopped and rested myself, as I felt much exhausted from travelling, so much winter and summer. I preached two or three times. Brother J.B.———was holding a protracted meeting. I gained strength; thank the Lord, and then left for home,and arrived in the city the last day of March 1842, having been two years, wanting a few days, almost incessantly travelling. I found my son, together with the rest of my family connections quite well; yet I could hear of the ravages of death, the relentless murderer, who never takes denials; my little grand-daughter, a promising child indeed, was taken with the rest. O! how soon delights may perish, and my heart responds—"The Lord's will be done."

My health being very much impaired, I knew not but that I should be the next one called away, but the Lord spared me for some other purpose, and upon my recovery I commenced travelling again, feeling it better to wear out than to rust out—and so expect to do until death ends the struggle—knowing, if I lose my life for Christ's sake, I shall find it again.

I now conclude—by requesting the prayers of God's people everywhere, who worship in His holy fear, to pray for me, that I ever may endeavor to keep a conscience void of offence, either towards God or man—for I feel as anxious to blow the Trumpet in Zion, and sound the alarm in God's Holy Mount, as ever;—

> Though Nature's strength decay,
>   And earth and hell withstand—
> To Canaan's land I'l urge my way,
>   At HIS Divine command.

But here I feel constrained to give over, as from the smallness of this pamphlet I cannot go through with the whole of my journal, as it would probably make a volume of two hundred pages; which, if the Lord be willing, may at some future day be published. But for the satisfaction of such as may follow after me, when I am no more, I have recorded how the Lord called me to his work, and how he has kept me from falling from grace, as I feared I should. In all things he has proved himself a God of truth to me; and in his service I am now as much determined to spend and be spent, as at the very first. My ardour for the progress of his cause abates not a whit, so far as I am able to judge, though I am now something more than fifty years of age.

As to the nature of uncommon impressions, which the reader cannot but have noticed, and possibly sneered at in the course of these pages, they may be accounted for in this way: It is known that the blind have the sense of hearing in a manner much more acute than those who can see: also their sense of feeling is exceedingly fine, and is found to detect any roughness on the smoothest surface, where those who can see find none. So it may be with such as I am, who has never had more than three months schooling; and wishing to know much of the way and law of God, have therefore watched the more closely, the operations of the Spirit, and have in consequence been led thereby. But let it be remarked that I have never found that Spirit lead me contrary to the Scriptures of truth, as I understand them. "For as many as are led by tha *Spirit* of God are the sons of God."—Rom. viii. 14.

I have now only to say, May the blessing of the Father, and of the Son, and of the Holy Ghost, accompany the reading of this poor effort to speak well of his name, wherever it may be read. AMEN.

P.S. Please to pardon errors, and excuse all imperfections, as I have been deprived of the advantages of education (which I hope all will appreciate) as I am measurably a self-taught person. I hope the contents of this work may be instrumental in leaving a lasting impression upon the minds of the impenitent; may it prove to be encouraging to the justified soul, and a comfort to the sanctified.

Though much opposed, it is certainly essential in life, as Mr. Wesley wisely observes. Thus ends the Narrative of JARENA LEE, the first female preacher of the First African Methodist Episcopal Church.

BETHEL AT PHILADELPHIA, PENN., UNITED STATES OF AMERICA.
FINIS.

Sara Coleridge (*Courtesy of the Houghton Library, Harvard University, from* Memoir and Letters of Sara Coleridge, *1874*)

Sara Coleridge, 1802–1852

Memoir and Letters (1873)

Sara Coleridge was born on December 22, 1802, at Greta Hall, near Keswick, the daughter of Samuel Taylor Coleridge and his wife, Sara (Fricker). Her girlhood was spent with her mother and brothers in the household of her uncle, the poet Southey, and also frequently in the company of the Wordsworths at Grasmere, where her father spent a number of the years of his separation from his family. Although she did not see her father for a period of about ten years when she was growing up, Sara became re-acquainted with him after her marriage and was a companion in his intellectual life as well as a favorite in his affections.

Her father, as well as his fellow poet Wordsworth, were awed by Sara's intellectual abilities. Her education (she was partly self-taught) included a knowledge of the classics, which enabled her to translate at her uncle Southey's initiative a three-volume work in Latin by a missionary in Paraguay, Martin Dobrizhoffer, and also included a mastery of French, Italian, German, and Spanish. Her editor-daughter, Edith Coleridge, also mentions her remarkable knowledge of theology, philosophy, and natural history—particularly botany and zoology. In 1825, she translated from the French, *Memoirs of the Chevalier Bayard, by the Loyal Servant.* Her own literary works were limited to children's stories, *Pretty Lessons for Good Children* (1834), and a fantasy, *Phantasmion,* published anonymously in 1837. Her real genius, however, was for scholarship and as one of the early editors of her father's work, including his *Biographia Literaria, Notes and Lectures on Shakespeare, Essays on his Own Times* and others, she showed genuine originality. A Wordsworth scholar and later correspondent with Sara Coleridge, Professor Henry Reed, wrote of her editing that it showed "an affluence of learning which, differently and more prominently presented, would have made her famous." Much of her correspondence, collected by her daughter, was written after the death of her husband and cousin, Henry Nelson Coleridge, who had been a great admirer of Samuel Taylor Coleridge and had become his literary executor. Sara Coleridge's intellectual life came into its own when she was a widow and after she assumed her husband's role as executor and editor of her father's works. Like Anne Bradstreet, she wrote a Memoir in the form of a letter to her children—to her daughter Edith—during her last illness and was unable to complete it before her death in May, 1852.

Sara Coleridge is another of England's "learned ladies." The image of the "learned lady" had changed considerably since the time of predecessors such as Margaret Cavendish and Lady Mary Montagu (whose work has been included above). No longer an eccentric recluse or a dazzling wit, the "Intellectual Lady"—as Sara Coleridge calls her—was rather self-consciously feminine and mild-mannered. In fact, Sara maintains that "all the women of first-rate genius" that she knew were "diffident, feminine, and submissive." Middle-class gentility seemed to have washed out some of the color and vitality of the earlier aristocratic women. However, Sara Coleridge was "submissive" only in manner and far too much has been made by her biographers of the image of her as "mild as Moonlight"—her doting father's description of her as an infant. Her letters show a woman whose intellect and critical abilities were entirely independent. In fact, she writes to a male friend who had found "intellectual ladies" unattractive that as a woman "no longer young" she had passed into a new "tough state of mind" where she no longer aimed to please the gentlemen but rather she aimed "to set them to rights, lay down the law to them." She concluded that "intellectualism" will "not be abandoned by us to please the gentlemen."

Even in her widowhood, her greatest period of intellectual activity, Sara Coleridge avoided fame and remained personally mild-mannered. Like some of her contemporary women writers, such as Charlotte Brontë, Elizabeth Gaskell, even Harriet Martineau, she stayed within the social conventions of her day. She was intensely interested in the work of other women and quick to admire their talents. Her letters, which discuss the work of the leading male writers such as Arnold, Carlyle, Ruskin, Dickens and poets, such as Keats, Shelley, and Tennyson, also acknowledge and honor women writers—some of them in the former century—such as Inchbald, Burney, Edgeworth, Jane Austen ("the princess of the novel"), and others. The writings of Miss Hannah More—much praised by the pious—she found not to her taste and insisted that More's literary genius was vastly overrated. In her own day she admired the work of Harriet Martineau, among others, and particularly the novels of Charlotte Brontë, *Jane Eyre* and *Shirley,* which she praised as "full of genius." Not surprisingly, when *Jane Eyre* first came out she had staunchly argued that it could only have been by a man and even in her subsequent recognition of its author, she spoke of its "masculine energy." But she found it full of "a spirit, a glow and fire."

In her correspondence with Professor Reed, Sara Coleridge recollects the important formative influences of Wordsworth and Southey—the former on the development of her intellect and the latter on the growth of her "character." But, she continues, "I never adopted the opinions of either *en masse,"* and she adds, that since her maturity, she has greatly modified many of their ideas and judgments. For one brought up amidst an extraordinarily gifted group of masculine personalities—her father, Southey, Wordsworth, De Quincey, among the major figures—all of whom admired her and indulged her gifts but who wanted her to grow up in the image they had created for her, Sara Coleridge achieved a remarkable independence of spirit and intellect. She said of Wordsworth, whose memory she held in great reverence that his poem "The Triad"—a portrait of herself, Dora Wordsworth, and Edith Southey—was a "mongrel" and the description in it "extravagant and unnatural." Like her assessment of his poetry in which she distinguishes the great from the mediocre, her critical abilities were free of sentimentality and her judgments were entirely her own.

EDITION USED:

Memoir and Letters of Sara Coleridge. Edited by her daughter [Edith
    Coleridge]. New York: Harper Brothers Publishers, 1874.

SUGGESTED READINGS:

Broughton, L. N. *Sara Coleridge and Henry Reed.* Itahaca, New York:
    Cornell University Press, 1937.
Griggs, Earl Leslie. *Coleridge Fille: A Biography of Sara Coleridge.* London:
    Oxford University Press, 1940.
Towle, Mrs. Eleanor A. *A Poet's Children: Hartley and Sara Coleridge.*
    London: Methuen and Co., 1912.

Memoir: Recollection of the Early Life of Sara Coleridge . . .

My young life is almost a blank in memory from that well-remembered evening of my return from our series of southern visits, till the time of my visit to Allan Bank, when I was six years old. That journey to Grasmere gleams before me as the shadow of a shade. Some goings on of my stay there I remember more clearly. Allan Bank is a large house on a hill, overlooking Easedale on one side, and Grasmere on the other. Dorothy, Mr. Wordsworth's only daughter, was at this time very picturesque in her appearance, with her long, thick, yellow locks, which were never cut, but curled with papers—a thing which seems much out of keeping with the poetic simplicity of the household. I remember being asked by my father and Miss Wordsworth, the poet's sister, if I did not think her very pretty. "No," said I, bluntly; for which I met a rebuff which made me feel as if I was a culprit.

My father's wish it was to have me for a month with him at Grasmere, where he was domesticated with the Wordsworths. He insisted upon it that I became rosier and hardier during my absence from mamma. She did not much like to part with me, and I think my father's motive, at bottom, must have been a wish to fasten my affections on him. I slept with him, and he would tell me fairy stories when he came to bed at twelve and one o'clock. I remember his telling me a wild tale, too, in his study, and my trying to repeat it to the maids afterward.

I have no doubt there was much enjoyment in my young life at that time, but some of my recollections are tinged with pain. I think my dear father was anxious that I should learn to love him and the Wordsworths and their children, and not cling so exclusively to my mother, and all around me at home. He was therefore much annoyed when, on my mother's coming to Allan Bank, I flew to her, and wished not to be separated from her any more. I remember his showing displeasure to me, and accusing me of want of affection. I could not understand why. The young Wordsworths came in and caressed him. I sat benumbed; for truly nothing does so freeze affection as the breath of jealousy. The sense that you have done very wrong, or at least given great offense, you know not how or why—that you are dunned for some payment of love or feeling which you know not how to produce or to demonstrate on a sudden—chills the heart, and fills it with perplexity and bitterness. My father reproached me, and contrasted my coldness with the childish caresses of the little Wordsworths. I slunk away, and hid myself in the wood behind the house, and there my friend John, whom at that time I called my future husband, came to seek me.

It was during this stay at Allan Bank that I used to see my father and Mr. De Quincey pace up and down the room in conversation. I understood not, nor listened to a word they said, but used to note the handkerchief hanging out of the pocket behind, and long to clutch it. Mr. Wordsworth, too, must have been one of the room walkers. How gravely and earnestly used Samuel Taylor Coleridge and William Wordsworth, and my Uncle Southey also, to discuss the affairs of the nation, as if it all came home to their business and bosoms—as if it were their private concern! Men do not canvass these matters nowadays, I think, quite in the same tone. Domestic concerns absorb their deeper feelings; national ones are treated more as things aloof, the speculative rather than the practical.

My father used to talk to me with much admiration and affection of Sarah Hutchinson, Mrs. Wordsworth's sister, who resided partly with the Wordsworths, partly with her own brothers. At this time she used to act as my father's amanuensis. She wrote out great part of the "Friend" to his dictation. She had fine, long, light-brown hair, I think her only beauty, except a fair skin, for her features were plain and contracted, her figure dumpy, and devoid of grace and dignity. She was a plump woman, of little more than five foot. I remember my father talking to me admiringly of her long light locks, and saying how mildly she bore it when the baby pulled them hard in play.

Miss Wordsworth, Mr. Wordsworth's sister of most poetic eye and temper, took a great part with the children. She told us once a pretty story of a primrose, I think, which she spied by the way-side when she went to see me soon after my birth though that was at Christmas, and how this same primrose was still blooming when she went back to Grasmere.

* * * My father had particular feelings and fancies about dress, as had my Uncle Southey and Mr. Wordsworth also. He could not abide the scarlet socks which Edith and I wore at one time. I remember going to him when mamma had just dressed me in a new stuff frock. He took me up, and set me down again without a caress. I thought he disliked the dress; perhaps he was in an uneasy mood. He much liked every thing feminine and domestic, pretty and becoming, but not fine-ladyish. My Uncle Southey was all for gay, bright, cheerful colors, and even declared he had a taste for the *grand,* in half jest.

Mr. Wordsworth loved all that was rich and picturesque, light and free, in clothing. A deep Prussian blue or purple was one of his favorite colors for a silk dress. He wished that white dresses were banished, and that our peasantry wore blue and scarlet, and other warm colors, instead of sombre, dingy black, which converts a crowd that might be ornamental in the landscape into a swarm of magnified ants. I remember his saying how much better young girls looked of an evening in bare arms—even if the arms themselves were not very lovely; it gave such a lightness to their general air. I think he was looking at Dora when he said this. White dresses he thought cold, a blot and disharmony in any picture, in-door or out-of-door. My father admired white clothing because he looked at it in reference to woman, as expressive of her delicacy and purity, not merely as a component part of a general picture.

My father liked my wearing a cap. He thought it looked girlish and domestic. Dora and I must have been a curious contrast—she with her wild eyes, impetuous movements, and fine, long, floating yellow hair—I with my timid, large blue eyes, slender form, and little, fair, delicate face, muffled up in lace border and muslin. But I thought little of looks then; only I fancied Edith S., on first seeing her, most beautiful.

I attained my sixth year on the Christmas after this my first Grasmere visit. It must have been the next summer that I made my first appearance at the dancing-school, of which more hereafter. All I can remember of this first entrance into public is that our good-humored, able, but rustical dancing-master, Mr. Yewdale, tried to make me dance a minuet with Charlie Denton, the youngest of our worthy pastor's home flock, a very pretty, rosy-cheeked, large-black-eyed, compact little laddikin. But I was not quite up to the business. I think my beau was a year older. At all events, it was I who broke down, and Mr. Yewdale, after a little impatience, gave the matter up. All teaching is wearisome; but to teach dancing, of all teaching the wearisomest.

The last event of my earlier childhood which abides with me is a visit to Allonby, when I was nine years old, with Mrs. Calvert. I remember the ugliness and meanness of Allonby (the town, a cluster of red-looking houses, as far as I recollect), and being laughed at at home for describing it as "a pretty place," which I did conventionally, according to the usual practice, as I conceived, of elegant letter-writers. The sands are really fine in their way, so unbroken and extensive, capital for galloping over on pony-back. I recollect the pleasures of these sands, and of the sea-side animation and vegetation; the little close, white Scotch roses; the shells; the crabs of every size, from Liliputian to Brobdingnagian, crawling in the pools; the sea-anemones, with their flower-like appendages, which we kept in jugs of salt-water, delighted to see them draw in their petals, or expand them by a sudden blossoming; the sea-weed, with its ugly berries, of which we made hideous necklaces. All these things I recollect, but not what I should most regard now—the fine forms of the Scotch hills on the opposite coast, sublime the distance, and the splendid sunsets which give to this sort of landscape a gorgeous filling up.

Of the party, besides J. and R. Calvert and M., their sister, were Tom and William M———, two sons of Mrs. Calvert's sister, Mrs. M———. We used to gallop up and down the wide sands on two little ponies, a dark one called

Sancho, and a light one called Airey, behind the boys. M. and I sometimes quarreled with the boys, and, of course, in a trial of strength, got the worst of it. I remember R. and the rest bursting angrily into our bedroom and flinging a pebble at M., enraged at our having dared to put crumbs into their porridge; not content with which inroad and onslaught, they put mustard into ours next morning, the sun having gone down upon their boyish wrath without quenching it. One of them said it was all that little vixen, Sara Coleridge; M. was quiet enough by herself.

I had a leaven of malice, I suppose, in me, for I remember being on hostile terms with some little old woman, who lived by herself in a hut, and who took offense at something I did, as it struck me, unnecessarily. She repaired to Mrs. Calvert to complain, and the head and front of her accusation was, "That'un (meaning me) ran up and down the mound before her door." Mrs. C. thought this no heinous offense; but it was done by me, no doubt, with an air of derision. The crone was one of those morose, ugly, withered, ill-conditioned, ignorant creatures who in earlier times were persecuted as witches, and tried to be such. Still I ought to have been gently corrected for my behavior, and told the duty of bearing with the ill-temper of the poor and ignorant and afflicted.

At this time, on coming to Allonby,I was rather delicate. I remember that Mrs. Calvert gave me a glass of port wine daily, which she did not give to the other children. Oh, me, how rough these young Calverts and M———s were! and yet they had a certain respect for me, mingled with a contrary feeling I was honored among them for my extreme agility—my power of running and leaping. They called me "Cheshire cat" because I "grinned," said they. "Almost as pretty as Miss Cheshire," said Tom M. to me one day, of some admired little girl.

Such are the chief *historical* events of my little life up to nine years of age. But can I in any degree retrace what being I was then?—what relation my then being held to my maturer self? Can I draw any useful reflection from my childish experience, or found any useful maxim upon it? What *was* I? In person, very slender and delicate, not habitually colorless, but often enough pallid and feeble looking. Strangers used to exclaim about my eyes, and I remember remarks made upon their large size, both by my Uncle Southey and Mr. Wordsworth. I suppose the thinness of my face, and the smallness of the other features, with the muffling close cap, increased the apparent size of the eye, for only artists, since I have grown up, speak of my eyes as large and full. They were bluer, too, in my early years than now. My health alternated, as it has done all my life, till the last ten or twelve years, when it has been unchangeably depressed, between delicacy and a very easy, comfortable condition. I remember well that nervous sensitiveness and morbid imaginativeness had set in with me very early. During my Grasmere visit I used to feel frightened at night on account of the darkness. I then was a stranger to the whole host of night-agitators—ghosts, goblins, demons, burglars, elves, and witches. Horrid ghastly tales and ballads, of which crowds afterward came in my way, had not yet cast their shadows over my mind. And yet I was terrified in the dark, and used to think of lions, the only form of terror which my dark-engendered agitation would take. My next bugbear was the Ghost in "Hamlet." Then the picture of Death at Hell-gate in an old edition of "Paradise Lost," the delight of my girlhood. Last and worst came my Uncle Southey's ballad horrors—above all the Old Woman of Berkeley. Oh, the agonies I have endured between nine and twelve at night, before mamma joined me in bed, in presence of that hideous assemblage of horrors—the horse with eyes of flame! I dare not, even now, rehearse these particulars, for fear of calling up some of the old feeling, which, indeed, I have never in my life been quite free from. What made the matter worse was that, like all other nervous sufferings, it could not be understood by the inexperienced, and consequently subjected the sufferer to ridicule and censure. My Uncle Southey laughed heartily at my agonies. I mean, at the cause. He did not enter into the agonies. Even mamma scolded me for creeping out of bed after an hour's torture, and stealing down to her in the parlor, saying I could bear the loneliness and the night-fears no longer. But my father understood the case better. He insisted that a lighted candle should be left in my room, in the interval between my retiring to bed and mamma's joining me. From that time forth my sufferings ceased. I believe they would have destroyed my health had they continued.

Yet I was a most fearless child by daylight—ever ready to take the difficult mountain-path and outgo my companions' daring in tree-climbing. In those early days we used to spend much of our summer-time in trees, greatly to the horror of some of our London visitors.

On reviewing my earlier childhood, I find the predominant reflection.

.   .   .   .

Letters

IV. Intellectual Ladies, Modern and Ancient

TO AUBREY DE VERE, Esq.:

Chester Place, August 20, 1847.—I had a very interesting talk last night with Mr. H. T., who is looking remarkably well. He put in a strong light the unattractiveness of intellectual ladies to gentlemen, even those who are themselves on the intellectual side of the world—men of genius, men of learning and letters. I could have said, in reply, that while women are young, where there is a pretty face, it covers a multitude of sins, even intellectuality; where there is not that grand desideratum to young marrying men, a love of books does not make the matter much worse in one way, and does make it decidedly better in the other: that when youth is past, a certain number of persons are bound to us, in the midst of all our plainness and pedantry; these old friends and lovers cleave to us for something underneath *all that,* not only below the region of good looks, skin, lip, and eye, but even far deeper down than the intellect, for our individual, moral, personal being, which shall endure when we shall be where all will see as angels ken, and intellectual differences are done away: that as for the *world of gentlemen at large*—that world which a *young* lady desires, in an indefinite, infinite way, to charm and smite—we that are no longer young pass into a new, old-womanish, tough state of mind; to *please* them is not so much the aim as to set them to rights, lay down the law to them, convict them of their errors, pretenses, superficialities, etc., etc.; in short, tell them a *bit of our mind.* This, of course, is as foolish an ambition as the other, even more preposterous; but it is so far better that even where the end fails, the means themselves are a sort of end, and a considerable amusement and excitement. So that intellectualism, if it be not wrong in itself, will not be abandoned by us to please the gentlemen.

God bless you, and prosper you in all your labors, for your country's sake and your own. But do not forget the Muses altogether. Those are intellectual ladies who *have* attractions for gentlemen worth pleasing, and who retain "the bland composure of perpetual youth" beside their refreshing Hippocrene.

To Professor Henry Reed, Philadelphia: Chester Place, May 19, 1851.—

But I must break away from this subject altogether into one of a different sort—"like"—indeed—because full of reference to the moral & spiritual. "Yet oh! how different!" The Poet Wordsworth & his Poetry differ from Theology as the speculative Intellect & Intelligence of man, from Practical Reason and the Will. I dare say that you and your friend Mr. Yarnall have lately been dwelling a good deal on the two-volume Memoir of Wordsworth—which I finished slowly perusing last night in my hours of wakefulness. For, alas! I sleep but every other night,—the intervening one is now almost wholly sleepless. Mr. H. C. Robinson requested that I would use the pencil or pen freely on the margins of his copy. The more notes the better. I fear he will be greatly disappointed by what I have written, and I almost wish it rubbed out, it is so trifling & in some instances not to the purpose—as I fear the owner of the book will think. I knew—and honor dear Mr. Wordsworth perhaps as well as I have ever known any one in the world—more intimately than I knew my Father, and as intimately as I knew my Uncle Southey. There was much in him to know and the lines of his character were deep and strong,—the whole they formed simple and impressive. His discourse as compared with my Father's was as the Latin language to the Greek, or to borrow a comparison which has been applied to Shakespeare and Milton, as statuary to painting: it was intelligible at once and easily remembered. But in my youth when I enjoyed such ample opportunities of taking in his mind, I listened to "enjoy" and not to "understand," much less to report and inform others. In our spring time of life we are poetical, not literary, and often absorb unconsciously the intellectual airs that blow, or stilly dwell, around us, as our bodies do the fragrant atmosphere of May, full of the breath of primroses and violets, and are nourished thereby without reflecting upon the matter, any more than we classify and systemize after Linnaeus or Jussieu the vernal blossoms which delight our outward senses. I used to take long walks with Mr. Wordsworth about Rydal & Grasmere and sometimes, though seldomer, at Keswick, to his Applethwaite cottage, listening to his talk all the way; and for hours have I often listened when he conversed with my Uncle, or in doors at Rydal Mount when he chatted or harangued to the inmates of his household or the neighbours. But I took no *notes* of his discourse either on the tablet of memory or on material paper: my mind and turns of thought were gradually moulded by his conversation and the influences under which I was brought by his means in matters of intellect, whilst in those which concerned the heart and the moral being I was still more, more deeply and importantly indebted to the character and daily conduct of my admirable Uncle Southey. Yet I never adopted the opinions of either *en masse,* and since I have come to years of secondary and more mature reflection I have been unable to retain many which I received from them. The impression upon my feelings of their minds remains unabated in force, but the formal views and judgments which I received from their lips, are greatly modified, though not more than they themselves modified and readjusted their own views and judgments from youth to age. I have felt deep interest in going through Dr. Wordsworth's *compilation* of fragments and scraps of the great man's life of thought and action, and think it does credit to the biographer's industry and to his discretion and good nature, though its merits as a literary performance are but negative. It does not positively misrepresent the subject, as Pickersgill's portrait, with neat shiny boots, velvet waistcoat, and sombre sentimentalism of countenance misrepresents him, but it exhibits him partially [,] disproportionately and brokenly, as one sees the oars of a boat, half in half out of the water; it puts his life-landscape also to my eye not a little out of perspective. Mr. Henry Taylor says, I think, quite justly, that the biographer has undertaken a subject of which he knows nothing, except externally & superficially, and has performed his task in a business-like way; and would have done better if he had confined himself to a business-like unpretending style throughout: the worst of his performance being the little attempts at independent poetical criticism & *purpureal patches* of high-flown moral & literary declamation which he introduces here & there. Dr. Ch. Wordsworth is an able writer in his own way, and as a controversial theologian displays great vivacity—sometimes approaching to wit, and considerable information, with I suppose a sufficiency of logical dexterity; but of poetry and speculative spirituality I believe him to have very little, at first hand; his relative estimate of his great Uncle's poetical production seems to me to prove that he has but a dim and partial intuition of the Wordsworthian genius. I doubt whether he sees or feels the measureless distance between such *essential* poetry as that of Wordsworth in its true generic character, its vigorous youth & manhood, and such verse as that of Mr. Keble, which gives evidence of a refined and poetical cast of thought, but not I should say, except in a slight degree, of creative power or poetic imagination. It is only a certain proportion of the large mass of persons who read poems and like to have favourite subjects of thought adorned—or to express myself humbly—*smartened* up with conventional poetic diction, who really like poetry *per se* or thought essentially poetical, and which would evaporate in any attempt to exhibit it in prose. To these Dr. W. does not seem to belong, and if so, he must be incapable of appreciating what is *immortal* in his Uncle's productions; the vital portion, by virtue of which the mass will continue to exist in the minds of men. Are you not amused by his thinking it necessary to apologize for the "Lines on revisiting the Wye &c" and buttress them up by the "Evening Voluntaries"? as if one should call upon Pugin to strengthen some of our old Cathedrals by his modern additions. Certainly if Wordsworth's Muse would be convicted of an irreligious Pantheism by that noble and exquisitely modulated poetic strain, Pantheistic she is and practically must be, whatever the *man* Wordsworth, in the late decline of his genius, thought fit to say in verse. The "Evening Voluntaries" can never piece out Lines on revisiting the Wye, "The Leechgatherer" the "Old Cumberland Beggar," "Ode on intimations of Immortality," and *id genus omne* of his poems, whatever it may tell us of Mr. Wordsworths state of feeling and convictions in the latter years of his life.

PORTRAIT OF LADY ANNE BLUNT IN ARAB COSTUME (BY MOLONY).

Lady Anne Blunt (*Courtesy of the Houghton Library, Harvard University, from* A
Pilgrimage to Nejd, *1881*)

Lady Anne Blunt, 1837–1917

A Pilgrimage to Nejd, the Cradle of the Arab Race (1881)

Lady Anne Isabella King Noel was born on September 22, 1837, daughter of the first Earl of Lovelace and Ada Augusta (Lord Byron's daughter). As Lord Byron's granddaughter, she inherited some of the family notoriety but also some of her famous grandparent's talents. Unlike her grandfather she was not a poet, but like him she was an imaginative traveller into other lands. She was also a gifted translator and scholar and a superb linguist with an outstanding knowledge of classical Arabic. Her translation from Arabic of "The Seven Golden Odes," which her husband Wilfred Scawen Blunt rendered into poetry, made a great classic work available for the first time to the non-Arabic speaking world. Her two accounts of her journeys in the Middle East and Asia—*Bedouin Tribes of the Euphrates* (1879) and *A Pilgrimage to Nejd* (1881)—were based on her observation, her journals, and her husband's notes. Blunt contributed parts of the factual chapters, styling himself as her "editor," but the narratives have the mark of Lady Anne. "Observations of the exotic, male-dominated Arabia," as one of her commentators notes, "are filtered through an aristocratic woman's consciousness." Her husband, who became renowned as a writer, poet, diplomat, and statesman, takes a second place in these travel memoirs.

Lady Anne belongs to the English tradition of the Victorian traveller, who was fascinated with the adventure and mystery of Africa and Asia. Among the men were the famous Richard Burton, William Palgrave, Charles Doughty, and, later, T. E. Lawrence. The women included Burton's wife, Lady Isabel, Lucie Duff Gordon who lived in Egypt, Isabella Bishop (Bird) who wrote of her travels in Tibet, Lady Brassey, author of *A Voyage in the "Sunbeam,"* Mary Kingsley, a traveller in India, and others.

Lady Anne's particular contribution to this travel tradition is the depth of her involvement with the other culture she discovers. In the last decade of her life, after a separation from her husband, she lived half of each year in Cairo where she bred Arabian horses and where she was able to use her knowledge of the language to absorb the culture of the Middle East. She shared her husband's interest in the cause of Arab self-determination and his critical assessment of British policies in Egypt and India. She also shared his particular affinity for the Bedouin tribes, whom she describes in her travel memoirs as a people who were fiercely independent, physically and spiritually noble, and bound by a rigid code of honor. Her husband's consuming political involvements, his fame, and his well-known infidelities gradually separated them, and Lady Anne withdrew into her own life though they met again in 1915 and a few times thereafter before her death in Cairo in 1917. She had become a Roman Catholic in 1880, a conversion she later explained in a letter to her husband as occurring after a vision had appeared to her in Persia in 1879 at "a time of great danger." Lady Anne's grandson, Noel Anthony Lytton, in his biography *Wilfred Scawen Blunt* (1961), tries to give a balanced portrait of his grandmother, rejecting the martyr image (fostered by his mother, Lady Anne's daughter, Judith), and rejecting the equally extreme portrait of the reincarnation of the prudish Lady Byron that other biographers had created. He remembers Lady Anne as a tiny woman, independent and handsome, an avid horsewoman, who at seventy-seven rode astride for the first time, instead of sidesaddle as she had done all her life.

The journey that produced *Pilgrimage to Nejd* was taken in 1878-79. After travelling in Europe, Spain, and Algeria in 1874, the Blunts went to Egypt and Syria. In 1877, they travelled down the Euphrates river ot Baghdad. After a trip back to England where they worked on their book *Bedouin Tribes,* they returned and began the trip across the Nejd in December, 1878. It took them three months to cross the one thousand miles of desert into central Arabia. They left Damascus with Blunt's Arabic "brother," Mohammed Ibn Aruk, as guide and with a small entourage including a cook and two camel drivers. After crossing the virtually untravelled desert and encountering the Wahhabi, the fanatic "Puritans of Islam," they were received hospitably in the city of Hail by Mohammed ibn Rashid, the Wahhabi leader. Their visit there included a rare opportunity to see the famous stud of Arabian horses. From there they travelled by caravan to Baghdad, accompanying Persian pilgrims making the Hajj. Although they had been preceded by Palgrave along some of this route, their impressions were very different and far more open than his to the people and culture. Although they wanted to continue their journey overland to India, they had to abandon that plan and instead they made a less well-prepared expedition, which started in March and ended in April with their arrival at Bushir on the Persian Gulf at the British Residency, where they looked like "vagabonds, blackened with the sun, and grimed with long sleeping on the ground."

The Indian servants who greeted the Blunts upon their arrival at the Residency in Bushir almost turned them away because they could not believe they were "English gentlefolks." Both Lady Anne and her husband would have accepted this rejection as a badge of honor and as a recognition of their remarkable cultural absorption. In the same way, when Lady Anne describes her role as a marriage broker for Mohammed in the selections here included, we see that she not only performs the service as a patron but also as a friend. In her description of the awe and wonder she feels at the beauty of the vast desert she shows her receptiveness to a landscape remote from her own. Above all, her travel memoirs give us a portrait of a woman who has a unique identity apart from her husband despite their partnership in many adventures. A biography giving her the individual consideration that she merits and placing her in the Victorian tradition, which has continued into the twentieth century with Isak Dinesen's *Out of Africa,* has not yet been written but it certainly due.

EDITION USED:

A Pilgrimage to Nejd, the Cradle of the Arab Race. Preface by the editor,
   Wilfred Scawen Blunt. 2 vols. London: John Murray, 1881.

SUGGESTED READINGS:

Blunt, Lady Anne. *Bedouin Tribes of the Euphrates.* Edited with a preface
   by Wilfred Scawen Blunt. 2 vols. London: Frank Cass, 1968.
_____ . *The Celebrated Romance of the Stealing of the Mare.* Translated
   by Lady Anne Blunt and done into verse by Wilfred Scawen Blunt.
   London: Reeves and T., 1892.
_____ . *The Seven Golden Odes of Pagan Arabia known also as the Moalla-
   kat.* Translated by Lady Anne Blunt; English verse by W. S. Blunt.
   London: Chiswick Press, 1903.
Blunt, Wilfred Scawen. *My Diaries: Being a Personal Narrative of Events,
   1888-1914.* New York: Knopf, 1932.
Finch, Edith. *Wilfred Scawen Blunt: 1840-1922.* London: Jonathan Cape,
   1938.
Lytton, Noel Anthony. *Wilfred Scawen Blunt: A Memoir by His Grandson.*
   London: L. Macdonald, 1961.
Rogers, William N. *"Lady Anne Blunt and Wilfred Scawen Blunt: Aristocrats
   as Arabian Travellers." Exploration": Journal of the MLA Seminar
   on the Literature of Exploration.* 2 (1974): 24-35.

A Pilgrimage to Nejd

[Volume I]
Chapter VII

"And Leah was tender eyed but Rachel was beautiful."—BOOK OF GENESIS

The Ibn Arûks of Jôf—Mohammed contracts a matriomonial alliance—Leah
and Rachel—We cheapen the bride's dower—A negro governor and his suite—
A thunder-storm

We stayed three days with Nassr and his sons, and his sons' wives and their
children, in their quiet farm house. It was a rest which we much needed, and
proved besides to be an interesting experience, and an excellent opportunity
of learning more of Arab domestic life than we had done on our previous
journeys. Not that the Ibn Arûks of Meskakeh are in themselves of any
particular interest. Like their relations of Tadmur, they have been too long
settled down as mere townspeople of the land, marrying the daughters and
adopting many of the sordid town notions, but they were honest and
kind-hearted, and the traditions of their origin, still religiously preserved, cast
an occasional gleam of something like romance on their otherwise matter of
fact lives. Nassr, the best of the elder generation, resembled some small
Scottish laird, poor and penurious, but aware of having better blood in his
veins than his neighbours—one whose thought, every day in the year but one,
is of how to save sixpence, but who on that one day shows himself to be a
gentleman, and the head of a house. His sons were quiet, modest, and
unpretending, and, like most young Arabs, more romantically inclined than
their father. They even had a certain appreciation of chivalrous ideas;
especially Turki, the elder, in whom the Bedouin blood and Bedouin
traditions predominated almost to the exclusion of commercial instincts,
while in his brother Areybi, these latter more than counter-balanced the
former. We liked both the brothers, of course preferring Turki, with whom
Wilfrid made great friends.

Mohammed is less distantly related to these people than I had supposed. His ancestor, Ali ibn Arûk, was one of the three brothers who, in consequence of a blood feud, or, as Wilfrid thinks more likely, to escape the Wahhabi tyranny of a hundred years ago, left Aared in Nejd, and came north as far as Tadmur, where Ali married and remained. Another brother, Abd el-Kader ibn Arûk, had stopped at Jôf, settled there, and became Nassr's grandfather. As to the third, Mutlakh, the descendants of the two former know nothing of his fate, except that, liking neither Tudmur nor Jôf, he returned towards Nejd. Some vague report of his death reached them, but nobody can tell when or how he died. Nassr came from Jôf to Meskakeh not many years ago.

Nassr is now the head of the family, at least of that branch of it which inhabits the Meskakeh oasis. But there lives in an adjoining house to his, his first cousin, Jazi ibn Arûk, brother to our friend Merzuga, and father to two pretty daughters. These, with a few other relations, make up a pleasant little family party, all living in their outlying farm together.

Of course our first thought on coming amongst them was for a wife for Mohammed, at whose request I took an early opportunity of making acquaintance with the women of the family. I found them all very friendly and amiable, and some of them intelligent. Most of the younger ones were good looking. The most important person in the harim was Nassr's wife, a little old lady named Shemma (candle), thin and wizened, and wrinkled, with long grey locks, and the weak eyes of extreme old age; and, though she can have been hardly more than sixty, she seemed to be completely worn out. She was the mother of Turki and Areybi; and I had heard from Mohammed that Nassr had never taken another wife but her. In this, however, he was mistaken, for on my very first visit, she called in a younger wife from the adjoining room, and introduced her at once to me. The second wife came in with two little boys of two and three years old, the eldest of whom (for they all have extraordinary names) is called Mattrak, "stick;" in spite of which he seemed an amiable, good-tempered child. In this he resembled his mother, whose respectful manner towards her elder, Shemma, impressed me favourably; she had, besides, a really beautiful face. The little boy, Mattrak, I recognised as a boy I had seen in the morning with old Nassr in our garden, and supposed to be his grandson. Nassr was doing his best to spoil the child, after the fashion of old men among the Arabs. I had then given Mattrak a little red frock, one I had bought for Sotamm's boy, Mansur, when we thought we were going to the Roala, and in this the child was now strutting about, showing off his finery to two very pretty little girls, his sisters. These two ran in and out during my visit, helping to bring bowls of dates, and to eat the dates when brought. Next appeared Turki's two wives, a pretty one and a plain one, and Areybi's one wife, pretty, and lately married. All these seemed to be on better terms with one another than is usually the case among mixed wives and daughters-in-law. They were extremely anxious to please me, and I, of course, did my best to satisfy their hospitable wishes about eating. They offered me dates of countless kinds,—dry ones and sticky ones, sweet and less sweet, long dried ones, and newer ones, a mass of pulp; it was impossible for one person to do justice to them all.

Shemma treated all the young people with the air of one in authority, though her tone with them was kind. She, however, spoke little, while the others talked incessantly and asked all sorts of questions, requiring more knowledge of Arabic than I possessed to answer. In the middle of the visit, Nazzch, Nassr's married daughter, own sister to Turki and Areybi, arrived with her daughter, and an immense bowl of dates. She had walked all the way from the town of Meskakeh, about three miles, carrying this child, a fat heavy creature of four, as well as the dates, and came in, panting and laughing, to see me. She was pleasant and lively, very like her brother Turki in face, that is to say, good-tempered rather than good-looking. Any one of these young ladies, seen on my first visit, might have done for Mohammed's project of marriage, but, unfortunately, they were all either married or too young. I asked if there were no young ladies already "out," and was told that there were none in Nassr's house, but that his cousin Jazi had two grown-up daughters, not yet married; so I held my peace till there should be an opportunity of seeing them.

Mohammed, in the meantime, had already begun to make inquiries on his own account, and the first day of our visit was not over before he came to me with a wonderful account of these very daughters of Jazi. There were three of them, he declared, and all more beautiful each than the others, Asr (afternoon), Hamú, and Muttra—the first two unfortunately betrothed already, but Muttra still obtainable. I could see that already he was terribly in love, for with the Arabs, a very little goes a long way; and never being allowed to see young ladies, they fall in love merely through talking about them. He was very pressing that I should lose no time about making my visit to their mother, and seemed to think that I had been wasting my time sadly on the married cousin. Mohammed has all along declared that he must be guided by my opinion. I shall know, he pretends, at once, not only whether Muttra is pretty, but whether good-tempered, likely to make a good wife. He had been calculating, he said, and thought forty pounds would be asked as her dower. It is a great deal to be sure, but then she was really "asil," and the occasion was a unique one—a daughter of Jazi!—a niece of Merzuga!—a girl of such excellent family!—an Ibn Arûk! and Ibn Arûks were not to be had every day!—forty pounds would hardly be too much. He trusted all to my judgment—I had so much discernment, and had seen the wives and daughters of all the Anazeh Sheykhs; I should know what was what, and should not make a mistake. Still, he would like Abdallah to go with me, just to spy out things. Abdallah, as a relation, might be admitted to the door on such an occasion, though he, Mohammed, of course could not; he might, perhaps, even be allowed to see the girl, as it were, by accident. With us, the Ibn Arûks, the wives and daughters are always veiled, a custom we brought with us from Nejd, for we are not like the Bedouins; yet on so important an occasion as this, of arranging a marriage, a man of a certain age, a dependant, or a poor relation, is sometimes permitted to see and report. I promised that I would do all I could to expedite the matter.

Accordingly, the next day Turki was sent for, and a word dropped to him of the matter in hand, and he was forthwith dispatched to announce my visit to the mother of the daughters of Jasi—Mohammed explaining, that it was etiquette that the mother should be made acquainted with the object of my visit, though not necessarily the daughters. Then we went to Jazi's house, Turki, Abdallah, and I.

Jazi's house is close to Nassr's, only the garden wall dividing them, and is still smaller than his, a poor place, I thought, to which to come for a princess; but in Arabia one must never judge by externals. At the door, among several women, stood Saad, Jazi's eldest son, who showed us through the courtyard to an inner room, absolutely dark, except for what light might come in at the doorway. It is in Arabia that the expression "to darken one's door," must have been invented, for windows there are none in any of the smaller houses. There was a smell of goats about the place, and it looked more like a stable than a parlour for reception. At first I could see nothing, but I could hear Saad, who had plunged into the darkness, shaking something in a corner, and as my eyes got accustomed to the twilight, this proved to be a young lady, one of the three that I had come to visit. It was Asr the second, a great, good-looking girl, very like her cousin Areybi, with his short aquiline nose and dark eyes. She came out to the light with a great show of shyness and confusion, hiding her face in her hands, and turning away even from me; nor would she answer anything to my attempts at conversation. Then, all of a sudden, she broke away from us, and rushed across the yard to another little den, where we found her with her mother and her sister Muttra. I hardly knew what to make of all this, as besides the shyness, I thought I could see that Asr really meant to be rude, and the polite manners of her mother Haliyeh and her little sister Muttra confirmed me in this ide. I liked Muttra's face at once; she has a particularly open, honest look, staring straight at one with her great dark eyes like a fawn, and she has, too, a very bright fresh colour, and a pleasant cheerful voice. I paid, then, little attention to Asr's rudeness, and asked the little girl to walk with me around their garden, which she did, showing me the few things there were to be seen, and explaining about the well, and the way they drew the water. The garden, besides the palm trees, contained figs, apricots, and vines, and there was a little plot of green barley, on which some kids were grazing. Muttra told me that in summer they live on fruit, but that they never preserve the apricots or figs, only the dates. I noticed several young palm trees, always a sign of prosperity. The well was about ten feet square at the top, and carefully faced with stone, the water being only a few feet below the surface of the ground. Water, she told me, could be found anywhere at Meskakeh by digging, and always at the same depth. I was pleased with the intelligence Muttra showed in this conversation, and pleased with her pretty ways and honest face, and decided in my own mind without difficulty that Mohammed would be most fortunate if he obtained her in marriage. It was promising, too, for their future happiness, to remark that Haliyeh, the mother, seemed to be a sensible woman; only I could not understand the strange behaviour of the elder sister Asr. Abdallah, in the meanwhile, standing at the door, had made his notes, and come to much the same conclusion as myself; so we returned with an excellent report to give to the impatient suitor waiting outside.

Mohammed's eagerness was now very nearly spoiling the negociation, for he at once began to talk of his intended marriage; and the same thing happened to him in consequence, which happened long ago to Jacob, the son of Isaac. Jazi, imitating the conduct of Laban, and counting upon his cousin's anxiety to be married, first of all increased the dower from forty pounds to sixty, and then endeavoured to substitute Leah for Rachel, the ill-tempered Asr for the pretty Muttra.

This was a severe blow to Mohammed's hopes, and a general council was called of all the family to discuss it and decide. The council met in our tent, Wilfrid presiding; on one side sat Mohammed, with Nassr as head of the house; on the other, Jazi and Saad, representing the bride, while between them, a little shrivelled man knelt humbly on his knees, who was no member of the family, but, we afterwards learned, a professional go-between. Outside, the friends and more distant relations assembled, Abdallah and Ibrahim Kasir, and half a dozen of the Ibn Arûks. These began by sitting at a respectful distance, but as the discussion warmed, edged closer and closer in, till every one of them had delivered himself of an opinion.

Mohammed himself was quite in a flutter, and very pale; and Wilfrid conducted his case for him. It would be too long a story to mention all the dispute, which sometimes was so warmly pressed, that negociations seemed on the point of being broken off. Jazi contended that it was impossible he should give his younger daughter, while the elder ones remained unmarried. "Hamú, it was true, was engaged, and of her there was no question, but Asr, though engaged too, was really free; Jeruan, the shock-headed son of Merzuga, to whom she was betrothed, was not the husband for her. He was an imbecile, and Asr would never marry him. If a girl declares that she will not marry her betrothed, she is not engaged, and has still to seek a husband she likes. But this would not do. We cited the instance of Jedaan's marriage with an engaged girl, and the unfortunate sequel, as proving that Jeruan's consent was necessary for Asr, and Mohammed chimed in, "Ya ibn ammi, ya Jazi, O Jazi! O son of my uncle how could I do this thing, and sin against my cousin? How could I take his bride? Surely this would be a shame to us all." In fine, we insisted that Muttra it should be or nobody, and Asr's claim was withdrawn. Still it was pleaded, Muttra was but a child, hardly fifteen, and unfit for so great a journey as that to Tudmur. Where indeed was Tudmur? who of all the Jûfi had ever been so far? Mohammed, however, replied that if youth were an obstacle, a year or two would mend that. He was content to wait for a year, or two, or even for three years, if need were. He was an Ibn Arûk, and trained to patience. As to Tudmur, it was far, but had we not just come thence, and could we not go back? He would send one of his brothers at the proper time, with twenty men, thirty, fifty, to escort her. So argued, the marriage project was at last adopted, as far as Muttra was concerned. But the question of "settlements" was not as easily got over. Here it was very nearly being wrecked for good and all. Wilfrid had all along intended to pay the dower for Mohammed, but he would not say so till the thing was settled, and left Mohammed to fight out the question of jointure to as good a bargain as they could make. This Mohammed was very capable of doing, despite the infirmity of his heart, and strengthened by Abdallah, who took a strictly commercial view of the whole transaction, a middle sum was agreed on, and the conference broke up. . . .

January 11.—Every morning since we have been here there has been a fog, and to-day (Saturday), as I have already said, it has rained heavily. The rain came with thunder and lightning, as I believe is almost always the case in this part of the world. I am much surprised to learn, in talking of the lightning, that nobody at Meskakeh has heard of people being killed by it, and Mohammed confirms the statement made here, by saying that the same is the case at Tudmur. He seemed astonished when I asked him, at lightning being thought dangerous, and says that accidents from it never occur in the desert. This is strange. The surface soil of Meskakah is very nearly pure sand, and the rain runs through it as quickly as it falls, remaining only in a few hollows, where there is a kind of sediment hard enough to hold it.

In the afternoon the weather cleared, and we made a little expedition to the top of the low tell just outside Nassr's farm. The tell is of sandstone rock, orange coloured below, but weathered black on the upper surface. It is not more than a hundred feet high, but standing alone, it commands a very extensive view, curious as all views in the Jôf district are, and very pretty besides. In the fore-ground just below lay the farm, a square walled enclosure of three or four acres, with its palms and ithel trees, and its two low mud houses, and its wells, looking snug and trim and well to do. Beyond, looking westwards, three other farms were visible, spots of dark green in the broken wilderness of sand and sandstone rock, and then behind them Meskakeh, only its palm-tops in sight, and the dark mass of its citadel rising over them in fantastic outline. The long line of the palm grove stretched far away to the south, disappearing at last in a confused mass of sand-hills. These specially attracted our notice, for they marked the commencement of the Nefûd, not indeed the great Nefûd, but an outlying group of dunes tufted with ghada, and not at all unlike those passed through by the Calais and Boulogne railway. Our route, we know, lies across them, and we are to start to-morrow.

While I sat sketching this curious view, Wilfrid, who had climbed to the top of a tall stone, crowning the hill, came back with the news that he had discovered an inscription. We have been looking out, ever since our arrival in the sandstone district, for traces of ancient writing, but have hitherto found nothing except some doubtful scratches, and a few of those simple designs one finds everywhere on the sandstone, representing camels and gazelles. Here however, were three distinctly formed letters, Π, H, Ϙ, two of them belonging to the Greek alphabet.

It was evident, too, by the colour of the incisions, that they had been there for very many years. On these we have built a number of historical conjectures relating to Meskakeh, and its condition in classical times. When we came home again, we found that Mohammed had been to make the last arrangements with Jôhar for our journey. The great man had raised objections at one point of the negociations, but these had been settled by a *dahab* or gold piece, and he has now agreed to send a man with us, a professional guide for crossing the Nefûd. It seems that there are two lines by which Hail may be reached, one of thirteen and the other of ten days' journey. The first is better suited, they say, for heavy laden camels, as the sand is less deep, but we shall probably choose the shorter route, if only for the sake of seeing the Nefûd at its worst. For the Nefûd has been the object of our dreams all through this journey, as the *ne plus ultra* of desert in the world. We hear wonderful accounts of it here, and of the people who have been lost in it. This ten days' journey represents something like two hundred miles, and there are only two wells on the way, one on the second, and another on the eighth day. The guide will bring his own camel, and carry a couple of waterskins, and we have bought four more, making up the whole number to eight. This will have to suffice for our mares as well as for ourselves, and we shall have to be very careful. We have laid in a sufficient stock of dates and bread, and have still got one of the kids left to start with in the way of meat, the other has just been devoured as I have said, and cannot be replaced. Provisions of every kind are difficult to procure at Meskakeh; it was only by the exercise of a little almost Turkish bullying that Jóhar has been able to get us a camel load of corn.

The rain is over and the moon shining. All our preparations are made for crossing the Nefûd, and in a few hours we shall be on our way. We shall want all our strength for the next ten days.

[Volume II], Chapter II, Our Persian Campaign

... About an hour before sunset we came to a broad river, broader and deeper than the Tibb, and here Ghafil decreed a halt. If we had been a strong enough party to shift for ourselves, and if we could have crossed the river alone, we should now have gone on and left our persecutors behind; but in our helpless state this was impossible, and we had no choice but to dismount. It was an anxious moment, but I think we did what was wisest in showing no sign of distrust, and we had no sooner stopped than we gave one a horse to hold, and another a gun, while we called on others to help us unload the camels, and get out coffee and provisions for a general feast. This seemed to most of them too good an offer to be declined, and we had already distributed a sack of flour and a sack of rice amongst them, which the two women had promised to bake into loaves for the whole party, when Ghafil and the one-eyed man, who had been down to look for a ford, arrived upon the scene. They were both very angry when they saw the turn things had taken, and were at first for forbidding the people to eat with us, alleging that we were kaffirs (infidels), so at least the people informed us later, but this was more than they could insist on. They would not, however, themselves eat with us or taste our coffee, and remained apart with those of the party which had not made friends with us. The women were on our side, and the better sort of the young men. Still it was a terribly anxious evening, for even our friends were as capricious as the winds, and seemed always on the point of picking an open quarrel. Later, they all went away and left us to our own devices, sitting round a great bonfire of brushwood they had built up, "to scare away lions," they said. We managed to rig up our tent, and make a barricade of the camelbags in such a way that we could not be surprised and taken at a disadvantage. I did not shut my eyes all night, but lay watching the bonfire, with my hand on my gun. Hajji Mohammed once in the darkness crept out and got near enough to overhear something of their talk, and he assures us that there was a regular debate as to whether and when and how we should be murdered, in which the principal advocate of extreme measures was the one-eyed man, a great powerful ruffian who carried a sort of club, which he told us he used to frighten the lions, beating in on the ground. The noise, he declared, sounded like a gun and drove them away. With this tale of horror Hajji Mohammed returned to comfort us; not was it wholly a delusion, for in the middle of the night, Wilfrid being asleep, and Hajji Mohammed, whose watch it was, having fallen into a doze, I distinctly saw Ghafil, who had previously come under pretext of lions or robbers to reconnoitre, prowl stealthily round, and seeing us all as he thought asleep, lift up the flap of the tent and creep under on Wilfrid's side. I had remained motionless, and from where I lay I could see his figure plainly against the sky. As he stooped I called out in a loud voice, "Who goes there!" and at the sound he started back, and slunk away. This woke Hajji Mohammed, and nobody slept again, but I could see Ghafil prowling like an hyaena round us the best part of the night.

Hajji Mohammed has behaved very well, though he owns himself much frightened. So am I, only I conceal my alarm better than he does. Indeed I am sure that putting on a bold face is our only chance of safety, for nothing but cowardice now prevents Ghafil and his set from attacking us. We are well armed, and he knows he could not do it with impunity. As long as we are on horseback, I believe we run no great risk, but the night is a disagreeable time. If we had only open desert in front of us we could set them all at defiance.

Beatrice Webb (*Permission of The London School of Economics and Political Science*)

Beatrice Webb, 1858–1943

My Apprenticeship (1926)

Beatrice Potter Webb was the next-to-last of nine daughters; her father was a liberal minded industrialist, Richard Potter, the only man, his daughters said, who really believed women were better than men and acted on that belief. Despite that, his wife, Laurencina Heyworth Potter, felt herself kept by marriage and childbearing from the intellectual life she wanted to lead. Beatrice grew up "in the shadow of [her] baby brother's birth and death"; the Potters' only son was born in 1863 and died in 1865, leaving his mother inconsolable. The last daughter, Rosy, was born in 1865, and Laurencina Potter turned her attention to the baby, again rejecting Beatrice. Near the end of her mother's life, Beatrice finally gained her attention and began in turn to understand her mother's disappointments; her death must have seemed another injustice.

Beatrice Potter's sense of justice was not directed only to herself, however. Mainly self-educated, living in a home visited frequently by leading business and political figures, she early became aware of social issues and began to question the morality of capitalism. The first major influence on her intellectual development was a frequent visitor to the Potter house, the philosopher Herbert Spencer. His concept of society as an organism whose ills could be approached only in a spirit of scientific investigation gave Beatrice Potter her vocation, the new career of social investigator. The assumed neutrality of the scientific spirit was foreign to Beatrice Potter's temperament, however, and she sought for a way to give context and meaning to the work she had chosen. She found this meaning—to Spencer's dismay—in socialism. In *My Apprenticeship*, she details the stages of her acceptance of that creed, stages which are no doubt neater in her remembrance than in actuality. The final stage coincided with her meeting with Sidney Webb, then beginning to be known as a member of the Fabian socialist group and as a writer on economics. The son of a lower-middle-class London family, a small man with a large head, who spoke with a Cockney accent, he was in every obvious way an unsuitable match for a handsome heiress who held an accepted place in London society. They met in 1890, the year before the publication of her book, *The Co-Operative Movement in Great Britain,* and were married in 1892, when her father's death made it possible. Together they wrote a massive history of Trades Unionism (published in 1894); *Industrial Democracy* (1897); a multivolume history of local government in England, and many other books and pamphlets. More important, together they founded and developed the London School of Economics and the magazine, *The New Statesman*. From 1905 to 1909, Beatrice Webb was a member of the Royal Commission on the Poor Laws; her *Minority Report* is a key document in English social history, arguing for universal social insurance and giving the outline for the welfare state.

Beatrice Webb's acceptance of socialism led to the work which gave her her significance in English political history. She continued throughout her life, however, to seek a spiritual creed that would be equally satisfying. In the multivolume diary that she kept throughout her life, she details this search through prayer and in 1926, the year *My Apprenticeship* was published, she described herself as "perpetually brooding over my inability to make clear even to myself, let alone to others, why I believe in religious mysticism, why I hanker after a Church—with its communion of the faithful, with its religious rites, and it religious discipline, and above all with its definite code of conduct" (Preface, *Our Partnership*, p. vii).

My Apprenticeship is a constant conversation between the older writer and the younger woman, as Webb alternates diary entries with reflection to create a remarkable autobiography which also, as she had planned that it would, presents a history of the Victorian era, and "the spirit of the times."

EDITION USED:

My Apprenticeship. London: Longmans, 1926

SUGGESTED READINGS:

Mackenzie, Norman, ed. *The Letters of Sidney and Beatrice Webb.*
    Cambridge: Cambridge University Press, 1978.
Mackenzie, Norman and Jeanne. *The Fabians.* New York: Simon and
    Schuster, 1977.
Muggeridge, Kitty and Adam, Ruth. *Beatrice Webb: A Life 1858-1943.*
    London: Secker and Warburg, 1967
Webb, Beatrice: *The Cooperative Movement in Great Britain.* London:
    Sonnenschein, 1891.
_____ . *Diaries, 1912-1924.* Ed. Margaret Cole. London: Longmans, 1952.
_____ . *Diaries, 1924-1932.* Ed. Margaret Cole. London: Longmans, 1956.
Webb, Beatrice. *Our Partnership.* ed. Barbara Drake and Margaret Cole.
    London: Longmans, 1948.

My Apprenticeship

CHAPTER II: In Search of a Creed [1862-1882; aet. 4-24]

The youngest but one of the nine daughters, creeping up in the shadow of my baby brother's birth and death, I spent my childhood in a quiet special way among domestic servants, to whom as a class I have an undying gratitude. I was neither ill-treated nor oppressed: I was merely ignored. For good or for evil I was left free to live my own little life within the large and loose framework of family circumstance. . . .

Out of doors there were "secret" places in the shrubberies where I arranged and rearranged stones and sticks; grottos in the woods where I puddled leaky pools in trickling streams; all the time building castles in the air in which the picture of a neglected child enjoying her own melodramatically forgiving death-bed was succeeded by the more cheerful vision of courting lovers. How and when I learnt to read I do not remember. Long before I drifted into the schoolroom for spells of regular lessons, continuous reading, self-selected from the masses of books stacked in the library, study and schoolroom bookcases, or from the miscellaneous pamphlets, periodicals and newspapers scattered throughout the house, had become my main occupation; a wholesome alternative to castle-building but not conducive to robust health. Indeed, almost continous illness, bouts of neuralgia, of indigestion, of inflammation of all sorts and kinds, from inflamed eyes to congested lungs, marred my happiness; and worse than physical pain was boredom, due to the incapacity of ill-health, the ever-recurring problem of getting rid of the time between the meals, and from getting up to going to bed; and, worst of all, the sleepless hours between going to bed and getting up. I have a vivid memory of stealing and secreting a small bottle of chloroform from the family medicine-chest as a vaguely imagined alternative to the pains of life and ennui of living; and of my consternation when one day I found the stopper loose and the contents evaporated.[1] Meanwhile the procession of governesses, English, French and German, did not trouble me. For the most part I liked

1. "My childhood was not on the whole a happy one," I wrote in 1884; "ill-health and starved affection, and the mental disorders which spring from

them and they liked me. But after a few weeks or months of experimenting in regular schoolroom hours, and disagreeable tussles with arithmetic or grammar, I always took to my bed, the family doctor prescribing "no lessons, more open-air exercise, if possible a complete change of scene." When the last of my elder sisters "came out," and my youngest sister had to be provided with a nursery governess, all pretence at formal education was abandoned.

But by this time I had invented a device of my own for self-culture—reading the books of my free choice, and in my private manuscript book extracting, abstracting and criticizing what I had read. To these immature reviews of books were added from time to time, as the spirit moved me, confessions of personal shortcomings or reflections on my own or other people's affairs.

I imagine that the majority of lonely but mentally alert children get into the habit of scribbling their thoughts and feelings, either to rid themselves of painful emotion or in order to enjoy the unwonted pleasure of self-expression. When this habit is combined with native wit, original observation and a quaint use of words these scribblings may easily rise into literature. I have no such treasure to unlock. Unlike one or two of my sisters, I was born without artistic faculty, either for dancing or acting, for painting or music, for prose or poetry. The talents entrusted to my care were a tireless intellectual curiosity together with a double dose of will-power. . . .

It was during the six years of irresponsible girlhood (1876-1882) that I tried the religion of science and found it wanting. Memory is a risky guide in tracing the ups and downs of belief and unbelief; gaps in the argument are apt to be filled in, and the undulating line of feeling becomes artificially straightened. As being free from the fallacy of "being wise after the event," I prefer the contemporary entries in the MS. diary. But this string of quotations from the subjective musings of a girl conveys its own false implications; inevitably these extracts emphasize the hidden over the outer life. Somewhere down in the depths the Ego that affirms and the Ego that denies were continuously wrangling over the duty and destiny of man; but it was only now and again that their voices were heard above the din of everyday life. For the most part consciousness was listening to the promptings of physical instinct and personal vanity, to the calls of family affection and casual comradeship—above all, to the exciting messages of the master-wave of intellectual curiosity.

these, ill-temper and resentment, marred it. Hours spent in secret places, under the shade of shrub and tree, in the leaf-filled hollows of the wood and in the crevices of the quarries, where I would sit and imagine love scenes and death-bed scenes and conjure up the intimacy and tenderness lacking in my life, made up the happy moments. But dreary times of brooding and resentfulness, sharp pains of mortified vanity and remorse of untruthfulness, constant physical discomfort and frequent pain absorbed the greater part of my existence; and its loneliness was absolute." [MS. diary, April 8, 1884.]

Thus, during the spring and summer months of most years, riding, dancing, flirting and dressing-up absorbed current energy; six months out of these six years were spent in the Rhineland, reading German literature and listening to German music; another six months in Italy, in churches and galleries revelling in Italian art. Nor were family events unexciting. My sister Kate, after all apprenticeship under Octavia Hill, had become a rent-collector in White-chapel; and it was when staying with her in London that I first became aware of the meaning of the poverty of the poor. The three other elder sisters had found their mates; and with the marriage of my sister Margaret, though she remained an affectionate sister, I lost my one intimate friend. As against this loss there was the rapidly growing intellectual comradeship with my mother during the latter years of her life, . . .

The following entries in the diary, scattered over five or six years and given in order of date, may be taken as notes of the controversy between the Ego that denies and the Ego that affirms the validity of religious mysticism.

This book, begun as a diary, ends in extracts and abstracts of books. One's interest in one's own character ceases to be so absorbing, as one grows in knowledge. Christianity certainly made one more egotistical, more desirous to secure one's own salvation. Whatever may be the faults, or rather the shortcomings, of the new religion, it accomplishes one thing; it removes the thoughts from that wee bit of the world called self to the great whole—the individual has no part in it; it is more than silent as to his future existence. Man sinks down to comparative in-significance; he is removed in degree but not in kind from the mere animal and vegetable. In truth, it requires a noble nature to profess with cheerfulness this religion; and the ideal it presents to us is far higher than any presented by the great religions of the world. [September 13, 1877.]

Mr. Spencer's *First Principles* has had certainly a very great influence on my feelings and thoughts. It has made me feel so happy and con-tented. . . . I do admire that still, reverent consciousness of the great mystery; that fearless conviction that no advance in science can take away the beautiful and elevating consciousness of something greater than humanity. One has always feared that when the orthodox religion vanished, no beauty, no mystery would be left, but nothing but what could and would be explained and become commonplace—but instead of that each new discovery of science will increase our wonder at the Great Unknown and our appreciation of the Great Truth. [MS. diary, December 15, 1878.]

The religion of science has its dark side. It is bleak and dreary in sor-row and ill-health. And to those whose lives are one continual suffering it has but one word to say—suicide. If you cannot bear it any longer, and if no ties of duty turn you from extinguishing that little flame of your existence—depart in peace: cease to exist. It is a dreadful thought. It can never be the religion of a "suffering humanity." The time may come, and I believe will come, when human life will be sufficiently happy and full to be unselfish. But there are long ages yet to be passed, and generations of men will still cry in their misery for another life to compensate for their life-long sorrow and suffering. [MS. diary, March 8, 1878.]

As it may be interesting in future years to know what my religious convictions were at nineteen, I might as well state roughly what are my vague beliefs. I do not see that there is sufficient evidence, either for believing in a future life or in a personal creator of the universe. I at present believe (by no means without inward fear at my audacity) that Christianity is in no way superior in kind, though in degree, to the other great religions; that it was a natural product of the human mind; that Christianity is not the highest religion conceivable; and that the idea of working out your own salvation, of doing good, and believing blindly, in order to arrive at eternal bliss, is, through its intense selfishness, an immoral doctrine. I believe also that, as soon as our religion becomes truly unselfish, the enormous interest in speculations as to the future existence of the individual will die out. But what seems to me clear is that we are at a very early period of man's existence, and that we have only just arrived at the true basis of knowledge: and that bright and glorious days are in store for our successors on this earth. [MS. diary, March 31, 1878.] . . .

One often has felt in life that there are two courses open to one; an endeavor after nobler and purer living, *i.e.* an earnest attempt to silence and put down what is vile in you; or the alternative principle of fixing your eye steadfastly on all that is wise and noble, and developing with all your power your better self; not heeding the little slips, perhaps sometimes into very dirty places. I do not think that many have sufficient nervous power to do both; and Goethe tells you to choose freedom of development. In life you should seek a really congenial career, as a life-occupation, and then you should keep your heart and mind open to the outer world with various interests and activities.

Until you have found this career you should wander up and down regarding no place as too low and dirty, no society too licentious and frivolous—perhaps in lowest society you may light on some human soul who will impart to you some vital truth. [MS. diary, December 14, 1878.]

The one thought that I have been pondering over is—does my want of happiness come from my want of belief in the old faith which has helped so many thousands along this weary way? Or is it simply physical melancholy which attaches itself to my pet grievance, and which, if I had been without education and culture, would have attached itself to some passing trifle? And when one looks around and sees good Christians fussing and fretting about little holes in their purses, little disappointments of their vanity and their greed, one begins to think that each human being has his share of "distemper"—but perhaps the patient is on the whole happier who has it out in surface irritations than he who believes it to be a sign of an inward and incurable complaint, peculiar not only to himself alone but to the whole human race.

I cannot help having a half-conscious conviction that, if the human race is mortal, if its existence is without aim, if that existence is to end, at however remote a period, in a complete dissolution, like that which overcomes the individual, then life indeed is not worth living—not worth living to the mass of mankind. [MS. diary, March 30, 1879.] . . .

It is impossible for a woman to live in agnosticism. That is a creed which is only the product of one side of our nature, the purely rational, and ought we persistently to refuse authority to that other faculty which George Eliot calls the emotive thought? And this, when we allow this faculty to govern us in action; when we secretly recognize it as our guide in our highest moments. Again, what is the meaning of our longing for prayer, of our feeling happier and nobler for it? Why should we determine in our minds that the rational faculty should be regarded as the infallible head in our mental constitution? The history of the human mind, shown in the works of the greatest of the race, proves that what has been logically true to one age has been logically untrue to another; whereas we are all able to sympathize and enter into the almost inspired utterances of the emotive thought of philosophers and poets of old. . . . But perhaps the real difficulty is that the emotional faculty, though it gives us a yearning, a longing for, perhaps even a distinct consciousness of, something above us, refuses to formulate and to systematize; and even forces us to see moral flaws in all the present religious systems. I suppose with most people it is the sense of what is *morally* untrue which first shakes your faith in Christianity; it is moral disapprobation of some of its dogmas which forces you to question rationally the rest. And this would be still more the case in an attempt to join the Catholic Church. You would be obliged to stifle your sense of what was right as well as that of what was true. [MS. diary, February 2, 1881.] . . .

[The Sunday after my mother's funeral.]

Now that I have experienced what the death of a dear one is, and have watched it and waited for it, a deep yearning arises for some religion by which to console grief and stimulate action. I have, if anything, less faith in the possibility of another life. As I looked at our mother dying

I *felt* it was a final dissolution of body and soul—an end of that personality which we call the spirit. This was an instinctive conviction: on this great question we cannot reason. But, though my disbelief in what we call immortality was strengthened, a new and wondrous faith has arisen within me—a faith in goodness—in God. I must pray, I do pray and I feel better for it; and more able to put aside all compromise with worldliness and to devote myself with single-heartedness to my duty. . . .

Rationally, I am still an agnostic, but I know not where my religious feeling, once awakened from the dreams of a vague idealism, and acknowledged as helpful in times of trial, sorrow and endeavor—where this religious feeling will lead me: whether I may not be forced to acknowledge its supremacy over my whole nature. [April 23, 1882.]

Mother's death opened out a new world to me in thought and action [I write a month later.] It stamped, by a new experience, the conviction which had been slowly growing from the first dawning of conscious thought within me, a conviction that the world was either an infernal chaos, or that all life was a manifestation of goodness; and death, disease and misery horrible only to our imperfect vision.

The death of one dear and near to me did not strike me as sadder than the death of the thousands who vanish unknown around us. Either "the all" is so inexpressibly sad that there is no room for an increase of sadness through personal affliction; or else there is a mysterious meaning which, if we could divine it and accept it, would hallow all things, and give even to death and misery a holiness which would be akin to happiness. And the result of this ultimatum, presented by the thoughtful to the practical part of my nature, was a partial reversion to religion; I was satisfied that this would be the last word of thought unaided by experience gathered in action. The question remained, how am I to live and for what object? Is the chopped-up happiness of the world worth anything if the first alternative be true. Physical annihiliation is impracticable. One's own life and one's own nature are facts with which one must deal; and with me they must be directed by some one consistent principle.

Even if the instinctive faith in a mysterious goodness is a fiction of the mind, would it not on the whole be happier to live by the light of this delusion, and blind oneself wilfully to the awful vision of unmeaning misery? Perhaps it would be difficult to direct a life on this negative basis. In truth one has a faith within one which persists in the absence of direct contradiction. [January 2, 1883.]

Thus the long-drawn-out controversy, between the Ego that affirms and the Ego that denies the validity of religious mysticism, ended, not in a reversion to the creed of Christianity, not even in an affirmation by the intellect of the existence of a spiritual power with whom man could enter into communion, but in an intuitive use of prayer as, for one of my temperament, essential to the right conduct of life. . . .

But this metaphysical resting-place was not reached until middle life. At this point in my narrative it suffices to record the fact that, during the ten years intervening between my mother's death (1882, aet. 24) and my father's death and my own marriage (1892; aet. 34)—crucial years during which I acquired the craft of a social investigator, experienced intense emotional strain, and persisted in continuous intellectual toil under adverse circumstances—it was the habit of prayer which enabled me to survive, and to emerge relatively sound in body and sane in mind.

Can I describe in a few sentences the successive steps in my progress towards Socialism?

My studies in East End life had revealed the physical misery and moral debasement following in the track of the rack-renting landlord and capitalist profit-maker in the swarming populations of the great centres of nineteenth-century commerce and industry. It is true that some of these evils—for instance, the low wages, long hours and insanitary conditions of the sweated industries, and the chronic under-employment at the docks—could, I thought, be mitigated, perhaps altogether prevented, by appropriate legislative enactment and Trade Union pressure. By these methods it might be possible to secure to the manual workers, so long as they were actually at work, what might be regarded from the physiological standpoint as a sufficient livelihood. Thus, the first stage in the journey—in itself a considerable departure from early Victorian individualism—was an all-pervading control, in the interest of the community, of the economic activities of the landlord and the capitalist.

But however ubiquitous and skilful this state regulation and Trade Union intervention might become, I could see no way out of the recurrent periods of inflation and depression—meaning, for the vast majority of the nation, alternate spells of overwork and unemployment—intensified, if not actually brought about by the speculative finance, manufacture and trading that was inspired by the mad rush to secure the maximum profit for the minority who owned the instruments of production. Moreover, "man does not live by bread alone"; and without some "socialism"—for instance, public education and public health, public parks and public provision for the aged and infirm, open to all and paid for out of rates and taxes, with the addition of some form of "work or maintenance" for the involuntarily unemployed—even capitalist governments were reluctantly recognizing, though hardly fast enough to prevent race-deterioration, that the regime of private property could not withstand revolution. This "national minimum" of civilized existence, to be legally ensured for every citizen, was the second stage in my progress towards socialism.

There remained to be considered the psychological evils of a community permanently divided into a nation of the rich and a nation of the poor, into a minority always giving orders and a vast majority always obeying orders. For the example of the United States showed that a rise in wages and an improvement in technique, far from promoting economic equality, might, through increasing efficiency, and the consequently augmented yield of rent and interest, produce even greater inequalities in wealth and personal power between one citizen and another than prevailed in less favored capitalist countries. "Choose equality and flee greed," said Menander; for, as Matthew Arnold had explained to an unheeding generation, "our inequality materializes our upper class, vulgarizes our middle class, brutalizes our lower."[2] At this point I remained for some time, because I could see no alternative to the authority of the profit-making employer.

Now it was in the constitution and activities of the consumers' co-operative movement, as developed by the British working class, with its production for use, and its elimination of the profit-maker, that I perceived a possible alternative to modern business enterprise, and one which would, at the same time, increase the security of livelihood and equalize the opportunity for self-development among the whole people. It was, in fact, by the recognition that the essential feature in the co-operative movement was not the advantages that it brought in the way of economical house-keeping and the thrifty accumulation of continual small savings, but the invention of a new type of industrial organization—the government of industry by the community of consumers, for their common benefit as consumers—that my difficulties were removed.

To this organization of commerce and industry by democracies of consumers, I added the complementary organization of democracies of workers by hand and by brain, organized in Trade Unions or in professional societies, in order to protect personal dignity and individual freedom by giving to the community of workers in each vocation such participation in the administration of their service as might prove to be practicable and desirable. It was, indeed, with a view to discovering the exact sphere of vocational organization in the government of industries and services that I decided, early in 1889, to make the British Trade Union Movement my next field of enquiry. . . .

In the ensuing year, whilst I was writing my little book, I got some further illumination in discussions with a leading member of the Fabian Society, out of which emerged (among other and more personally significant transformations!) the recognition that the municipality, and even the state itself, in so far as they undertook the provision of commodities and services for their citizens, were, from the economic standpoint, also associations of consumers,

2. See the essay on "Equality" in *Mixed Essays,* by Matthew Arnold, p. 92.

based upon an obligatory instead of upon a voluntary membership. Thus, the conception of the organization of "production, distribution and exchange" by the consumers, not for individual profit but for the common good, could be extended from merely voluntary groupings, associated for the purchase of household requisites, to the obligatory association of all the residents of a city, for every civic purpose; and I saw a new meaning in the steady growth of municipal enterprise and other forms of Local Government. . . . Further study of the constantly developing consumers' co-operative movement in all the European countries opened a vista of the eventual supersession of the export trade by a system of deliberately arranged reciprocal imports, organized by communities of consumers, whether states, municipalities or co-operative societies; each importing country thus obtaining from other countries *merely what it found it desirable to order*—thus avoiding all questions of protective tariffs or "dumping." . . .

It was this vision of a gradually emerging new social order, to be based on the deliberate adjustment of economic faculty and economic desire, and to be embodied in an interlocking dual organization of democracies of consumers and democracies of producers—voluntary as well as obligatory, and international as well as national—that seemed to me to afford a practicable framework for the future co-operative commonwealth. . . .

The enquiry into the Co-operative Movement was carried out under the deepening gloom of my father's last illness; and at times I despaired of completing my task. In the pages of my diary, during the autumn of 1889, I watch myself falling back for encouragement on a growing faith in the possibility of reorganizing society by the application of the scientific method directed by the religious spirit.

> Unfit for work: alone with poor dear father and his shadowlike mind and irresponsible character. Depressed, I take up a volume of Matthew Arnold's poems and read these words as the expression of the ideal life towards which I constantly strive:

> > Of toil unsevered from tranquillity!
> > Of labor, that in lasting fruit outgrows
> > Far noisier schemes, accomplished in repose
> > Too great for haste, too high for rivalry!

> This state of toil unsevered from tranquillity I sometimes feel I have attained. Still, one is troubled (alas, too often troubled) with the foolish dreams of personal success and with a deep depression of personal failure. I love my work; that is my salvation; I delight in this slow stepping towards truth. Search after truth by the careful measurement of facts is the enthusiasm of my life. And of late this has been combined with a

realization of the common aim of the great army of truth-seekers: the ennobling of human life. It has been enriched by the consciousness of the supreme unity of science, art, morality; the eternal trinity of the good, the beautiful and the true, knit together in the ideal towards which humanity is constantly striving, knowingly or unknowingly, with failure or success according to the ebb and flow of pure motive and honest purpose. [MS. diary, August 17, 1889.]

Constantly during the last week, as I have eagerly read every detail of the Strike, [the famous Dock Strike of August, 1889] I have been depressed by my own powerlessness to suggest any way out of the difficulty I have been disheartened by a consciousness that my little mite of knowledge is not of much avail—that the great instinctive movements of the mass are perhaps, after all, more likely to effect than the carefully reasoned judgments of the scientific (or pseudo-scientific?) observer. . . . Then I have realized that if we are to get a basis for action through knowledge of facts, that knowledge must be far more complete and exhaustive than it is ever likely to be in my time; certainly than it is likely to be in my case. For instance, the little knowledge I gained of the London Docks is practically useless. In order to offer an opinion of any value, one would need to thoroughly master the facts about trade at the docks; to realize exactly the methods of management; to compare these with other methods of management so as to discover deficiencies and possibilities. Is that kind of exhaustive knowledge, even granting the opportunity and the ability and the strength to acquire it, open to a mere observer? Is it not the exclusive opportunity of the great organizer? On the other hand, this realization of the extent of the knowledge required shows me that in my desire to master commercial and financial facts as a key to the labor problem I was guided by a true instinct; that on my capacity to master these facts will rest my power to influence for good the condition of my people.

. . . .

Finished up my work for the summer, and leave for a fortnight's change to-morrow [this was the visit to the Trades Union Congress at Dundee]. The summer has passed quickly away with the content of a fully occupied life. The work has been hard and to a great extent mechanical, and in my spare time I have usually been too tired to enjoy beauty, so that my existence has been for the most part a mere routine of sleep, work, food and exercise. Poor dear father, his companionship is saddening, inexpressibly depressing in its soullessness. And yet, now and again there are glimpses of calm reason and warm feeling which makes me wonder whether the general habit of the family of cajoling and flattering him, of ignoring all responsible thought or action in him, is right and sound? If there be an immortal principle in him are we degrading it? But the assumption is that he is a creature whose effectual life is gone but that love and duty bids us make him physically easy and mentally content; that there is no room for moral progress or retrogression; that morally he is dead. Sometimes I think that the repulsiveness of the conclusion must mean untruth in the premises. At other times I see in our method of treatment simply a logical view of the facts of human life; a realization of the inevitable. [MS. diary, August 31, 1889] . . .

The very demon of melancholy gripping me, my imagination fastening on Amy Levy's story, a brilliant young authoress of seven-and-twenty, in the hey-day of success, who has chosen to die rather than stand up longer to live. We talk of courage to meet death; alas, in these terrible days of mental pressure it is courage to *live* that we most lack, not courage to die. It is the supreme courage of fighting a battle for an unknown leader, for an unknown cause, that fails us now and again. Poor Amy Levy! If there be no other faith for humanity but to eat, drink and be merry, for to-morrow we die, she has done well and wisely in choosing death, for to our natures such contentment, such merriment is not possible; we are the "unfit," and the sooner we leave our room to others, the better. But if this be only a passage to other things, a pilgrimage among other pilgrims whom we may help and cheer on the way, then a brave and struggling life, a life in which suffering measures progress, has the deepest meaning—in truth, embraces the whole and the sole reason for human existence. [MS. diary, October 11, 1889.]

Five months' work here and at last I have got the table of contents of my book. Now I can let my imagination play at construction instead of restricting all my energies to investigation. My spirits began to rise as I see the whole subject mapped out before me and know exactly the extent of my discoveries and the boundaries of the ground that must be covered. In a week or so I shall have sketched out each chapter and shall have before me my plan of campaign for the next six months. [MS. diary, November, 1889.]

The final entry in the diary for the year 1889 was written during a crisis in my father's illness which we all thought would be the last. It is a long account of his life, the better part being used as material in the first chapter of this book. Here I give the concluding paragraphs as they stand in the MS. diary because they reveal, more vividly than I can from memory, the happy relationship throughout life between the father and his nine daughters.

Companionship with him was a liberal education in human nature and in the affairs of the world; near relationship to him was a tie of extraordinary tenderness and charm owing to the absolute self-devotedness of his character. His own comfort, his own inclinations were unconsidered before the happiness of his wife, the welfare of his children. With him the domestic instinct was a passion to which all else was subordinated. . . .

Darling father! How your children have loved you: loving even your weaknesses, smiling over them tenderly like so many mothers. How we have all combined to blind you to the realities of your illness: nine diplomatists sitting round the old diplomatist, hiding things, smoothing things; and you all the while perhaps the most polished diplomatist of the lot; accepting the illusion as pleasanter than the fact: delighting in the diplomacy that you have taught us. With what gentle dignity you have resigned your grasp on life, though not without an internal struggle, but all hidden from view.

"I know you did it for my good, dear child, but it is a little hard."

These were his only words when, a year after his first stroke, I refused absolutely to post his letter ordering his brokers to buy for speculation. He tried it again, but this time I checkmated him by writing privately to the brokers urging them on their honor to discourage it: I remember the queer expression when he read their letter—the passing look of irritation—then the bright glance at me when he perceived my move—the affectionate tone in which he next addressed me on some indifferent matter: the silent acknowledgment of my good intention, the inward chuckle over the smartness of his offspring; and from that moment the absolute and entire resignation of his affairs into Daniel's hands; betaking himself exclusively to the contracted routine of a shadow-like existence. His content would have been painful if one had not felt that it was reasoned out on his large unselfish philosophy of life; an idealized Epicureanism: the happiness of the world (*i.e.* of those around you) and of yourself as a unit of the world.

And now that he lies helpless, the vitality flickering to extinction: his limbs motionless, his breathing labored, the last pleasure in his sleep, food and cigarette gone, he still brightens up to welcome his "bright-eyed daughter"; to compliment a middle-aged married woman on her good looks: to enquire how each husband is doing; to ask how much he will leave to his children. In the long hours of restlessness he broods over the success of his children, and finds reason for peace and satisfaction. "I want one more son-in-law" (a proof that he feels near his end, as he has discouraged the idea of matrimony for me, put it off as something I could easily attain), "a woman is happier married: I should like to see my little Bee married to a good strong fellow," and the darling old father dreams of the "little Bee" of long ago; he does not realize that she has past away, leaving the strong form and determined features of the "glorified spinster" bending over him as a mother bends over her sick child. [MS. diary, November 26, 1889.]

"THE OTHER ONE"

My father lingered on for another two years, barely conscious of his surroundings. But within a few weeks of his call for "one more son-in-law" there came "The Other One"!

This culminating event of my life—for did it not lead to the rapid transformation of "My Apprenticeship" into "Our Partnership," and therefore to the ending of this book?—clearly deserves a preface. And this preface shall consist in a recollection of a mysterious penumbra, making me aware of a new and significant Presence in my environment at least a year before I was introduced to the little figure with a big head who was to become the man of my destiny, the source of unhoped-for happiness; and, be it added, the predominant partner of the firm of Webb! . . .

> Sidney Webb, the socialist, dined here [Devonshire House Hotel] to meet the Booths. A remarkable little man with a huge head and a tiny body, a breadth of forehead quite sufficient to account for the encyclopaedic character of his knowledge. A Jewish nose, prominent eyes and mouth, black hair, somewhat unkempt, spectacles and a most bourgeois black coat shiny with wear. But I like the man. There is a directness of speech, an open-mindedness, an imaginative warm-heartedness which will carry him far. He has the self-assurance of one who is always thinking faster than his neighbors; who is untroubled by doubts, and to whom the acquisition of facts is as easy as the grasping of things; but he has no vanity and is totally unself-conscious. Hence his absence of consciousness as to treading on his neighbor's corns. Above all, he is utterly disinterested, and is, I believe, genuine in his faith that collective control and collective administration will diminish, if not abolish, poverty. [MS. diary, February 14, 1890.]

> Every day my social views take a more decidedly socialist turn, every hour reveals fresh instances of the curse of gain without labor; the endless perplexities of the rich, the never-failing miseries of the poor. In this household [there are] ten persons living on the fat of the land in

order to minister to the supposed comfort of one poor old man. All this faculty expended to satisfy the assumed desires of a being well-nigh bereft of desire. The whole thing is a vicious circle as irrational as it is sorrowful. . .

[MS. diary, April 22, 1890.]

Anna Julia Haywood Cooper (*Courtesy of the Houghton Library, Harvard University, from* A Voice from the South . . . , *1892*)

Anna Julia Haywood Cooper, 1859–1964

Autobiographical Letter (n.d.); The Third Step: Autobiographical (1925?)

Anna Julia Haywood Cooper was a scholar of languages, principal of the M Street High School in Washington, D.C., from 1901 to 1906, and a member of its faculty from 1911 to 1930. In 1925, at the age of sixty-six, she received a Ph.D. from the Sorbonne with a thesis on French attitudes toward slavery during the Revolution. Four years later, she founded an advanced adult education institute for employed blacks in Washington, Frelinghuysen University. She was president from 1929 to 1941; the school closed in 1964, the year of her death at 105. From the 1880's, when she began to teach and lecture, Anna Julia Cooper dedicated herself to two ideals: scholarship, and the furtherance of education for blacks, especially for black women. Her informed, witty, brisk comments on questions of women's role in America and on attitudes toward the higher education of women make her collection of essays, *A Voice from the South by a Black Woman of the South* (1892) an important feminist document, as well as a record of significant moments in the history both of blacks and of women.

Anna Julia Cooper was the daughter of a slave mother, as she recounts in her autobiographical sketch. Her selection, at age six, to be a student at a newly founded Episcopal school, St. Augustine's Institute in Raleigh, North Carolina, set the pattern for her life: her mission was to educate. Married at eighteen to the Reverend George Cooper, a teacher at the school, she was widowed at twenty. Leaving North Carolina she went to Oberlin, one of the first colleges to admit blacks. She graduated in 1884, taught at Wilberforce University from 1885 to 1887, and then moved to Washington, which was her home and the center of her career until her death.

M Street High School, where much of her career was spent, is a uniquely important institution in the history of American education. The only high school then offering academic training to black students in the nation's capitol, it evolved from the Preparatory High School, organized in 1870 as a project of white abolitionists. Because of government jobs, larger numbers of black families in Washington than in other cities could seek higher education for their children, and the Preparatory High School, though segregated, was by law to have the same curriculum as other academic high schools in the city. The school (located after 1891 on M Street N.W.) faced a serious and potentially destructive crisis in 1901, the first year of Anna Julia Cooper's term as principal. The Board of Education of the District of Columbia attempted to institute a separate curriculum for the M Street School, one offering vocational rather than academic training. Anna Cooper resisted this attempt to devalue the school and its students at the risk of her own position. In her history of the school (later renamed the Dunbar High School), Mary Gibson Hundley points to Anna Cooper as the woman "of rare courage and vision" who ensured that the school would continue to prepare black students for higher education. It was she, too, who first gained accreditation for the school and searched out scholarships for its students in such places as Harvard and Brown. None of this can have been easy, and the firm no-nonsense tone of assurance with which Anna Cooper speaks in her autobiographical writings represents her triumph over the limitations placed on an educated black woman, a triumph she intended others to share.

Despite the pressures from both black and white administrators in the school system, Anna Julia Cooper never lost sight of her mission—for herself as well as for the students she taught. Her determination to go on for a higher degree led her first to Columbia University and ultimately to France, which she, like many black Americans then and later, saw as in sharp contrast to the United States in its support of black scholars and intellectuals.

Having gained the scholarly recognition she sought, at an age when she might have retired, she created a new institution to offer others the chance to do what she had done.

While she was principal at the M Street High School, Anna Cooper wrote the words to the school's Alma Mater. In them, even within the circumscribed form of such a piece, she makes clear her own mission and the sources of her strength: "With faith in thy mission, in self in the All/ And loyally serving humanity's call/ For Justice, God's justice even-handed open-eyed,/ For love universal, no creature denied/ Thy precept in action self-poise, self-control/ Never answering to will, steady onward to goal. . . .

EDITION USED:

"The Third Step: Autobiographical." Privately printed, 1925. Manuscript
   letter, undated. Both from the Anna Julia Haywood Cooper Collection,
   Moorland-Spingarn Research Center, Howard University, Washington,
   D.C.

SUGGESTED READINGS:

Hundley, Mary Gibson. *The Dunbar Story, 1870-1955.* New York: Vantage
   Press, 1965.
Terrell, Mary Church. *Colored Woman in a White World.* Washington, D.C.:
   Ransdell, 1940.

Manuscript letter from the Anna Julia Haywood Cooper Papers, n.d.

I was born in Raleigh, North Carolina. My mother was a slave and the finest woman I have ever known. Tho untutored she could read her Bible and write a little. It was one of my happiest childhood memories explaining for her the subtle differences between q's and g's or between b's and l's. Presumably my father was her master, if so I owe him not a sou and she was always too modest and shamefaced ever to mention him. I was born during the civil war and served many an anxious slave's superstition to wake the baby up and ask directly "Which side is goin' to win de war?" "Will de Yankees beat de Rebs and will Linkum free de Niggers." I want to say that while it may be true in infancy we are nearer Heaven, if I had any vision or second sight in those days that made my answers significant to the troubled souls that hung breathless on my cryptic answers such powers promptly took their flight with the dawn of intelligent consciousness. In the later struggle for existence I could not have told you how the simplest encounter with fate would end.

At hardly more than kindergarten age it was my good fortune to be selected for a scholarship by Dr. J. Brinton Smith, founder of St. Augustine's Normal School at Raleigh, N. C. (now St. Augustine's College) in the nucleus he was planning to train as teachers for the colored people of the South. That school was my world during the formative period, the most critical in any girl's life. Its nurture and admonition gave not only shelter and protection from the many pitfalls that beset the unwary but even more emphatically the daily round of Church Services, Morning and Evening Prayer with the Psalter recited every month, the Old and New Testaments listened to once a year through the first and second Lessons for the day, the Epistles and Gospels at Holy Communion each Sunday and Holy Day, the Church's calendar beginning with Advent and revolving around the life of its Head as consciously and vitally as Earth around its sun, the whole atmosphere contributed growth and nourishment beyond the power of mortals to estimate.

The collects memorized weekly and recited in concert, the beauty and dignity of the Prayer Book English, I may say, elevated and fixed a standard not only of reverent and decorous worship but of good taste even in secular behavior, the truest and deepest canons of Education. It developed in one a feeling of "belonging" wherever the Te Deum is sung—a feeling which has been thru out an "open Sesame" to the Communion of Souls. Whether a sojourner in Oberlin or Washington or foreign lands, at the communion rail in Westminster Abbey, London or in humble St. George's Chapel, Washington, I can say with the Psalmist, "My lives have fallen in pleasant places and I have a goodly heritage."

With grateful acknowledgment of the spiritual ministrations of the Vicar of St. George's, under whose care I have been providentially brought at this period of my life, I am, Sincerely, Anna J. Cooper.

"The Third Step (Autobiographical)"

"Que Dieu vous protege et benisse vos courageux desseins."
May God protect you and bless your courageous designs.

These are the words and this the prayer of M. l'Abbé Felix Klein, French author whose book, *Au Pays de la Vie Intense,* dedicated to President Theodore Roosevelt and containing a chapter on a visit to the M Street High School and an hour with a class in Vergil taught by its principal, caused a general raising of eyebrows in the United States and a few red faces in Washington, D. C.

The "Courageous designs" referred to was the audacious plan I had concocted to transfer my credits and thesis for the doctorate from Columbia University in New York to the University of Paris, France. It came about in this way. Following the Washington School Upheaval of 1906 . . . legal experts of D. C. found it expedient to promulgate a new doctrine, that reorganization of the school system involved the reappointment of all teachers—a thousand in a day. Thus it happened that the principal of M St. High School and several others were "overlooked"—not put out but left out in the shuffle, so to speak. . . .

The next four school years I held the chair of languages (French, German, Greek, Latin) at Lincoln University, Jefferson City, Missouri. It was pleasant to spend the summers of these four years in Oberlin, the college of so many happy memories, and I promptly applied to President King to matriculate for my next degree, the doctorate. He informed me however, that Oberlin's charter did not confer the Ph.D. and I contented myself with stimulating courses in belles lettres.

The fall of 1910 . . . Dr. Davidson, the new Superintendent in Washington sent for me . . . and I was duly appointed teacher of Latin in the Washington High School.

The following vacation months of July and August 1911, 1912, 1913 were employed at La Guilde Internationale, Paris, pursuing courses in French Literature, History, Phonetics. Provided with *certificats* for each of these courses . . . I matriculated for the long dreamed of Ph.D. at Columbia University, New York City, July 3, 1914.

Here I put in four summer sessions of close study, completing two full courses each session. This met the required number of 32 credits . . . but I still had the year's residence requirement to meet and a thesis which meant loss of subsistence income from September to June. . . .

Minimum residence? Ah, there's the rub. How was I to establish a year's residence in New York City from September to June without losing my job and utterly abandoning several important irons I had in the fire? First there was the brood of five motherless children ranging in age from an infant of 6 months to the ripe age of 12 years. I had taken them under my wing with the hope and determination of nurturing their growth into useful and creditable American citizens. Then too I had been at some pains to find a place in Washington that would be a home to house their Southern exuberance—a place with room enough all around so that their "expansion" would not be as thorns in the side of our Washington public.

A place was found and with it was discovered a unique combination of the perfect gentleman with a Christ-like attitude toward little children "regardless of race, color, creed or national origin," General LeFevre, a truly great American, who sold me the place that had been his home in old Le Droit Park which in the historic past had been forbidden ground for colored people except as servants. The place had been used as a chicken yard by its white tenants and I immediately set about landscaping, threw an octagon sun room across the square cornered porch, changed the wooden pillars to graceful Italian columns and installed a concrete balustrade all around, none of which brought me any nearer the residential requirements at Columbia University.

With butter at 75 cents per lb. still soaring, sugar severely rationed at any price and fuel oil obtainable only on affidavit in person at regional centers, the Judge at Children's Court—on occasion I had to report there—said to me: "My, but you are a brave woman!" Not as brave as you may imagine, was my mental rejoinder—only stubborn, perhaps, or foolhardy, according to the point of view. Either way my design was taking shape about the residence bugaboo: I. I would bide my time and like Micawber, wait for some thing to turn up. II. If the big chance should come to take a year off, I would not spend it in little old New York. Meanwhile, for "Home Work" I started on the Glossary for Le Pelerinage de Charlemagne. . . . [Her proposed dissertation was a college edition of this eleventh century work.]

The two or three vacations of waiting were filled with out of town work as usual: War Camp Community Service in Indianapolis, Playground Director at Wheeling, when finally the hour struck. The answer to prayer came—but not according to preconceived plans and specifications. It was a "frowning Providence" readily diagnosed even by the unlearned as the "Flu"—the real thing truly that pointed a way for my year's residence abroad.

'Twas the night before Christmas. After a hectic day of last minute shopping and preparations, late at night I was busy sorting out gifts and filling the children's stockings, when suddenly, things began to swim before me and grow black. I left the stockings to the oldest girl and staggered off to bed. The next day and many after I was not able to raise my head above the pillow and when I did get back to school I realized I was not at my best and decided to ask for a year's sick leave. This ostensibly was granted but the string to which it was attached turned out later to have elastic claws. After much figuring, rearranging and refurbishing of rules to make the punishment fit the crime, it transpired that the substitute's compensation for every day of my absence was larger than my own per diem pay on the principle that the larger the divisor for a given dividend the smaller the quotient. This was a minor headache compared with the bombshell that exploded when this cable reached me in Paris: "Rumored you will be dropped if not back in 60 days!"

You've guessed it. I had posted to France after sending ahead my application and transcript of credits from Columbia University to the Sorbonne, Paris U. It was astonishing and a bit amusing how earnest the Secretary to the Dean at Columbia became when I disclosed my intention to put in the year's residence in France. In anticlimax she argued it was impossible, unnecessary, undesirable. I countered for a while and then ceased firing, yielding the palm to preponderance of vociferation rather than to conviction. This was the first summer session following the attack of influenza . . . [After various special examinations and the submission of notes on the *Pelerinage*] I remembered to write my great and good friend the Abbé Felix Klein and received in reply his adorable prayer and blessing: May God protect you and your courageous designs.

I was on my way but far from plain sailing . . . The most formidable hurdle of all was getting my thought boiled down to a topic acceptable to the Faculté des Lettres de L'Université de Paris. President Poincaré had been making headlines that seemed to me significant of France's attitude toward Racial Equality. A monument had just been erected at Dakar *"A la Gloire de L'Armée Noire,—"le patriotisme ardent des tirailleurs tombés sur tous les Champs de bataille de France."* I had accumulated some notes and comments of my own on the Franco Japanese Treaty of 1896—The Naturalization laws of France: a) for Japanese, b) Hindus, c) Negroes, and of course the discussions in the National Assemblies during the French Revolution; the writings and speeches of and about La Société des Amis des Noirs . . . I concluded that by delving deeper into original sources and official documents to be found in the Archives at Paris I might produce something worth while on the French conception of dignity of all Races. Accordingly with some trepidation I submitted my first tryout for a subject: L'Attitude de la France à l'Egard dé l'Egalité des Races.

"Madame Cooper est informée que le sujet . . . ne peut être accepté sous une forme aussi vague. En principe votre sujet est accepté. . . . Too vast and too vague! How hem it in. How pin it down. How make it concrete, definite, pointed. I still felt the urge to compliment France, and was entirely sincere in my belief that the torch I hoped to see grow bigger and brighter had its lightning spark in her Liberté, Fraternité, Egalité.

> "Trop vaste"? Definite Title: Slavery
> "Trop vague"? Time Limit: The Revolution
> "L'Attitude de la France *a l'egard de L'Esclavage pendant la Revolution*".

[The subject was approved as "The Attitude of France in the Question of Slavery between 1789 and 1848" and she began her work.] However a friend close to authoritative sources at home cabled me: "Rumored dropped if not return within 60 days." Ouch! Just as I was settling down to work at the archives where you have to be checked to go in and doubled checked to get out!

On the credit side for my 50 days residence however they had prepared for me an exhaustive dossier of sources bearing on my subject and I would gladly have spent more than the promised year delving in so rich a mine. But 60 days! I began counting off my Saturdays and Sundays, the Christmas holidays, George Washington's birthday. Only 10 days remained for me to wind up my affairs and report "present" at Dunbar High School, Washington, D. C. A desperate Cinderella with no fairy godmother to turn to! But again yes; a friend in need, the friend indeed. . . Monsieur l'Abbé. A trip to Mendon to explain the situation. If I did not return at once, I'd lose not only my job as a present means of support but also all hope of future security on retiring. Would he recommend some collaboratrice whom I could employ to copy aux Archives the subjects I had already checked in the dossier and relay the same to the Library of Congress at Washington where I would work after school hours and week ends. I could arrange . . . to continue my year's work in the Washington Library, returning to Paris for the Soutenance [defense] of my Thesis when completed. (Yes; come I would, I fiercely promised myself, "If I have to swim!")

When I walked into my class room 5 minutes before 9 on the morning of the 60th day of my absence, I did not sense the true inwardness of the gleeful applause that greeted me till sometime afterwards when I learned that these little friends of mine had had all the excitement of fans holding ringside seats at a race; for the substitute had confided to them "I'll be your permanent teacher if Mrs. Cooper does not get back by next Thursday."

Plugging away every leisure moment and putting in full time in summer vacation and holidays . . . I had my stuff fit to be typed by Thanksgiving. This time I prostrated myself before the Throne and asked for leave under Rule 45 for "Emergency" stating the emergency to present my thesis before a Jury at the Sorbonne. . . . My immediate supervisor wanted to know why the "emergency" could not be squeezed into the ten days of Easter holiday. Well we could not manipulate the Law of France to accommodate a High School in Washington. So again scrapping Thanksgiving, Christmas, Easter and all Saturdays and Sundays, I took the bit in my teeth deciding "If they drop me this time it shall be for doing as I darn please. If I perish, I perish."

With my typed MSS. in my hand bag I once again crossed the Atlantic, following the Beam. . . . [Her defense of her thesis was scheduled for March 23]

Somewhere off the quadrangle I had read in passing: *Thèse pour le Doctorat 23 Mars à 9 heures Salle de Richelieu Mlle. Cooper.* But the only directing I had received was "Tout pres de l'Eglise" in very rapid and very careless French. As I entered for the first time the awesome portals of the Salle du Doctorat I was met by an elderly personage in black gown who addressed me as Mademoiselle and inquired what college was designated by my Master's hood of crimson and gold. He conducted me to a table at front on which a carafe of water, a goblet and a bowl of sugar for what purpose I was too painfully preoccupied to try to guess. . . . The audience, which was behind me and did not disturb me in the least, rose and I stood up as the three judges filed in by a door at the rear of the high platform on which they seated themselves.

Anticipating that Sagnac would lead off with a general question on the thesis itself, I had written out in French and memorized a resume of my basic thought as to the influence of the Encyclopedists and 18th century philosophy on attitudes in France regarding the Rights of Man, the barbarity of slavery, etc. . . . After about an hour on the main theme Sagnac passed the defendant over to M. Cestre who had to meet a class elsewhere at 11. In his kindly hands my fears ceased clawing at my heart. Without consciousness of the unusual I followed his lead as if in informal conversation when he mentioned John C. Calhoun, Thomas Jefferson, State Sovereignty, Nullification. When he rose to be excused I knew that I had at least one vote for "passing."

From 11 to 12 the Bête Noir [Prof. Bouglé, the judge whose questions she feared most]. My best bolstering boost was that Bouglé's Thesis, *Egalité,* had been carefully studied and I knew it almost as well as I knew my own. He could not trip me on that if once I caught his question. Only once did my ear stumble and it was on the word densité. I hesitated "densité" dans cité— "Pardon Monsieur. Je n'ai pas compris votre question." However, that was all straightened out and by the very irony of fate, when, after three solid hours of grilling questions and grueling fear, the mentor at my back rapped a third time for the audience to rise on the return of the judges, and I remained standing for the sentence to be pronounced, it was Monsieur Bouglé who delivered the verdict, of which all that I could make out or can now recall, was "bien satisfaite" and "que vous êtes Docteur."

Vida Scudder (*Permission of the Wellesley College Archives*)

Vida Scudder, 1861–1954

On Journey (1937);
My Quest for Reality (1952)

Vida Scudder was a literary scholar, a woman of deep religious faith, and a political radical who urged the reconciliation of Christianity and socialism. Born in India, she was the daughter of a missionary, David Scudder (who died when she was an infant), and Harriet Dutton Scudder, of an old New England and literary family. Vida Scudder's career blended the legacy of the long Scudder missionary tradition with the intellectual commitments and responsibilities of the Duttons.

As she tells us in her first autobiography, *On Journey*, Scudder's career was lived within a series of interlocking circles of educated women. A graduate of Smith, Scudder went on after college to be a founder of the College Settlement Association. Denison House, the settlement house in Boston she helped to establish, was staffed by college-bred women who, like her, felt a responsibility to service. For Scudder, however, that sense of responsibility was accompanied by doubt—about both the possibility and the legitimacy of trying to transcend class divisions.

At Wellesley College, where she taught in the English department from 1887 to 1928, there was no such class conflict. There, instead, Scudder's sense of mission led her to try to bring to her students her awareness of social problems as well as her love of literature. Wellesley offered her the pleasure of scholarship and intellectual companionship, but she was concerned that these pleasures might draw her away from her responsibility to social change. Just as she tried to direct the college's attention to social problems, so also within the Episcopal Church, which she had joined in the 1870's, she tried to broaden the church's acceptance of the social gospel. Her belief that socialism and Christianity were compatible, and her hope for their reconciliation, led her into such groups as the Church League for Industrial Democracy. She was also a founding member of the Society of Companions of the Holy Cross, a group of Episcopal laywomen who were devoted to prayer and contemplation and to the examination of crucial social issues. It was to her Companions that she dedicated her second autobiography, *My Quest for Reality*, a series of brief comments and meditations on experience written in 1952 when she was over ninety.

The evolution of Scudder's thought, as a Christian socialist and as a literary radical, forms a significant chapter in American intellectual history, as well as in the history of women's roles in movements for social change. Like such other Wellesley faculty of her generation as Ellen Hayes and Emily Greene Balch, Scudder believed that the academic life demands, rather than precludes, social responsibility. She gave a speech at the Lawrence strike in 1912 which deeply disturbed those who wished to maintain a wall around the academy. Widely reported, it was long remembered: in a 1957 memoir, Mary Heaton Vorse, the labor journalist whose commitment to the cause of labor began at Lawrence, recalled the impact of "Miss Scudder, who made that speech on the Commons. . . . [She] felt passionately about what was being done."

Influenced by Ruskin, and later by the Fabians, Vida Scudder's work is also important for its effort to interpret literature from a social as well as an aesthetic perspective. The censure imposed on her at Wellesley for participating in the Lawrence strike was the suspension for a year of her course, "Social Ideals in English Literature." What a remarkable testimony that is to the success of the course and to the attractiveness of her blending of social and aesthetic ideas.

Revival of interest in Scudder in the 1970's is in part the result of new scholarship on the significance of the women's colleges; she is also receiving attention because of the defense she made in literature and in life of the importance of female friendships. She should have been rediscovered earlier, in that ferment of social activism which characterized university life in the 1960's, as her life and work are a model for an activist intellectual.

EDITIONS USED

On Journey. New York: E.P. Dutton, 1937.
My Quest for Reality. Privately printed, 1952.

SUGGESTED READINGS:

Corcoran, Theresa, S.C. "Vida Dutton Scudder: Impact of World War I on
      Radical Professor." *Anglican Theological Review* (Spring, 1975).
Frederick, Peter J. "The Professor as Social Activist." *The New England
      Quarterly* (September, 1970):
Scudder, Vida. *Listener in Babel.* Boston: Houghton Mifflin, 1903.
      _____. *Socialism and Character.* Boston: Houghton Mifflin, 1912.

On Journey

Part II: The Middle Years, 1887-1912

CHAPTER V:
"THE TERRIBLE CHOICE"

I

An outstanding fact in private experience during those long years, is that I was perpetually drawn in three directions at once, and racked in consequence. I could echo from my heart the phrase of Browning's great Pope, from the monologue in "The Ring and the Book" which I always taught with special admiration: "Life's business being just the terrible choice."

Always I coveted the single-track mind. Worthwhile people never scattered their energies; Bacon the statesman never wrote Shakespeare's plays. But my own energies were scattered far and wide. While I so eagerly played my part in the developing social movement, delight in my profession had grown stronger every year, and by the turn of the century, academic ambition of a not ignoble type was keen in me. But what can you do if, in the memorable phrase of the then President of Bryn Mawr, you are irresistibly impelled to take your next step in two directions? The tumultous sphere of social reform claimed me no less than the calm college world.

Even in that world, I encountered conflict. Some teachers rejoice in pedagogy for its own sake; others hunger for research; a few have a genuinely creative function, straining to be fulfilled. In European universities, where not more than six lectures a week are usually required of a professor, research and teaching—I don't know about creative work—are less at odds; and even in the United States reconciliation is possible: witness the prolific output of many teachers; the academic life, after all, is one. But where was unity for me? By this time—I speak now of the early twentieth century—St. Francis had touched the springs of my life. The call of Lady Poverty rang clear, I longed to make an ultimate surrender. The comfort and security of my life, the beauty of the Wellesley campus, the charm of my pleasant home, filled me intermittently with loathing. I suppose the blood of my missionary father was running hot in my veins.

When in New York, usually on settlement business, I would often stay in the home of my uncle, E.P. Dutton, the publisher, a stately house where the foot sank deep into rugs, where good pictures graced the walls, where all was ordered softly to suit the two dear elderly people who lived a curiously quiet life, my little aunt being a semi-invalid. From there I would go down to the push carts, the crowds, the grim excitement of Rivington Street. I found the contrast excruciating. Always I have remembered a response of my devout uncle, one of the most sincerely religious men I ever knew. I had reproached him gently for his pew in aristocratic St. Thomas's and had persuaded him to go with me one Sunday to St. George's, where Dr. Rainsford was then in his prime. My uncle did not enjoy the service. He complained that a stout and, to speak frankly, smelly man was shown into the same seat. "I was not comfortable," said he.

"Christ was not always comfortable," returned his impatient and slightly irrelevant niece.

"No," said the dear uncle slowly, thinking the matter out: "No-o. But He became uncomfortable in order that we might be comfortable." Not a bad summary of some old theories of the Atonement.

I could not away with it. But in my modest home on the Boston Back Bay, my mother, aunt, and I lived simply indeed but in dainty peace. Was there much to choose between my life and my uncle's?

So I envisaged the parting of the ways; and for at least a couple of years lived in distressed and not wholly healthful indecision. But I suspect that choices are usually made rather for one than by one; the decisive moment never came. I kept right on with my diverse interests, till time for retirement arrived, and the "academic" dropped me, not I it. Nor did I drift, exactly. I constantly sought submission to Hardy's "Immanent Will," and I consulted spiritual advisers, Bishop Hall of Vermont, and Father Huntington of the Order of the Holy Cross. This last wise and holy man said in effect: "To accept a conventional life with humility may be your share in expiation for the sins of the world." I think he went on to speak of the Nailed Hands on the Cross. I did not dare appropriate his words, being aware that cowardice and self indulgence blended with an honest sense of duty to hold me in that pleasant, hated life. And I knew that the inner expiation of which he spoke called for a steady vicarious suffering which despite my restlessness I was not likely to sustain. Yet there has been abiding comfort as well as challenge in what he said.

His immediate allusion was of course to my primary duty toward my mother; he would never have encouraged me to behave like St. Francis, and fling my clothes in her face. She had only me. I think she would gladly have spared me to the mission field, but she never understood my radicalism, and I did not force it on her. Now a certain text, "Whoso loveth father or mother more than Me", always tormented me; and had I been of more heroic fiber, I might have behaved differently. But common sense came to my aid. To abandon my profession for the undefined realm of social activities, would have meant exchange of sure usefulness for doubtful values; I was American enough to want definite and fruitful action ahead. Moreover, my college salary had become important. I had never considered money; I believe I was over forty years old before ever I made out a check. My mother once told me that our income, apart from my salary, amounted to twelve hundred dollars a year, and while I somehow can't quite believe that, our resources were certainly modest; we moved serenely, shaping our lives by the simple maxim in which I was so well drilled that I practice it to this day: Never let the sun set on an unpaid debt. But times were changing; earned income had become a necessity.

I hated my salary. Queer hatred, which would well become a citizen of Utopia, but hardly one in this commercialized world. I think I was feeling the first instinctive stirrings of such speculation about right relations of work and reward as have much concerned me of late years; I recollect still the sense of irrelevance and distaste with which I went to the appointed office to draw my first pay. Yet to live rather on money earned than on money inherited seemed comparatively respectable to me. So my divided life continued, and on the natural human leval, I have nothing to regret. I got another bit of comfort from that picturesque and original person, Patrick Geddes. One night at Denison House he got to talking on my precise problem, and recommended rotation of crops, insisting that the human soil was as much enriched by variety in cultivation as any other. I believe he was both right and wrong. I know that the division of my energies destroyed my chance of amounting to much on any one line; but oh, what fun I have had! It is true, however, that in sustaining three distinct interests—for I was busily writing books all through these years—I deliberately renounced personal ambition.

The time had come when to reach distinction in the academic world I should have secured a Ph.D. My first interlude, when in '93-'95 I took two years away from the College, gave me the opportunity. But I devoted the first half of that period chiefly to settlements; in the second half, I got over to France for courses at the Sorbonne, but I ignored systematic study for a degree. Truth to tell, I was impatient then, as sometimes now, with Ph.D. research. What I cared for was to keep my students as well as myself in the presence of significant racial experience, embedded in forms of undying beauty; I thought that was what America needed, and I was indifferent to rummaging about in literary byways in pursuit of unimportant information. (Having written that naughty sentence, I hasten to remark that I am not unappreciative of Ph.D. work on higher levels, when students have been equipped with the contacts of which I speak.) So I did not then sacrifice much; but I did renounce concern for status, since I heartily endorsed the policy demanding that women, new as they were to the academic world, should qualify on accredited lines for collegiate positions. But no Ph.D. for me; and, in that world, a permanently subordinate place.

As for social activities, they demand the whole of you. Didn't I know it? My best impulses, compounded of shame and of adventurous urge toward trail-making, pointed that way. They were illumined, those impulses, they shone on the path trodden not only by the contemporaries I most honored, but by the saints of God. I resisted. This did not mean that I severed myself completely from that glorious company, only that my share in the life must be insignificant, my contacts occasional. As time went on, I realized that I was only on the fringe of that great world of social endeavor. Tremulously I felt that I might have claimed my place there. But not if at the same time I was, for instance, developing a course on Arthurian romance at Wellesley. By degrees, relations with working people, alas, grew fewer; the old prison walls of class again closed round me. I found to my disgust that I was putting more time on uptown committees and on administrative planning, than on actual human fellowship. This I never ceased to mourn.

Remained, the writing of books. Had I shaped my life according to taste, this would have been my chief pursuit. For the wish to write was irrepressible, and by the time I reached my early thirties I knew that I had plenty to say. I had, frankly, not only impulse from within, but ambition to make my mark in American letters, as fatuously enough I thought that I might possibly do. And I wrote, vigorously, joyously; but under what pressure, in time how jealously snatched from other matters! One can do good journalistic work perhaps under these conditions, but one can't write the books of one's dreams. A five-foot shelf of volumes I have written stands, to my credit or discredit, in my book case; I shall speak of them now and then. They have brought me marvelous friends, more than one book has come from deep within me. But they have been conditioned by circumstance, written often with a view to some special need of others, seldom from the pure and free creative passion. And only once or twice under conditions of freedom. I am content; "for I know that nothing happens without Mystery."

II

Life does not move along parallel lines; it is rather an interweaving of threads; and the threads put in my hands by the Fates, along which my fingers moved so blindly, were intricate to handle. Sometimes they knotted, sometimes they interfered with one another. My social and academic interests did not easily work out into a smooth pattern. Two instances of disagreeable conflict must be chronicled.

At about the turn of the century, I caught the distaste for "tainted money" infectious among radicals at that time, and joined, if I did not instigate, a vehement protest made by sundry members of the Wellesley faculty against accepting money from the profits of Standard Oil. The decorous Rockefeller Foundation was far in the future; the scandal of the normal methods of capitalistic competition was shocking many consciences for the first time. Henry Demarest Lloyd's book, "Wealth against Commonwealth," had fanned the flame. Now Wellesley was a struggling college, dedicated to the pious education of young women; and that the (much solicited) offer of money could be other than cause of thanksgiving was an inconceivably disloyal notion, to our trustees as to our honored President, Miss Hazard. I was not the only one to shrink from that money, but I was the most violent, and I signed, I forget whether for myself or with two or three others, a Memorial more extreme than that sent by the larger group. Many a discussion ensued on the perennial subject of academic freedom. (I recall publishing an article on the issue, in the "Century" I believe.) And in a book, entitled "A Listener in Babel," I included a fairly accurate transcript of the excited war of opinions waged on that battle field. . . .

Our little movement of revolt and inquiry was naturally disconcerting to the Wellesley trustees. From that time on, I perennially bothered them, and myself, by the ever recurrent question of loyalty. I consulted my rector, later Bishop Brent, as to the propriety of resigning from the college. "Stay where you are till they force you out," said he. "The deeper loyalty demands it; loss of the radicals would spell death for the colleges." I stayed, though with increasing discomfort, and I was not tipped out. Here I would like to record the habitual liberality of Wellesley toward its most troublesome teachers—a policy only once broken, in my experience, when in wartime Emily Greene Balch failed of reappointment, by a narrow margin of two votes among the trustees. Great was my pleasure, and great I know the pleasure of Miss Pendleton, when on the return of Miss Balch from Geneva after long and honored service in the Woman's International League of Peace and Freedom, she was asked to give the official address at the College on Armistice Day, *Autre temps, autres moeurs*.

Naturally, I disliked making the trustees unhappy. One of them wrote me, anent this "tainted money" business, an indignant letter which I long preserved. It took me sharply to task for stressing the curse which must rest on enterprises built on a foundation of social injustice. Do not flowers grow on the blood-stained field of battle? Shall we audaciously seek to improve the methods of the Almighty? . . . Of course the money was accepted; the only concern of the trustees was whether our agitation should reach the ears of the donor and cause him to withdraw his offer. Either he never heard or didn't care; the money was spent on a much needed central heating plant, with an ugly tower which intrudes into our fair landscape to this day. We radicals were at least glad that the money didn't go into salaries, but I don't think our situation was really improved by the fact. My colleague, Margaret Sherwood, presented in her arresting novel, "Henry Worthington, Idealist," the predicament of the young academic radical. Some of us discussed resigning; but we all stayed on, largly because we perceived that short of fleeing into a hermitage, we could not escape the taint of communal guilt. And even a hermit must wear clothes, perhaps made by sweated labor.

When the time came to retire on a Carnegie pension, the old problem, quiescent but never solved, was acutely renewed for me. I wanted to refuse that money, and I could have done so and not starved. But I took it. I decided that my legal claim on it involved moral responsibility for its use. So I spend it year by year, on radical social causes mostly religious in character and inspired if not endorsed by the Church; thereby seeking to hack off the branch I sit on. I have been amused, and easy in my conscience; only, if the Revolution proceeds with quickened tempo, and dividends continue to crumble, I may be forced any day to the sad expedient of endowing myself as a revolutionary force.

A sensitive radical in the college world is inevitably placed in a false and painful position, if only because the public will insist on holding his institution responsible for his opinions. Freedom is little more than a mirage, as soon as one is committed to group activity of any type. I had my share of the acute distress resultant on knowing that my presence was a practical disadvantage to the College which paid me for my services. The generosity with which I was treated enhanced this distress. I have been shown letters from irate parents threatening to withdraw their daughters on my account; I have been gently asked more than once to explain myself to the trustees; I have been informed of gifts refused because I was a member of the faculty. . . . But worse than any external criticism, and an enduring strain, was the tormenting uncertainty as to what loyalty involved. . . . I trod my way to Wellesley with caution; seeking always that finer truthfulness which demands not only statement of conviction but concern for the effect of such statement on other minds. Into the attempt to strike a balance between candor and reserve, the whole science of pedagogy enters.

Perplexities, and opportunities, came to the head toward the end of the years I am reviewing, in the famous Lawrence strike of 1912. The Tainted Money controversy had gone on within the familiar and comparatively sheltered precincts of middle-class thinking; this strike precipitated us into the storm-center of the class struggle. As "The Survey" said with prescient wisdom, it presented "a new thing in the industrial world, which must henceforth be taken into account." The young I.W.W. captured it from A.F. of L., and in comparison with their picturesque methods, charged as every one felt with revolutionary dynamite, the older organization, representing by that time a sort of aristocracy of labor, seemed mild and rational. Ettor and Giovanitti, and big Bill Haywood—the only leader I met personally—were the heroes, or villains, of the piece. Communists now take in some ways—not all—the place of I.W.W., and we are intimate with this type of industrial conflict. We know the hot dangerous passions, the bitter recriminations, the police brutality, the calling out of the militia, the outrages on both sides; and slowly we come to recognize that more often than not, violence does not begin with the strikers. Let Marion, Gastonia, Passaic bear witness; let Tampa never be forgotten. It was all new then, especially in staid New England, and the whole community was set vibrating. That strike will live in American history, as a salient early episode in the long story of the class war during the slow decay of a capitalistic order already alarmed and passionately on the defensive.

I went to Lawrence. I attended strike meetings, and was tremendously impressed by the able leadership which secured unity of action in that seething ferment where cross currents of racial and religious antagonism constantly interfered below the surface—I forget how many languages were spoken by the strikers. I visited the workers' homes, bad enough to justify almost any revolt in my indignant eyes. I lunched at the Franco-Belge Co-operative, recognizing in that group, well versed as they were in revolutionary techinique, the most competent among the strikers. And recognition grew on me of the amazing disciplines in comradeship and corporate action afforded to wage-earners by such grim warfare, offering as it does release from tread-mill monotony and sordid individual interests, into that consciousness of group life, with its stern call for adjustments and controls, which is the only hope of democracy. I saw then, as I have seen in every industrial struggle watched since, the evocation of sacrificial devotion such as the churches might well envy. I saw the horizons of those strikers extend under my eyes, while the leaders, many of whom stood to lose personally, urged heroic aims, pointing into the future when

> "The International Party
> Shall be the human race."

Rupert Brooke in a well-known sonnet described the young soldiers of the World War as "swimmers into cleanness leaping." I do not like war as a means of purification; but what that sonnet suggests is what I saw happening in Lawrence, and what I met only the other day in the flaming young spirit of Edith Berkmann, a later leader in Left-Wing revolt.

I am still glad that I went to Lawrence. But my contacts with the strike were slight. I spoke at a meeting. I was assured that it was not under the auspices of the I.W.W., but it might just as well have been. The conduct of the strike involved some dramatic features; one was a plan for sending away the children of the often hungry strikers and putting them under the care of friendly sympathizers at a distance. For some reason, that plan roused the ire of the manufacturers and was met by harsh and violent measures. The meeting of protest which I was asked to address was called by a women's committee, nominally of citizens. I have never been sorry that I assented; but even to have visited that infected town was a crime in the eyes of "The Boston Transcript."

I did not go alone. I was not the only radical at Wellesley. My valiant little comrade and colleague, Ellen Hayes, professor of astronomy, went also. Her cast of mind was more revolutionary than mine, for though I had read Marx by this time, I was not completely "sold" as she was to belief in the class struggle as the only means of salvation. The meeting was much bigger than we expected. I was wearing a hat with a modest white ostrich plume, I remember, and as we advanced to the platform I heard her murmuring something behind me about "the white plume of Navarre." Her speech was better liked than mine; for I pleaded with all my feeble power for obedience to law, and I think my remarks fell flat. I have dug that old speech out of my records; luckily I had written it in advance, and it ran all over the country:

> We who do not live in Lawrence must speak and feel with great
> caution—(What a way to begin!)
> Many hundred years ago, a young Hebrew working-man, later exe-
> cuted as a demagogue, said a strange thing: "Blessed are ye when men
> shall revile you and persecute you." Yesterday the words kept ringing
> in my ears.

Had the Lawrence strikers been persecuted? I put the case hypothetically, though everybody knew the facts.

> If their leader has been refused bail—if women have been roughly
> handled—if young girls have been dragged to the police court—

I went on to plead for non-resistance. The way out would be agitation for a minimum wage law, etc. etc.

> I speak for thousands beside myself when I say that I would rather
> never again wear a thread of woolen than know my garments had been
> woven at cost of such misery as I have seen and known past the shadow
> of doubt to have existed in this town.

This remark for some reason specially enraged certain newspapers. I continued, quoting the Vulgate version of the Beatitude—"Blessed are they who suffer for justice's sake,"—and proceeded:

> Is it for justice's sake that the strikers in Lawrence suffer? I do not
> know. But this I can say. I went home yesterday giving thanks that at
> least certain ends of justice are being served here. For in the meeting of
> the strike committee which I attended, I saw two great ends achieved;

ends for which we social workers and reformers spend our lives, too often in vain. The first was the end of Fraternity. Men of different tongues and alien cultures were bound into one dogged unity of purpose; and vibrations of brotherhood ran through that assembly, so strong that I believe they augur a future when in America those of differing races shall be indeed of one heart, one mind, one soul. And the other end is Vision. For on every man and woman there, had flashed the vision of a just society, based on fair rewards to Labor and on fraternal peace. I give thanks that these two noble ends are being attained through union of the Workers.

Exhortations followed: "See that you hold your task too sacred to be defended by dishonorable or violent means." Miss Hayes spoke in a different vein, and she had a hit at the D.A.R.—later described by Upton Sinclair as the "Daughters of No More American Revolutions"—who were already going strong. But she and the other speakers from Boston—George Willis Cooke and Mr. John Adams—spoke as I did chiefly of the educational values of the strike. Only the last speaker, who must have been a Labor man, remarked that Magna Carta was won by force, and that force would come into this picture sooner or later. On the whole, the reports of that meeting sound mild enough to me. But such was not the opinion of "The Boston Transcript". Pontificating after its usual pleasant habit, it demanded that Miss Hayes and I resign from Wellesley, adding that we should have resigned before going to Lawrence. And there ensued a tempest in our little academic teapot. "The Survey" sprang to my defense, saying that "such discussion as that of Professor Scudder furnishes the very foundation of free institutions in a democracy" (one could still talk about democracy in those days). But "The Market Reporter," organ of "the financial and real estates interests of Boston," went for Miss Hayes because she had made an uncomplimentary allusion to Krupp in Germany,—remember that we were in the year 1912: "All Germany," says this organ, "honors Herr Krupp for the splendid results of his genius given to his country and the world." Other industrial leaders in other countries are equally entitled to gratitude and honors for what they have accomplished for human progress in spite of ignorant labor opposition: "Karl Marx and his rattle-brained followers see nothing of all this."

The Wellesley trustees were deluged with letters from both sides. I suppose only those coming to my defense reached me, and I have a kind and touching sheaf of them, largely but by no means entirely from alumnae. Again, Wellesley stood by her principles. My resignation was not asked, and for reasons already given I did not proffer it. When similar storms occur, as they do again and again in other college teapots, I remember my own small adventure. And I want to say that I do not believe the trustees of any educational institution ever acted with more temperate kindness than the trustees and the officers of Wellesley. . . .

I was asked to submit an account of the whole affair to the trustees; and the request was made that I suppress for the coming year my course on "Social Ideals in English Letters." The only thing that grieved me was the attitude of my old friend and colleague, now Head of my department, Katharine Lee Bates. She acted, according to her lights, with kindness and wisdom; but our ways had diverged far. To her, anything calling down criticism on that central object of her loyalty, the College, savored of treason. Her first reaction was that I should resign. I loved the College too, but for me there would have been deeper disloyalty in any act on my part which should even seemingly discredit Wellesley's academic freedom. Katharine wrote on March 12:

> I felt with penitence, after our scraps of talk on Friday, that I had rather stubbornly pressed my point of criticism instead of assuring you of my fundamental support, and my essential fellowship, in the ideals toward which I hope the socialistic movement is working. I would defend anywhere and to anybody your right to express under proper circumstances your social creed, and the only circumstances that occur to me as improper are those which might mislead the public into claiming you with the forces of anarchy,—as seems to have been the case at Lawrence,—and the Wellesley classroom, where your given task as I understand it is to interpret English literature. That you should interpret there the social theories of Shelley and Morris is right; that you intend to urge your own views there I do not believe, though I think it likely that you unconsciously impress them on our immature thinkers more forcibly than you realize.
>
> The more I think of this whole matter, the more I am inclined to modify my original opinion that self-respect and generosity toward the college authorities require your resignation. . . . It is fortunate I think that your book is out at this time and under review.

A fine letter, and a friendship that bore the strain. But despite her loving words, she never again quite trusted my classroom judgment; and I want to think that this may have been in part the reason why on her retirement fourteen years later, she failed to recommend me as her successor. She did quite right, from her angle of vision; but I was saddened and grieved, much as I should have disliked the office.

So that was that. The book to which she alludes, called "Socialism and Character," I still think contained some of my best thinking, though it never attained even the small popularity of "Social Ideals in English Letters," the book summarizing the course I was asked to suspend. . . . I skipped my course for a year or two; then, feeling having subsided, took it up again.

As for "Socialism and Character," which I dedicated to the dearest of my students, Florence Converse, by this time my close friend, I suppose it was a queer book. I am sure it was premature. Years later, a young unchurched radical presented an interesting idea to me. The supreme achievement of Thomas Aquinas in the fourteenth century was, as we all knew, said he, synthesizing Aristotelian philosophy and the Catholic faith; the time would come, when a genius would arise to perform a like service by synthesizing the Catholic faith and Karl Marx. We are still waiting for that genius;[2] but in my stumbling way I was trying to do precisely that. For I was turning very gradually from my first guides, the Fabians, to the socialist thought of the Continent; and the doctrine of economic determinism, or the materialistic interpretation of history as it was then called, seemed to me in some of its aspects, as it seems still, extraordinarily consonant with a Sacramental understanding of the universe. Moreover, I wished to show that in the classless and functional society of the Marxian hope, Catholic doctrine would find itself at home as in no preceding culture, while character—that is to say, personality, which is the ultimate concern of Christian thought—would have such chance as never before was known at free self-realization. . . . The book found, as I have said, few readers, but it brought me more than one valued friend; there is something magical about friendship born of no human contact but of one's disembodied thought. One young man copied pages from that book on rice paper, which he carried in his breast pocket all through a strange pilgrimage he made in pre-war Russia. It was this same young man who, after the Kerensky revolution, wanted me to go to Russia with him on a sociological-religious evangelistic adventure. I am afraid he was not a very practical young man.

2. Now, in 1937, the attempt is beginning in many quarters.

My Quest for Reality

My attitude toward Evil? I welcome it. For I think it is waking us up. We have reached a critical stage in our Process. Today, both forces we deplore and forces we endorse and would fain cultivate, are astonishingly vital. I am startled at the relief I feel as I watch the terror threatening us. I feel life vibrating through both the secular and the religious world. And I rejoice and give thanks.

How complacent was the middle class civilization of my New England girlhood! Especially was this true of the comfortable people with whom my lot was cast. The honest merchants of my family profited with no uneasy moral quivers, and certainly with no conscious dominance by greed, from the "Free Enterprise", or, if you prefer, from the Capitalist system which had its best opportunities in the United States. Was it not identical with the Democracy which had escaped from that Feudal inheritance, an aristocracy of birth? . . . We were terribly sleepy, on the level where most Christians lived before the first World War. For that matter, we still are. If we look at contemporary life from the pages of the daily newspaper, what it offers is disconcerting alike to our morals and our taste. I'm thinking of its calm assumption of America's superiority . . . say over Russia . . . in ethics; also, if you like, of its vulgarity in its records of divorces and murders. I might also mention our callous appetite for Mystery Novels (an appetite I confess I share). Does the "Democracy" we profess deserve allegiance? The newspapers make my loyalty to America uncertain.

Of course there were stirrings of promise in my youth; Rauschenbusch was speaking, and Debs. I've told elsewhere how my own social awakening came at Oxford, largely through Ruskin and the Fabians: I share Gandhi's attitude toward "Unto This Last". But the social impulses waiting my return to America, though they were stirring, rarely rose above the level of plain philanthropy. But now! We live in terror. Confusion entangles us. We are eaught by dilemmas, suspicious of one another, uncertain whether we can look toward a racial future on this planet. We have waked up. And I repeat that I am glad. Tragedy, witness Shakespeare, witness Dante, always affords, I think, exhilaration and relief.

Submission to the process we must accept may connote either indolence or humility. Lots of evils are of transitory importance, to overcome them is exhilarating. . . . But what about that worst evil which coincides with the arrival of humanity on this planet? How about Sin? The Christian shudders at it, in himself and in society at large. I think that in no previous epoch was the accusation of Sin so flung at one another as today. Pretty much every nation and social group ascribes it to another; Russians accuse the Capitalist system as we Americans accuse Communism. Bewilderment results. But the Christian . . . (dare I say this?) . . . knows that the world would be very dull without Sin. Were struggle against that worst of evils abolished, I sometimes feel that all which is most worth while in civilization would disappear.

With some shame I'll say that I am specially relieved when I look at the Church. For how somnolent and decorous it was in my Protestant girlhood! The astounding assumptions of Christianity pass easily into platitudes if they are not applied. In the Churches of my youth they bore no relation to corporate life except as regards the Family. The economic order was serenely actuated by incentives flatly irrelevant to our holy faith and to the teachings of the New Testament. These last were taught in Sunday School and, as I said, were applied to family life, but otherwise they possessed only individual appeal . . . Don't think for a moment that I deny the Christian culture of my youth. Today, when emphasis on social reform is often urged with purely ethical and humanistic stress, we need to remember that corporate Christianity finds its only sure foundation in personal religion. Only those who have followed successfully the Quest of Reality can enter and stay in the Light in which corporate behavior can be rightly shaped. But to pause alone in that Light is fatal. I think all lasting social reform, or revolution if you like, rests on personal conversion, never on that fatally dangerous short-cut, totalitarian control. On the other hand, weakness in revivalist movements is usually found in their ignoring social application. Such Christian thinking was, in the main, with some marked promising pioneer exceptions, singularly unadventurous in the earlier years here in America. It needed to be shocked. It has that privilege now. We begin to see, what some pioneers were hinting, that personal conversion is thwarted and inert unless it demands corporate transformation . . . We are all trying now to discover what it would mean to apply the laws of the Kingdom of Heaven beyond personal life and the family circle. . . .

Corporate obedience to laws beyond those controlling natural life on all lower levels in Space and Time is no easy matter. It may rightly be called revolutionary, and the exploring path is perilous at every turn. Problems are sure to increase and methods to clash, more and more. But I think the light thrown by my automobile on a darkening evening road on which fog is brooding offers a good symbol, and I must say that I enjoy driving more and more because the fog grows thicker and shadows darker. I don't want ever to stop. I am a controversial person. I accept more and more the discipline of cultivating sympathy with all travelers even if they invite me to try another road. I think many leaders at cross-purposes both in politics and religion are sustained by honest conviction that they tread the right way; and perhaps so were their predecessors a few centuries . . . or even decades . . . ago. I must carefully avoid complacency as I stumble on, for unless one watches one's steps prayerfully at every turn one is sure to fall down. I think that the Spirit illuminates our foggy road more and more.

H. D. (Hilda Doolittle) (*By Islay Lyons, permission of David R. Godine, Publisher, from* Tribute to Freud, *copyright 1956, 1974 by Norman Holmes Pearson*)

H.D. [Hilda Doolittle], 1886–1961

Tribute to Freud (1956)

In his introduction to H.D.'s *Trilogy,* the three long poems which emerged from her experience of World War II, her friend Norman Holmes Pearson says that H.D. initialled certain lines as especially appropriate to various friends: "For herself she chose 'We are as voyagers, discoverers/of the not known.' " The notes she took during her sessions with Freud (published as "Advent" in Pearson's edition of *Tribute to Freud*) work out three stages of her voyage. "The first decade," she said began on "the Argo, *Floride,* a small French Line steamer sailing to Havre." That journey was in 1911, when H.D. left America for Europe.

H.D. was born in Bethlehem, Pennsylvania, to a "pure New England" father, Charles Doolittle, a professor of astronomy, and a "musician-artist" mother, Helen (Wolle) Doolittle, whose family were Moravian Brethren. In her sophomore year at Bryn Mawr, she became engaged to Ezra Pound. Her parents disapproved, and she left, going first to Philadelphia, then to New York, and eventually to London where Pound was already the center of a circle of writers and intellectuals. This group became H.D.'s circle of support and encouragement for her early writing. Within this circle H.D. met the other two men who were to figure significantly in her life, the novelist Richard Aldington, whom she married in 1913, and D.H. Lawrence. In 1913, Pound sent a group of her poems, signed "H.D., Imagiste" to Harriet Monroe, who printed them in *Poetry* magazine. The Imagist movement was Pound's creation and H.D. has continued to be known as an Imagist, praised for the "crystalline" purity of her images:

> Rose, harsh rose,
> marred and with stint of petals,
> meagre flower, thin,
> sparse of leaf,
> more precious than a wet rose,
> single on a stem—
> you are caught in the drift.

More significant than most of the early poetry, however, are such complex and reflective longer poems as the *Trilogy* ("The Walls Do Not Fall"; "Tribute to the Angels"; "The Flowering of the Rod"), written between 1944 and 1946 and *Helen in Egypt.* The Greek metaphors that mark her early poetry expand into mythic structures in these poems, and she uses here as well the myths of Egypt, especially the story of Isis and the resurrection myths. These poems seek more than the beauty of the exact word; they seek also to give answers to the great questions of war and of woman's life.

This transformation was related to two other journeys. "The second decade of my adventure [began] with the Argo, *Borodino,*" the boat on which she went from England on her first trip to Greece in the spring of 1920. With her was Bryher (Winifred Ellerman), the young British heiress and writer who was to be central to H.D.'s life from then on. She had discovered H.D. in 1919, when the poet was ill with influenza, about to give birth, and suffering from the breakup of her marriage to Aldington. Bryher offered love, support, and the invaluable gifts of appreciation that made it possible for H.D. to move beyond survival. It was on their visit to Corfu that H.D. saw the writings on the wall which became the central subject of her sessions of analysis with Freud.

"The third decade of my cruise or quest may be said to have begun in London with my decision to undertake a serious course of psychoanalysis." For this, she travelled to Vienna in 1933, in March, the month of her daughter's birth, and of the deaths of her mother and of D.H. Lawrence. H.D. had tried psychoanalysis before—the decision to go to Freud himself came from the converging crises of her need to understand her past and the imminence of war in Europe. The two were related: her older brother had died in World War I, and her father had died shortly after from the shock of his loss. Her marriage to Aldington had failed during that war, when he was in the British army, and it had been then, too, that she realized it was "impossible to continue my friendship with Lawrence."

To endure another war seemed almost impossible; she turned to Freud hoping to find a means to do more than survive, to find a faith that would sustain her through the catastrophe she knew was coming. The *Trilogy* records her experience and her vision of the war, ending triumphantly in "The Flowering of the Rod" with a symbol of resurrection, drawn from the Moravian imagery of her childhood, the flowering myrrh brought to the infant Christ in Bethlehem by a shepherd, Kaspar.

The assurance and discovery in the poems that "the walls do not fall," she attributed to Freud: "Without the analysis and the illuminating doctrine or philosophy of Sigmund Freud, I would hardly have found the clue or the bridge between the child-life, the memories of peaceful Bethlehem and the orgy of destruction, later to be witnessed and lived through in London. That outer threat of death drove me inward."[1]

In 1944 H.D. wrote her account of her experience with Freud, calling it "Writing on the Wall." In 1938, Freud had come to London as an exile; he died there in 1939.

1. Quoted by Norman Holmes Pearson, Foreword to H.D., *Hermetic Definition*

EDITION USED:

H.D. *Tribute to Freud.* Forward by Norman Holmes Pearson. New York: McGraw-Hill, 1974.

SUGGESTED READINGS:

Bryher, Winifred. *The Heart to Artemis: A Writer's Memoirs.* New York: Harcourt, Brace and World, 1962.

H.D. *Bid Me to Live.* New York: Grove Press, 1960.

_____. *Hermetic Definition.* With a foreword by Norman Holmes Pearson. New York: New Directions, 1972.

_____. Selected Poems. New York: Grove Press, 1957.

_____. *Trilogy.* With a foreword by Norman Holmes Pearson. New York: New Directions, 1973.

_____. *Helen of Egypt.* New York: Grove Press, 1961.

Contemporary Literature, X (1969). Contains several essays on H.D. by a variety of scholars.

Tribute to Freud

8

I had originally written *had gone,* but I crossed it out deliberately. Yes, he was dead. I was not emotionally involved. The Professor was an old man. He was eighty-three. The war was on us. I did not grieve for the Professor or think of him. He was so spared so much. He had confined his researches to the living texture of wholesome as well as unwholesome thought, but contemporary thought, you might say. That is to say, he had brought the past into the present with his *the childhood of the individual is the childhood of the race*—or is it the other way round?—*the childhood of the race is the childhood of the individual.* In any case . . . he had opened up, among others, that particular field of the unconscious mind that went to prove that the traits and tendencies of obscure aboriginal tribes, as well as the shape and substance of the rituals of vanished civilizations, were still inherent in the human mind. . . . But according to his theories the soul existed explicitly, or showed its form and shape in and through the medium of the mind, and the body, as affected by the mind's ecstasies or disorders. About the greater transcendental issues, we never argued. But there was an argument implicit in our very bones. We had come together in order to substantiate something. I did not know what. There was something that was beating in my brain; I do not say my heart—my brain. I wanted it to be let out. I wanted to free myself of repetitive thoughts and experiences—my own and those of many of my contemporaries. I did not specifically realize just what it was I wanted, but I knew that I, like most of the people I knew, in England, America, and on the Continent of Europe, was drifting. . . . At least, I knew this—I would (before the current of inevitable events swept me right into the main stream and so on to the cataract) stand aside, if I could (if it were not already too late), and take stock of my possessions. You might say that I had—yes, I had something that I specifically owned. I *owned* myself. I did not really, of course. My family, my friends, and my circumstances owned me. But I *had* something. Say it was a narrow birch-bark canoe. The great forest of the unknown, the supernormal or supernatural, was all around and about us. With the current gathering force, I could at least pull in to the shallows before it was too late, take stock of my very modest possessions of mind and body, and ask the old Hermit who lived on the edge of this vast domain to talk to me, to tell me, if he would, how best to steer my course.

We touched lightly on some of the more abstruse transcendental problems, it is true, but we related them to the familiar family-complex. Tendencies of thought and imagination, however, were not cut away, were not pruned even. My imagination wandered at will; my dreams were revealing, and many of them drew on classical or Biblical symbolism. Thoughts were things, to be collected, collated, analyzed, shelved, or resolved. Fragmentary ideas, apparently unrelated, were often found to be part of a special layer or stratum of thought and memory, therefore to belong together; these were sometimes skillfully pieced together like the exquisite Greek tear-jars and iridescent glass bowls and vases that gleamed in the dusk from the shelves of the cabinet that faced me where I stretched, propped up on the couch in the room in Berggasse 19, Wien IX. The dead were living in so far as they lived in memory or were recalled in dream. . . .

10

. . . For myself, I veer round, uncanonically seated stark upright with my feet on the floor. The Professor himself is uncanonical enough; he is beating with his hand, with his fist, on the head-piece of the old-fashioned horsehair sofa that had heard more secrets then the confession box of any popular Roman Catholic father-confessor in his heyday. This was the homely historical instrument of the original scheme of psychotherapy, of psychoanalysis, the science of the unravelling of the tangled skeins of the unconscious mind and the healing implicit in the process. *Consciously,* I was not aware of having said anything that might account for the Professor's outburst. And even as I veered around, facing him, my mind was detached enough to wonder if this was some idea of *his* for speeding up the analytic content or redirecting the flow of associated images. The Professor said, "The trouble is—I am an old man—*you do not think it worth your while to love me.*"

11

The impact of his words was too dreadful—I simply felt nothing at all. I said nothing. What did he expect me to say? Exactly it was as if the Supreme Being had hammered with his fist on the back of the couch where I had been lying. Why, anyway, did he do that? He must know everything or he didn't know any thing. He must know what I felt. Maybe he did, maybe that was what this was all about. Maybe, anyway, it was just a trick, something to shock me, to break something in myself of which I was partially aware—something that would not, must not be broken. I was here because I must not be broken. If I were broken, I could not go on here with the Professor. Did he think it was easy to leave friendly, comfortable surroundings and come to a strange city, to beard him, himself, the dragon, in his very den? Vienna? Venice? My mother had come here on her honeymoon, tired, having "done" Italy as a bride. Maybe my mother was already sheltering the child, a girl, that first child that lived such a very short time. It was the bread she talked of, Vienna and how she loved the different rolls and the shapes of them and ones with poppy-seeds and Oh—the coffee! Why had I come to Vienna? The Professor had said in the very beginning that I had come to Vienna hoping to find my mother. Mother? Mamma. But my mother was dead. I was dead; that is, the child in me that had called her mamma was dead. Anyhow, he was a terribly frightening old man, too old and too detached, too wise and too famous altogether, to beat that way with his fist, like a child hammering a porridge-spoon on the table. . . .

28

For things had happened in my life, pictures, "real dreams," actual psychic or occult experiences that were superficially, at least, outside the province of established psychoanalysis. But I am working with the old Professor himself; I want his opinion on a series of events. It is true, I had not discussed these experiences openly, but I had sought help from one or two (to my mind) extremely wise and gifted people in the past and they had not helped me. At least, they had not been able to lay, as it were, the ghost. If the Professor could not do this, I thought, nobody could. I could not get rid of the experience by writing about it. I had tried that. There was no use telling the story, into the air, as it were, repeatedly, like the Ancient Mariner who plucked at the garments of the wedding guest with that skinny hand. My own skinny hand would lay, as it were, the cards on the table—here and now—here with the old Professor. He was more than the world thought him—that I well knew. If he could not "tell my fortune," nobody else could. He would not call it telling fortunes—heaven forbid! But we would lead up to the occult phenomena, we would show him how it happened. That, at least, we could do—in part, at any rate. I could say, I did say that I had had a number of severe shocks; the news of the death of my father, following the death in action of my brother in France, came to me when I was alone outside London in the early spring of that bad influenza winter of 1919. I myself was waiting for my second child—I had lost the first in 1915, from shock and repercussions of war news broken to me in a rather brutal fashion.

The second child, for some reason, I knew, must be born. Oh, she would be born, all right, though it was an admitted scientific fact that a waiting mother, stricken with that pneumonia, double pneumonia, would not live. She might live—yes—but then the child would not. They rarely both live, if ever! But there were reasons for us both living, so we did live. At some cost, however! The material and spiritual burden of pulling us out of danger fell upon a young woman whom I had only recently met—anyone who knows me knows who this person is. Her pseudonym is Bryher and we all call her Bryher. If I got well, she would herself see that the baby was protected and cherished and she would take me to a new world, a new life, to the land, spiritually of my predilection, geographically of my dreams. We would go to Greece, it could be arranged. It was arranged, though we two were the first unofficial visitors to Athens after that war. This was spring, 1920. This spring of 1920 held for me many unresolved terrors, perils, heart-aches, dangers, physical as well as spiritual or intellectual. If I had been a little maladjusted or even mildly deranged, it would have been no small wonder. But of a series of strange experiences, the Professor picked out only one as being dangerous, or hinting of danger or a dangerous tendency or symptom. I do not yet quite see why he picked on the writing-on-the-wall as the danger-signal, and omitted what to my mind were tendencies or events that were equally important or equally "dangerous." However, as the Professor picked on the writing-on-the-wall as the most dangerous or the only actually dangerous "symptom," we will review it here.

29

The series of shadow-or of light-pictures I saw projected on the wall of a hotel bedroom in the Ionian island of Corfu, at the end of April, 1920, belong in the sense of quality and intensity, of clarity and authenticity, to the same psychic category as the dream of the Princess, the Pharaoh's daughter, coming down the stairs. For myself I consider this sort of dream or projected picture or vision as a sort of half-way state between ordinary dream and the vision of those who, for lack of a more definite term we must call psychics or clairvoyants. . . .

32

The Professor translated the pictures on the wall, or the picture-writing on the wall of a hotel bedroom in Corfu, the Greek Ionian island, that I saw projected there in the spring of 1920, as a desire for union with my mother. I was physically in Greece, in Hellas (Helen). I had come home to the glory that was Greece. Perhaps my trip to Greece, that spring, might have been interpreted as a flight from reality. Perhaps my experiences there might be translated as another flight—from a flight. There were wings anyway. I may say that never before and never since have I had an experience of this kind. I saw a dim shape forming on the wall between the foot of the bed and the wash-stand. It was late afternoon; the wall was a dull, mat ochre. I thought, at first, it was sunlight flickering from the shadows cast from or across the orange trees in full leaf and fruit and flower outside the bedroom window. But I realized instantly that our side of the house was already in early shadow. The pictures on the wall were like colourless transfers or 'calcomanias, as we pretentiously called them as children. The first was head and shoulders, three-quarter face, no marked features, a stencil or stamp of a soldier or airman, but the figure was dim light on shadow, not shadow on light. It was a silhouette cut of light, not shadow, and so impersonal it might have been anyone, of almost any country. And yet there was a distinctly familiar line about that head with the visored cap; immediately it was *somebody,* unidentified indeed, yet suggesting a question—dead brother? lost friend?

Then there was the conventional outline of a goblet or cup, actually suggesting the mystic chalice, but it was the familiar goblet shape we all know, with round base and glass-stem. This chalice is as large as the head of the soldier, or rather it simply takes up the same amount of space, as if they were both formal patterns stamped on picture-cards, or even (now that I think of it) on playing cards. I have said, with the Professor, that I would lay my cards on the table. These were those cards; so far, two of them. The third follows at once or I now perceive it. It is a simple design in perspective, at least suggesting perspective after the other two flat patterns. It is a circle or two circles, the base the larger of the two; it is joined by three lines, not flat as I say but in perspective, a simple object to draw, once the idea of tilting the planes to give the idea of space is understood. And this object is so simple yet so homely that I think again, "It's a shadow thrown." Actually, it could not have been as this shadow was "light"; but the exact replica of this pattern was set on the upper shelf of the old-fashioned wash-stand, along with toothbrush mug, soap-dish and those various oddments. It was exactly the stand for the small spirit-lamp we had with us. (*Spirit-lamp?*) And I know that, if these objects are projected outward from my own brain, this is a neat trick, a short-cut, a pun, a sort of joke. For the three-legged lamp-stand in the miscellaneous clutter of the wash-stand is none other than our old friend, the tripod of classic Delphi. So the tripod, this venerated object of the cult of the sun god, symbol of poetry and prophecy, is linked by association with this most ordinary little metal frame that fits into the small saucepan and is used as a support for it when we boil water for that extra sustaining cup of tea upstairs in our room. The tripod then is linked in thought with something friendly and ordinary, the third or second member of my travellers' set, used as base for the flat spirit-lamp and support for the aluminium container. The tripod now becomes all the more an object to be venerated. At any rate, there it is, the third of my cards on the table.

33

So far, so good—or so far, so dangerous, so abnormal a "symptom." The writing, at least, is consistent. It is composed by the same person, it is drawn or written by the same hand. Whether that hand or person is myself, projecting the images as a sign, a warning or a guiding sign-post from my own subconscious mind, or whether they are projected from outside—they are at least clear enough, abstract and yet at the same time related to images of our ordinary time and space. But here I pause or the hand pauses—it is as if there were a slight question as to the conclusion or direction of the symbols. I mean, it was as if a painter had stepped back from a canvas the better to regard the composition of the picture, or a musician had paused at the music-stand, perhaps for a moment, in doubt as to whether he would continue his theme, or wondering perhaps in a more practical manner if he could himself turn the page on the stand before him without interrupting the flow of the music. That is in myself too—a wonder as to the seemliness, or the safety even, of continuing this experience or this experiment. For my head, although it can not have taken very long in clock-time for these pictures to form there, is already warning me that this is an unusual dimension, an unusual way to *think.* that my brain or mind may not be equal to the occasion. Perhaps in that sense the Professor was right (actually, he was always right, though we sometimes translated our thoughts into different languages or mediums). But there I am seated on the old-fashioned Victorian sofa in the Greek island hotel bedroom, and here I am reclining on the couch in the Professor's room, telling him this, and here again am I, 10 years later, seated at my desk in my own room in London. But there is no clock-time, though we are fastidiously concerned with time and with a formal handling of a subject which has no racial and no time-barriers. Here is this hieroglyph of the unconscious or subconscious of the Professor's discovery and life-study, the hieroglyph actually in operation before our very eyes. But it is no easy matter to sustain this mood, this "symptom" or this inspiration.

And there I sat and there is my friend Bryher who has brought me to Greece. I can turn now to her, though I do not budge an inch or break the sustained crystal-gazing stare at the wall before me. I say to Bryher, "There have been pictures here—I thought they were shadows at first, but they are light, not shadow. They are quite simple objects—but of course it's very strange. I can break away from them now, if I want—it's just a matter of concentrating—what do you think? Shall I stop? Shall I go on?" Bryher says without hesitation, "Go on."

34

While I was speaking to Bryher, there is a sort of pictorial buzzing—I mean about the base of the tripod, there are small creatures, but these are in black; they move about, in and around the base of the tripod, but they are very small; they are like ants swarming, or very small half-winged insects that have not yet learnt to fly. Fly? They are flies, it seems—but no, they are tiny people, all in black or outlined as in, or with, shadow, in distinction to the figures of the three "cards" already described. They are not a symbol of themselves, they are simply a sort of dust, a cloud or a swarm of small midges that move back and forth, but on one level, as if walking rather than flying. Even as I consider this new aspect of the writing, I am bothered, annoyed—just as one is when suddenly in a country lane one is beset in the evening light by a sudden swarm of midges. They are not important but it would be a calamity if one of them got stuck in one's eye. There was that sort of feeling; people, people—did they annoy me so? Would they perhaps eventually cloud my vision or, worse still, would one of them get "stuck in my eye"? They were people, they were annoying—I did not hate people, I did not especially resent any one person. I had known such extraordinarily gifted and charming people. They had made much of me or they had slighted me and yet neither praise nor neglect mattered in the face of the gravest issues—life, death. (I had had my child, I was alive.) And yet, so oddly, I knew that this experience, this writing-on-the-wall before me, could not be shared with them—could not be shared with anyone except the girl who stood so bravely there beside me. This girl had said without hesitation. "Go on." It was she really who had the detachment and the integrity of the Pythoness of Delphi. But it was I, battered and disassociated from my American family and my English friends, who was seeing the pictures, who was reading the writing or who was granted the inner vision. Or perhaps in some sense, we were "seeing" it together, for without her, admittedly, I could not have gone on.

35

Yet, although now assured of her support, my own head is splitting with the ache of concentration. I know that if I let go, lessen the intensity of my stare and shut my eyes or even blink my eyes, to rest them, the pictures will fade out. My curiosity is insatiable. This has never happened to me before, it may never happen again. I am not actually analysing this as I watch the pictures, but it seems now possible that the mechanism of their projection (from within or from without) had something to do with, or in some way was related to, my feelings for the shrine at Delphi. Actually, we had intended stopping off at Itea; we had come from Athens, by boat through the Corinthian canal and up the Gulf of Corinth. Delphi and the shrine of Helios (Hellas, Helen) had been really the main objective of my journey. Athens came a very close second in affection; however, having left Athens, we were informed when the boat stopped at Itea that it was absolutely impossible for two ladies alone, at that time, to make the then dangerous trip on the winding road to Delphi, that in imagination I saw so clearly tucked away under Parnassus. Bryher and I were forced to content ourselves with a somewhat longer stay than was first planned in the beautiful island of Corfu.

But the idea of Delphi had always touched me very deeply and Bryher and I, back in that winter London of the previous spring—it was a winter London that spring—had talked of the famous sacred way. She herself had visited these places with her father before the 1914 war and I had once said to her, while convalescing from the 1919 illness, "If I could only feel that I could walk the sacred way to Delphi, I know I would get well." But no, now that we were so near, we could not go to Delphi. We were going in another direction, Brindisi, Rome, Paris, London. Already our half-packed bags, typewriter, books lay strewn about; we obviously *were* leaving. And we were not leaving Corfu in order to return to Athens, as we had talked of doing when we first landed at Corfu, with the thought of a possible arrangement, after all, with a party from one of the archaeological schools at Athens, from Athens itself, overland to Delphi. Travel was difficult, the country itself in a state of political upheaval; chance hotel acquaintances expressed surprise that two women alone had been allowed to come at all at that time. We were always "two women alone" or "two ladies alone," but we were not alone.

41

[The last figure of the vision forms quickly; the poet names her Niké.] Victory, Niké, as I called her exactly then and there, goes on. She is a common-or-garden angel, like any angel you may find on an Easter or Christmas card. Her back is towards me, she is simply outlined but very clearly outlined like the first three symbols or "cards." But unlike them, she is not flat or static, she is in space, in unwalled space, not flat against the wall, though she moves upward as against its surface. She is a moving-picture, and fortunately she moves swiftly. Not swiftly exactly but with a sure floating that at least gives my mind some rest, as if my mind had now escaped the bars of that ladder, no longer climbing or caged but free and with wings. On she goes. Above her head, to her left in the space left vacant on this black-board (or light-board) or screen, a series of tent-like triangles forms. I say tent-like triangles, for though they are simple triangles they suggest tents to me. I feel that the Niké is about to move into and through the tents, and this she exactly does. So far—so good. But this is enough. I drop my head in my hands; it is aching with this effort of concentration, but I feel that I have seen the picture. I thought. "Niké, Victory," and even as I thought it, it seemed to me that this Victory was not now, it was another Victory; in which case there would be another war. When that war had completed itself, rung by rung or year by year, I, personally (I felt), would be free, I myself would go on in another, a winged dimension. For the tents, it seemed to me, were not so much the symbolic tents of the past battle-fields, the near part or the far past, but tents or shelters to be set up in another future contest. The picture now seemed to be something to do with another war, but even at that there would be Victory. Niké, Victory seemed to be the clue, seemed to be my own especial sign or part of my hieroglyph. We had visited in Athens, only a short time ago, the tiny Temple of Victory that stands on the rock of the Acropolis, to your right as you turn off from the Propylaea. I must hold on to this one word. I thought. "Niké, Victory." I thought, "Helios, the sun . . ." And I shut off, "cut out" before the final picture, before (you might say) the explosion took place.

But though I admit to myself that now I have had enough, maybe just a little too much, Bryher, who has been waiting by me, carries on the "reading" where I left off. Afterwards she told me that she had seen nothing on the wall there, until I dropped my head in my hands. She had been there with me, patient, wondering, no doubt deeply concerned and not a little anxious as to the outcome of my state or mood. But as I relaxed, let go, from complete physical and mental exhaustion, she saw what I did not see. It was the last section of the series, or the last concluding symbol—perhaps that "determinative" that is used in the actual hieroglyph, the picture that contains the whole series of pictures in itself or helps clarify or explain them. In any case, it is apparently a clear picture or symbol. She said, it was a circle like the sun-disc and a figure within the disc; a man, she thought, was reaching out to draw the image of a woman (my Niké) into the sun beside him.

42

The years between seemed a period of waiting, of marking time. There was a growing feeling of stagnation, of lethargy, clearly evident among many of my own contemporaries. Those who were aware of the trend of political events, on the other hand, were almost too clever, too politically minded, too high-powered intellectually for me altogether. What I seemed to sense and wait for was frowned upon by the first group, though I learned very early not to air my thoughts and fears; they were morbid, they were too self-centered and introspective altogether. Why—my brother-in-law spent such a happy holiday in the Black Forest . . . and the food was so good—everybody was so hospitable and so very charming. If, on the other hand, I ventured a feeble opinion to the second group, I was given not chapter and verse so much as the whole outpouring of predigested voluminous theories. My brain staggers now when I remember the deluge of brilliant talk I was inflicted with; what would happen if, and who would come to power when—but with all their abstract clear-sightedness, this second group seemed as muddled, as lethargic in their own way, as the first. At least, their theories and their accumulated data seemed unrooted, raw. But this, I admit—yes, I know—was partly due to my own hopeless feeling in the face of brilliant statisticians and one-track-minded theories. *Where is this taking you,* I wanted to shout at both parties. One refused to admit the fact that the flood was coming—the other counted the nails and measured the planks with endless exact mathematical formulas, but didn't seem to have the very least idea of how to put the Ark together.

43

Already in Vienna, the shadows were lengthening or the tide was rising. The signs of grim coming events, however, manifested in a curious fashion. There were, for instance, occasional coquettish, confetti-like showers from the air, gilded paper swastikas and narrow strips of printed paper like the ones we pulled out of our Christmas bon-bons, those gay, favors that we called 'caps' as children in America. . . . The party had begun, or this was preliminary to the birthday or the wedding. I stooped to scrape up a handful of these confetti-like tokens as I was leaving the Hotel Regina one morning. They were printed on those familiar little oblongs of thin paper that fell out of the paper cap when it was unfolded at the party; we called them mottoes. These mottoes were short and bright and to the point. One read in clear primer-book German, 'Hitler gives bread,' 'Hitler gives work,' and so on. . . . The paper was crisp and clean, the gold clear as Danae's legendary shower, and the whole savored of birthday cake and candles or fresh-bought Christmas-tree decorations. The gold, however, would not stay bright nor the paper crisp very long, for people passed to and fro across Freiheitsplatz and along the pavement, trampling over this Danae shower, not taking any notice. Was I the only person in Vienna who had stopped to scrape up a handful of these tokens? It seemed so. One of the hotel porters emerged with a long-handled brush-broom. As I saw him begin methodically sweeping the papers off the pavement, I dropped my handful in the gutter.

44

There were other swastikas. They were the chalk ones now; I followed them down Berggasse as if they had been chalked on the pavement especially for my benefit. They led to the Professor's door—maybe, they passed on down another street to another door but I did not look any further. No one brushed these swastikas out. It is not so easy to scrub death-head chalkmarks from a pavement. It is not so easy and it is more conspicuous than sweeping tinsel paper into a gutter. And this was a little later.

Mira Behn (*From Mira Behn,* The Spirit's Pilgrimage, *Longmans Green and Co.,*
copyright 1960 by Madeleine Slade, Wide World Photograph)

Mira Behn [Madeline Slade], 1892–

The Spirit's Pilgrimage (1960)

In 1925 Madeline Slade boarded a ship in England which would take her to India and the new life for which she had spent a year in preparation. Her goal was the ashram at Sabarmati of Mahatma Gandhi, the spiritual and political leader who would ultimately free India nonviolently from British rule. There were many British and European followers of Gandhi, then and later. Madeline Slade is nevertheless one of the most striking, because of her history, and because of her total devotion to Gandhi's cause.

Madeline Slade was the daughter of an officer in the British Navy, the descendant of what his daughter saw as a "decidedly conventional" family, with an "aristocratic society touch about it" which did not suit her temperament. Her mother was also from an upper-class family, but a more unusual one, "never a slave to convention," and more congenial to Madeline. When her father was at sea, or posted briefly away from England, the family lived at Milton Heath, her grandfather's country estate. She grew up there and in London with all the privileges of her class in the high period of British imperialism. When she was fifteen, her father was made an admiral and was appointed Commander in Chief of the East Indies Station. The Slade family spent two years in Bombay (1909-1911), absorbed in the round of social duties expected of the residents of the Admiral's House. Insulated in this imperial preserve, they received no glimpse of the "real India," the India of poverty and oppression which was to absorb most of Madeline Slade's adult life.

Just before leaving for India, she had heard Beethoven's music for the first time, and it had revealed to her "a living sense of the Divine Power." Returning to England, she immersed herself in music and art and arranged concerts for a pianist known for his rendering of Beethoven. The war interrupted this life and she withdrew into herself, away from the "hate talk" of war, away as well from the German and Austrian music she loved. Shortly after the war, she learned of Romain Rolland's epic novel, *Jean Christophe,* based in part on the life of Beethoven. Reading it, she determined to meet Rolland, and set herself to learn French in order to be able to speak with him.

In 1923, she went to France, where her meeting with Rolland changed the direction of her life.

A preacher of pacifism during World War I, Rolland had turned to the East, and more importantly to India, to save the West from its suicidal militarism. He was at first interested in Rabindranath Tagore, and Rolland in his book, *Mahatma Gandhi,* contrasts that poet with Gandhi, the social reformer, as Indian analogues of Plato and St. Paul. Rolland admired Gandhi tremendously: the *satyagraha* technique of peaceable protest and pressure were exactly what he thought the West lacked and needed, but at this point in his career he still preferred Tagore. Rolland was himself an aesthete and an artist, not a man of action. Thus Madeline Slade's reading of his book was not simply an act of adoption of Rolland's ideas. Rather it was an act of decision and interpretation, and she chose the more heroic alternative. She chose Gandhi, and she transformed her life, abandoning her history to conform to that choice.

She stifled her first impulse to rush directly to India and instead set herself the difficult task of preparing alone, both physically and spiritually, for her new life. Only after a year of intensive discipline and training did she feel herself ready to ask for acceptance into the life she desired.

In India, Madeline Slade became Mira Behn and her devotion to Gandhi's cause was absolute. For her, Gandhi represented the only possible way of life, and she submerged herself in that way, in order to serve the cause of history. She remained in India for over thirty years, participating in the triumph of *satyagraha* and India's independence from British rule in 1947. On January 30, 1948, Gandhi was assassinated. Mira Behn was not with him; she was in Pashulok, a jungle area near Rishikesh, at the foot of the Himalayas, where she was supervising the construction of a cattle center. She stayed in India for almost ten years after Gandhi's death, trying to create projects which would further Gandhi's ideals. The bureaucracy of the new India frustrated her, however, and she left in 1960, returning to the Austria of Beethoven, going to live in the forests above Baden near Vienna.

EDITIONS USED:

The Spirit's Pilmigrimage. London: Oxford University Press, 1960

SUGGESTED READINGS:

Behn, Mira. *Gandhi's Letters to a Disciple.* With an introduction by John
     Haynes Holmes (1950).
Erikson, Erik. *Gandhi's Truth* (1969).
Gandhi, M. K. *An Autobiography* (1949).

The Spirit's Pilgrimage

Chapter XVI

I think it was October when I finally returned to Europe. I stayed only a day or two in Naples, and then went straight to Paris. I was impatient to get that little book of Romain Rolland's which was due to appear, and the very next day after reaching Paris I went to the publishers. The shop window was entirely filled with a small orange-colored book bearing the title *Mahatma Gandhi* in bold black letters. I entered the shop and bought a copy.

I started reading it that morning, and once having begun there was no stopping. In the middle of the day when I went out to a restaurant for lunch I took the little book with me, then back I went to my room, and by evening I had finished it.

Now I knew what that "something" was, the approach of which I had been feeling. I was to go to Mahatma Gandhi, who served the cause of oppressed India through fearless truth and nonviolence,[1] a cause which, though focused in India, was for the whole of humanity. I did not weigh the pros and cons or try to reason *why* this was the outcome of my prayers. The call was absolute, and that was all that mattered. I went back to London and reserved a berth in a P & O liner. I told my parents. They sensed the magnitude of my inspiration and did not argue with me. I soon realized, however, that I was being altogether too hasty. I must put myself through severe training before I could hope to be accepted. So I returned to the P & O office and exchanged my booking for one twelve months later.

It was necessary to think out in real earnest how to set about my year's training. Without any doubt I should learn spinning and weaving, but most especially spinning, because Mahatma Gandhi had made this the pivot of his constructive program for the masses, which in India meant the villagers —millions and millions of them who, since the introduction by the British of Lancashire cloth, had lost their age-old subsidiary occupation of cloth

1. In Gandhian phraseology this means active resistance to evil without use of physical force, and cheerful acceptance of the consequences of one's actions.

production and consequently remained unemployed for several months in the year, as the Indian climate is such that agriculture has long off-seasons. Another reason why he fastened on cotton spinning was that it could touch every house in the village. Weaving was the job of only a few, but spinning had been the job of all the women and girls—it takes many spinning wheels to feed one loom. So the spinning wheel had now become the emblem of India's masses and their fight for freedom. At the same time spinning and the wearing of khadi (hand-spun and hand-woven cloth) had become obligatory for political leaders and constructive workers, making a bond of sympathy between them and the dumb millions.

Learning how to spin, therefore, was at the top of my program. But as no one spins cotton in the West, I had to do my training with wool. For this I was very luckily situated, as right at the bottom of Bedford Gardens were "The Kensington Weavers," run by Dorothy Wilkinson and her sisters, old friends of the family. I bought a spinning wheel and carding brushes and started spinning wool at home, while for the weaving I went to the school. Then I had to become a vegetarian and a teetotaler, and start learning the language. I should likewise teach myself to sit cross-legged on the floor and sleep there also, and of course I must read all I could about India. In regard to the change of diet I decided to proceed gently, as it would be foolish to spoil one's health at such a time. First I gave up alcohol and then progressively limited my food to a purely vegetarian diet. The language was a more difficult problem. Who could teach me and what language should it be? As with the French, Father had come to my aid. He wrote to the then Permanent Under Secretary of State at the India Office, who was a friend of his, and asked his advice. We were told it should be Urdu, and an Indian student in London was recommended as teacher. So I bought the *Munshi,* an excellent Urdu grammar, and it was arranged for the Indian student to come and give me lessons. I found them extremely difficult and made very slow progress. French had been hard, for I am not a natural linguist, but this was enough to make one's hair stand on end! The sitting and sleeping on the floor developed quite well, though I am afraid it gave Mother much pain to have to remove my comfortable bed. As for the reading, I immediately subscribed to Mahatma Gandhi's weekly, *Young India,* and located a shop near the British Museum where I could get some books.

Part of this year of training I spent in Paris at my old quarters in the rue Notre Dame-des-Champs. I wrote to Romain Rolland telling him of what had come to me through the reading of his book. In Paris I also found Indian students with whom I could continue my Urdu studies. It was during this time that I first read the *Bhagvadgita* and some of the *Rigveda*—both in French.

Back in London, and right in the midst of my training, the report appeared in the newspapers that Mahatma Gandhi had started a twenty-one-day fast for

Hindu-Moslem unity, and it was doubtful whether he would survive the ordeal. This was agonizing. There was nothing I could do but pray in silence. Day by day the news grew more alarming. Those twenty-one days seemed never ending, but I kept on at my studies without slackening. When at last the news came that the fast had been successfully broken, and all was well, my thankful joy was such that I could remain silent no longer. I must write and send some thanksgiving offering. But what to send? I had run out of money with those orchestral concerts and had sold my piano, but there was a small diamond brooch which my grandfather had given me on my twenty-first birthday. I would sell that and send the proceeds. I sent a letter, along with a check for twenty pounds, expressing my thankfulness for the successful fulfillment of the fast, and explaining how I had read Romain Rolland's book, how I had in the beginning wanted to come to India at once and then, realizing that I should first put myself through a year's training, I was now carrying out that task. I hardly expected an answer, but I knew the endorsed check would come back through the bank. I went on with my training with renewed vigor. Some time later, when I happened to be sitting one day at the telephone table at Bedford Gardens, someone placed a worn-looking post card in front of me. The handwriting was unfamiliar and rather indistinct. I turned it over and looked at the signature—*M. K. Gandhi.* Reverentially I picked it up and read it through. This is what it said:

> Dear Friend,
>
> I must apologize to you for not writing to you earlier. I have been continuously travelling. I thank you for £20. sent by you. The amount will be used for popularizing the spinning wheel.
>
> I am glad indeed that instead of obeying your first impulse you decided to fit yourself for the life here and to take time. If a year's test still impels you to come, you will probably be right in coming to India.
>
> On the train,   Yours sincerely,
> 31-12-24   M. K. Gandhi.

With new confidence and joy I went on with my training, and when I was just halfway through, I wrote again asking whether I might actually join Sabarmati Ashram, and enclosed some samples of wool I had spun. In August a reply came which put all fears and suspense at rest:

> 148, Russa Road,
> Calcutta.
> 24 July 1925.
>
> Dear Friend,
>
> I was pleased to receive your letter which has touched me deeply. The samples of wool you have sent are excellent.
>
> You are welcome whenever you choose to come. If I have advice of

the steamer that brings you, there will be someone receiving you at the steamer and guiding you to the train that will take you to Sabarmati. Only please remember that the life at the Ashram is not all rosy. It is strenuous. Bodily labour is given by every inmate. The climate of this country is also not a small consideration. I mention these things not to frighten you but merely to warn you.

Yours sincerely,

M. K. Gandhi.

The heat of the summer I spent in Switzerland, working with the peasants in their fields in order to be in as good physical trim as possible, because I could see there would be a lot of hard manual work once I reached my destination.

The P & O on which my passage was booked was due to sail from Marseille on October 25th, so by the end of the summer I returned to London to make preparations. I had already written to Delhi for khadi, which now arrived and was made into plain white frocks. I kept a minimum of warm things for the voyage, and the rest of my clothes I distributed along with everything else except a certain number of books and what little jewelry I possessed. I had a nice collection of about four hundred really good books, from which I made a selection which filled two trunks. The jewelry, such as it was, I had decided to take for presentation to the Cause. Being the younger daughter, and known to have no interest in fashion and society, not much jewelry had come my way. This was the first time I felt sorry about it, as now there was so little to give.

Up to the last I went on spinning and weaving intensively and, having achieved some proficiency, I managed to spin, dye, and weave a woolen scarf for Romain Rolland's sister. This I would take with me when I went on my farewell visit to Villeneuve.

The year of training was drawing to an end. The two trunks of books, and perhaps one other with odds and ends, were sent off to the P & O office to go round by sea, and my plan was to go to Paris and Villeneuve and so south to Marseille where I could pick up the P & O liner.

It is remarkable how the English, by tradition, are habituated to keeping their deeper feelings to themselves, restraining any outward sign of emotion. There were, therefore no tears or other visible manifestations of the wrench that the parting meant, especially with Mother. Everyone was quiet and gentle. Mother and Rhona saw me off at the London station, and Father, who was in Paris at the time, said goodbye to me there. From the beginning no one had ever tried to dissuade me from my decision. Everyone seemed to realize that it was a spiritual necessity and accepted it as inevitable. The only advice that Father gave me was as we separated, when he merely said, "Be careful." And it was not an easy thing for a man connected with the highest

British officials and ministers to have a daughter going to join the archrevolutionary of the British Empire!

From Paris I went to Villeneuve to bid farewell to Romain Rolland and his sister. To this day remains in my memory the picture of them standing together on the doorstep of the little Villa Olga as I left them—the look in those wonderful eyes of his, and the ring in his voice as he said, "How lucky you are!"

Chapter XVII

I boarded the P & O liner on October 25, 1925, and the voyage began. The weather was fair and the moon was waxing. Each evening, as it rose in the east and shed on the ocean a path of light along which the ship traveled, I gazed upon it as an emblem of what I was approaching. And day by day I wrote down my thoughts and feelings to be posted to Villeneuve as soon as I reached India. On November 6th the ship came alongside the dock in Bombay. As had been promised, friends were there to meet me. They took me to the Nairojees' house on Malabar Hill, where the brother and sisters, grandchildren of Dadabhai Nairojee, pressed me to stay and rest for at least twenty-four hours. But I had no thought for anything but to reach Sabarmati without delay. In the afternoon, Devadas Gandhi, Mahatma Gandhi's fourth and youngest son, came in and he too pressed me to stay, but, seeing my determination to go on at once, he finally arranged for my departure by the Ahmedabad train that night.

The train steamed into the Ahmedabad station next morning, November 7th, exactly on time, and as it drew to a standstill, a smiling bespectacled person looked in at the window. In half a minute another, also smiling but of quite a different character, looked over his shoulder, and a third was in the background. They all seemed to know that I was the person they were looking for, and introduced themselves—Mahadev Desai (secretary and right-hand man of Mahatma Gandhi); Vallabhbhai Patel (later to become first Home Minister of Free India); and Swami Anand (manager of the weekly *Young India*). Even at that moment of concentrated anticipation I noted the masterful manner of Vallabhbhai, who turned to Mahadev and said, "You two look after the luggage and I'll take her off in the car." And before I knew where I was I found myself being swept away in the car, this new acquaintance sitting by my side. I looked at his clean-shaven face and was struck by its power curiously intermingled with a kindly and humorous expression. The car turned into a courtyard and drew up in front of a house.

"This is not the Ashram, is it?" I exclaimed.

"No, no," he said, "this is the All-India Spinners' Association Office."

As he spoke, someone came out and had a few words with him through the window, all in Gujerati, and I could not understand anything. I looked inquiringly at him as we drove off again.

"That was the All-India Spinners' Association Secretary," he said, "Shankarlal Banker."

Now we passed out of the city and over a bridge to the other side of the Sabarmati River. I was gazing out of the window in tense suspense. I saw buildings ahead.

"Is that the Ashram?" I eagerly asked.

"Not yet," he replied, and I noticed the quizzical look in his expression. Then in a few minutes he remarked, "You see those trees and some buildings beyond? That's the Ashram."

By this time I had lost any sense of physical being. All was concentrated in the thought of what was approaching. In a minute or two the car drew up at a gate under a big tamarind tree. We got out and went along a narrow brick path which passed through a custard-apple orchard. Then a little garden gate led to a small enclosure where a simple building stood. We stepped up onto the veranda. I felt encumbered with the bag in my hand and hurriedly handed it to my companion. He took it and, standing a little to one side, ushered me into the room. As I entered, a slight brown figure rose up and came toward me. I was conscious of nothing but a sense of light. I fell on my knees. Hands gently raised me up, and a voice said: "You shall be my daughter." My consciousness of the physical world began to return, and I saw a face smiling at me with eyes full of love, blended with a gentle twinkle of amusement. Yes, this was Mahatma Gandhi, and I had arrived. He went back to his white gaddi behind a little desk, and I sat down on the floor in front of him.

People began coming in and out of the room, and I noticed everyone spoke of "Bapu." Here there was no Mahatma Gandhi, only Bapu, meaning in Gujerati, Father. But in this case it had a meaning all its own, just as he whom it described was unique.

Bapu now said, "Come along, let's go to see Ba [Mother]," and he took me onto the veranda and on into the kitchen.

Bapu introduced me jokingly in Gujerati, but I could understand he was telling Ba she would have to bring out her best English. Ba, very small and dignified, folded her hands and said sweetly, "How do you do." But she kept looking at my feet.

"She is looking at your shoes," said Bapu, "because our custom in India is to take off our shoes before coming into a kitchen."

I rushed out onto the veranda and took mine off at once. Bapu laughed.

Thus my new education began. . . .

Chapter XVIII

By God's infinite blessing I had arrived, not on the outer edge of Bapu's activities, but right in the intimate heart of his daily life. The impact on my emotions was tremendous. From early morning to the last thing at night I lived for the moments when I could set eyes on Bapu. To be in his presence was to be lifted out of oneself. Not that there was anything imposing about his physical appearance, or striking about his manner of speech; indeed it was the perfect simplicity of both which held one. Here one was face to face with a Soul which, in its very greatness, made the body and speech through which it manifested itself glow with gracious and natural humility. At the same time there was a sense of spiritual strength, quietly confident and all-pervading, while the whole presence was made intensely human and appealing by the purehearted and irresistible humor which kept peeping like golden sunshine through the leaves of a deep forest.

I was so busy in those days with lessons, cooking, cleaning and the rest that I used hardly to see Bapu except at the morning and evening Prayers, and then for the most precious half-hour at the end of the day, when Bapu used to lie down on his bed under the open sky in the garden, and I was allowed to sit on the ground by his side while Ba rubbed oil on his head, and someone else (at that time Surendraji) rubbed ghee, the clarified butter of India, on the soles of his feet. The conversation was in Gujerati, and Bapu spoke English only when addressing me. Often some visitor who happened to be staying in the Ashram would come for a talk at that time; then the language used was sometimes Hindustani. I listened attentively but could as yet follow very little.

Though Bapu himself was all and more than all I had pictured, the Ashram proved a different matter and I had to make a big effort to readjust my expectations. I had imagined to myself that the inmates would be a compact group, wholeheartedly of one mind about Bapu's ideals. Instead of that I found a heterogeneous collection of one or two hundred people, men, women and children of all ages and all degrees of faith, from fanatical ascetics to skeptical family women. What was more, the ascetics were few in number, and the family types were in the majority. One thing that was clear was that most of the women were there not because they had themselves felt a call to join the Ashram, but because their husbands or relatives had thrown in their lot with Bapu. As to the young people and children, they of course were there because of their parents. Among the men there was considerable variety in the reasons which had led them to Bapu. Because Bapu himself was all-sided, he attracted people of the most varied types. Some were drawn especially by the revolutionary and political aspect, some by the social and economic aspect, and some by the ascetic and religious aspect. But one and all were drawn by the magnetic power of Bapu's spirit, and had thrown up everything else to join the cause.

Thus the Ashram was not at all of the monastic type, but was a miniature cross-section of the everyday world, on which Bapu was experimenting with the most lofty and drastic conceptions of moral, physical and economic reforms. Moral standards were poised at a height where the slightest wavering by an inmate from the strictest truth, honesty and rectitude was noted down and made the subject of public discussion between Bapu and the rest of the Ashramites. Physical standards regarding diet, labor, and hours of rising and going to rest were rigidly severe, and economic ideals required that everyone should use only hand-spun and hand-woven cloth, and other hand-made articles as far as possible, besides living a life of the utmost simplicity, even by Indian standards.

Naturally, the reactions on this heterogeneous group were as varied as the temperaments involved and led to high tension of the nerves, except in the case of Bapu, who usually sailed peacefully through the repeated disturbances, though even he became affected when the storms were very severe.

I did not realize all this at once, but it did not take me long to comprehend that the Ashram was composed of highly explosive material. I also sensed that my arrival had added yet another variation to the problems already there, and one about which the Ashramites were naturally none too sanguine. Where was I to fit in? I was myself sufficiently highly strung at that period and spontaneously joined the ascetic group with not a little fanatical zeal. . . .

Chapter XIX

[Soon after Mira Behn's arrival, Ghandi began a penitential fast.] No sooner was Bapu out of the fast and on the way to recovery, than it was time for him to prepare for the yearly visit to Wardha in the Central Provinces where the learned ascetic, Acharya Vinoba Bhave, was at that time running a Brahmachari Ashram for celibates. Bapu used to go there for about ten days' rest each year before attending the Open Session of the Indian National Congress. I was on tenterhooks as to whether I should accompany the party, and dared not think what it would be like to remain behind without Bapu. However, the final decision was that I should go. The Congress Session that year was to be at Kanpur, where the nights would be cool in the middle of winter, and Bapu asked me if I had sufficient warm rugs. As a matter of fact I had only one very thin one, so something had to be done. Bapu thought for a little, and then sent for Tulsi Mahar. "You come from Nepal," said Bapu, "and you must have a warm rug or two." "Of course," said Tulsi Mahar. "Then you give her one," replied Bapu, pointing to me. Off went Tulsi Mahar and returned with a beaming face, holding out with both hands a splendid warm, soft rug woven in black and white wool.

So far I had only seen Bapu at work in the Ashram. Now when we moved out to go to Wardha and Kanpur, a new and amazing realization burst upon me, and that was the peculiar hold Bapu had upon the masses. At every station, pressing, surging crowds thronged the platform, and the air throbbed with the cry "Mahatma Gandhi ki Jai!" (Victory to Mahatma Gandhi). The faces did not reflect the excitement of people out to catch a glimpse of a celebrity, but the eager, thirsting look of devotees seeking to set eyes on some holy person, a savior on whom they had pinned all their hopes with a faith which they would not have been able to explain or express in so many words, but which drew them irresistibly. At the smaller stations, where the peasantry from the surrounding countryside gathered, this was most striking. Their eyes had an inspired glow about them as the peasants pressed toward the carriage window with folded hands and no thought in the world but to obtain the *darshan*[1] of him they were seeking. I watched in wonderment, and was deeply moved. Then I looked at Bapu to see his reaction. There he sat perfectly quiet and still, with hands folded in acknowledgment of the salutations, and with a stern look upon his face. This impressed me still more—the throbbing, surging mass of humanity on one side, and the still, small, stern figure on the other.

Up to now I had not witnessed this stern side of Bapu's nature. It was, as I came to know by continual observation, his invariable reaction to excessive expression of emotions, especially when they demonstrated admiration and devotion toward himself.

When we reached the Wardha Ashram I found quite a different type of center to Sabarmati, and I could not help being enthusiastic about it, as it was very much the kind of Ashram that I had pictured to myself before reaching India. It was a small compact group of men all earnestly believing in the principles of the institution. Bapu's ideals and experiments were being carried out with great thoroughness, and onto them had been added theories and methods evolved in the austere and searching soul of Vinoba, whom the inmates looked up to as their Guru (preceptor). Quietness of atmosphere, unity of endeavor, hard work, and spiritual purposefulness were the qualities which impressed one. Bapu noticed my enthusiasm, and when I talked to him about it and asked whether we could not have more such discipline and earnestness in Sabarmati, he pointed out how he could not break up the families of the devoted co-workers who had gone through the South-African ordeal with him, how they must all strive together toward the ideal, and how it was not in his nature to pick and choose, selecting only the best and casting away the rest. On the contrary he must take all along with him, even to the

1. Sight.

weakest. Though Bapu was severe in his admission of outsiders, such was the ever-growing pressure of new aspirants that his sternness could not always hold out against his all-accepting heart. Hence Sabarmati was made up of that heterogeneous group, that miniature cross-section of the everyday world.

I began to realize that a laboratory for experimenting with theories for the betterment of the world must be comprised of such a cross-section, and not a carefully chosen selection of unusual people. I began to understand also another fundamental difference between Bapu and other spiritual leaders. Bapu would, on no account, accept anyone as a disciple, and flatly refused to be looked upon as a Guru. "The conception of Guru," he would say, "is so lofty that there is no one in these days competent to live up to the ideal. There may have been such super-beings in the past, and even today there may be some purest *Rishis* [seers] existing in unknown caves in the Himalayas who are worthy of being accepted as Gurus, but this ancient conception of Guru and disciple is not for us ordinary mortals of this degenerate age. So seek God and look to Him alone as Guru, for He will never fail you if you seek Him with a true heart."

Dorothy Day (*By Stanley Vishnewski, permission of the* Catholic Worker)

Dorothy Day, 1897–

The Long Loneliness (1952)

Dorothy Day occupies a unique place in contemporary American culture: she is seen by large numbers within and without the Catholic Church as a symbol of the survival of conscience. The absolute consistency of her beliefs and actions, her persistent allegiance to the idea that society can be changed through radical personalist action, has created a movement without parallel in this country. The Catholic Worker movement, founded in the early 1930's, is inextricably identified with Dorothy Day, but she is not and refuses to be its leader. Committed to the principles of communitarian anarchism, she has been the interpreter of the movement's ideas and a force for social change within the United States, through the assertion of faith, not power.

Dorothy Day was born in Bath Beach, Brooklyn. Her father was a journalist and the family moved from New York to California and, after the San Francisco earthquake, to Chicago where she grew up, protected by her family from the risks of the city. Her brother's work on a labor movement paper gave her her first awareness of the slums and the struggles of those who lived there. She read Kropotkin in high school and felt that he had given "a direction to [her] life." Two years on scholarship at the University of Illinois, where she joined the Socialist Club, deepened her conviction that her life was to be dedicated to the cause of the workers, and led her to reject religion, but college itself provided no direction. Moving to New York with her family, she worked for the Socialist *New York Call* and later for *The Masses,* took a room on Cherry Street on the Lower East Side, and joined the young radicals who hoped for revolution. In 1918 she picketed the White House as part of a suffragist demonstration and was jailed; in the same year she wearied of the life she was leading, began and dropped nurses' training, and, in 1919, went to Europe. She often felt herself drawn to the Catholic Church, to "put [herself] in the atmosphere of prayer," and in Chicago in 1923, working on the radical journal, *The Liberator,* she lived with a Catholic family and envied them their faith. Attracted to many faiths, she could attach herself to none; radical by temperament, she found no ideology that satisfied both her spiritual needs and her sense of social responsibility. In 1924 her novel, *The Eleventh Virgin,* was published and the movie rights sold, allowing her to buy a small bungalow on Staten Island, the setting of the selection included here. The island offered a time for reflection and peace; it also brought a love affair with Forster Battingham, an anarchist. Through that love, and the birth of their daughter, Tamar, in 1927, Dorothy Day came to the crisis and the choice described here.

To join the Catholic Church was an individual solution but not an answer to her sense of social responsibility. That answer did not come until 1930 when she "found Peter Maurin,—Peter, the French peasant, whose spirit and ideas will dominate . . . the rest of my life." It was he, a wandering, talkative, self-trained theologian and manual worker who brought to Dorothy Day the vision that shaped the Catholic Worker movement. Maurin demonstrated in his own life the coexistence of religious orthodoxy and a radical commitment to social change, lived out in voluntary poverty, which Dorothy Day had sought. Recognizing that she had found what she had looked for for many years, Dorothy Day embarked on the new pilgrimage that became the Catholic Worker movement.

The first copies of the *Catholic Worker* newspaper were sold in New York's Union Square on May 1, 1933. It cost a penny a copy; the subscription price in the 1970's is twenty-five cents a year. The history of the movement and of the paper are closely entwined. As Stanley Vishnewski has said, the paper has not only reported news but made it; the news it has made comes from the *Worker*'s firm and undeviating commitment to anarchism and to pacifism— positions it held through the Spanish Civil War, World War II, and the war in Vietnam.

In describing the paper in her introduction to *On Pilgrimage: The Sixties,* Dorothy Day talks of its editors, who comprise the residents of the many "houses of hospitality" that have developed in the United States and abroad in the pattern of that established in New York by Peter Maurin and Dorothy Day. The houses offer food, clothing, and shelter to anyone in need, free of judgment or demand. They also provide a gathering place for people committed to the search for social justice. As Peter Maurin originally intended, they are places where works of mercy are practiced by mutual aid and cooperation, rather than through state assistance. These editors of the *Catholic Worker* "are mostly Catholic, and if they are not, they agree that without brotherly love there can be no love of God. They profess voluntary poverty and sharing—living together in city and country with the poor and the wounded in spirit."

Dorothy Day describes her own role as "travelling and visiting readers of the paper," a description which characteristically underplays the meaning her travels have had for her readers—for laboring men and women seeking justice, for the homeless poor of the cities, for migrant farm workers—whose lives she has shared in perfect equality, and whose sorrows and imprisonments she has also shared. She never speaks when she will not act, and the deep commitment to living God's love that has illuminated her words over the years in the *Catholic Worker* has led her to picket lines, demonstrations, and jail.

It is not only those who suffer from poverty and physical deprivation who have benefited from the clarity and consistency of her vision, however. For many years she has also made belief possible for numbers of scholars and intellectuals who find in her a way to combine religious faith with a commitment to the more skeptical world of ideas. For many of this number, months or years spent early in their careers at the Catholic Worker house in New York City or at the farm at Tivoli, provided a shape and structure for their later lives.

In explaining the title of her book, Dorothy Day acknowledges the loneliness common to all lives. Responding to an elderly woman who had complained of loneliness: "I thought again, 'The only answer in this life, to the loneliness we are all bound to feel, is community. The living together, working together, sharing together, loving God and loving our brother, and living close to him in community so we can show our love for Him.'" For those who have shared the Catholic Worker life, that has been their experience; for many more, Dorothy Day's faith and vision have made this an ideal worth the striving.

EDITION USED:

The Long Loneliness. New York, Harper, 1952.

SUGGESTED READINGS:

Day, Dorothy. *Loaves and Fishes.* New York: Curtis Books, 1963.
_____. *On Pilgrimage: The Sixties.* New York: Curtis Books, 1972.
Miller, William D. *A Harsh and Dreadful Love: Dorothy Day and the Catholic Worker Movement.* New York: Liveright, 1973.

The Long Loneliness

Having a Baby

I was surprised that I found myself beginning to pray daily. I could not get down on my knees, but I could pray while I was walking. If I got down on my knees I thought, "Do I really believe? Whom am I praying to?" A terrible doubt came over me, and a sense of shame, and I wondered if I was praying because I was lonely, because I was unhappy.

But when I walked to the village for the mail, I found myself praying again, holding in my pocket the rosary that Mary Gordon gave me in New Orleans some years before. Maybe I did not say it correctly but I kept on saying it because it made me happy.

Then I thought suddenly, scornfully, "Here you are in a stupor of content. You are biological. Like a cow. Prayer with you is like the opiate of the people." And over and over again in my mind that phrase was repeated jeeringly, "Religion is the opiate of the people."

"But," I reasoned with myself, "I am praying because I am happy, not because I am unhappy. I did not turn to God in unhappiness, in grief, in despair—to get consolation, to get something from Him."

And encouraged that I was praying because I wanted to thank Him, I went on praying. No matter how dull the day, how long the walk seemed, if I felt sluggish at the beginning of the walk, the words I had been saying insinuated themselves into my heart before I had finished, so that on the trip back I neither prayed nor thought but was filled with exultation.

Along the beach I found it appropriate to say the *Te Deum.* When I worked about the house, I found myself addressing the Blessed Virgin and turning toward her statue.

It is so hard to say how this delight in prayer grew on me. The year before, I was saying as I planted seeds in the garden, "I *must* believe in these seeds, that they fall into the earth and grow into flowers and radishes and beans. It is a miracle to me because I do not understand it. Neither do naturalists understand it. The very fact that they use glib technical phrases does not make it any less of a miracle, and a miracle we all accept. Then why not accept God's mysteries?"

I began to go to Mass regularly on Sunday mornings.

When Freda went into town, I was alone. Forster was in the city all week, only coming out week ends. I finished the writing I was doing and felt at loose ends, thinking enviously of my friends going gaily about the city, about their work, with plenty of companionship.

The fact that I felt restless was a very good reason to stay on the beach and content myself with my life as a sybaritic anchorite. For how could I be a true anchorite with such luxuries as the morning paper, groceries delivered to the door, a beach to walk on, and the water to feast my eyes on? And then the fresh fish and clams, mushrooms, Jerusalem artichokes, such delicacies right at hand. I invited Lefty to supper and discussed with him the painting of the house. I read Dickens every evening.

In spite of my desire for a sociable week in town, in spite of a desire to pick up and flee from my solitude, I took joy in thinking of the idiocy of the pleasures I would indulge in if I were there. Cocktail parties, with prohibition drinks, dinners, the conversation or lack of it, dancing in a smoky crowded room when one might be walking on the beach, the dull, restless cogitations which come after dissipating one's energies—things which struck me with renewed force every time I spent days in the city. My virtuous resolutions to indulge in such pleasure no more were succeeded by a hideous depression when neither my new-found sense of religion, my family life, my work nor my surroundings were sufficient to console me. I thought of death and was overwhelmed by the terror and the blackness of both life and death. And I longed for a church near at hand where I could go and lift up my soul.

It was pleasant rowing about in the calm bay with Forster. The oyster boats were all out, and far on the horizon, off Sandy Hook, there was a four-masted vessel. I had the curious delusion that several huge holes had been stove in her side, through which you could see the blue sky. The other vessels seemed sailing in the air, quite indifferent to the horizon on which they should properly have been resting. Forster tried to explain to me scientific facts about mirages and atmospheric conditions, and, on the other hand, I pointed out to him how our senses lie to us.

But it was impossible to talk about religion or faith to him. A wall immediately separated us. The very love of nature, and the study of her secrets which was bringing me to faith, cut Forster off from religion.

I had known Forster a long time before we contracted our common-law relationship, and I have always felt that it was life with him that brought me natural happiness, that brought me to God.

His ardent love of creation brought me to the Creator of all things. But when I cried out to him, "How can there be no God, when there are all these beautiful things," he turned from me uneasily and complained that I was never satisfied. We loved each other so strongly that he wanted to remain in the love of the moment; he wanted me to rest in that love. He cried out against my attitude that there would be nothing left of that love without a faith.

I remembered the love story in Romain Rolland's *Jean Christophe,* the story of his friend and his engrossing marriage, and how those young people exhausted themselves in the intensity of their emotions.

I could not see that love between man and woman was incompatible with love of God. God is the Creator, and the very fact that we were begetting a child made me have a sense that we were made in the image and likeness of God, co-creators with him. I could not protest with Sasha about "that initial agony of having to live." Because I was grateful for love, I was grateful for life, and living with Forster made me appreaiate it and even reverence is still more. He had introduced me to so much that was beautiful and good that I felt I owed to him too this renewed interest in the things of the spirit.

He had all the love of the English for the outdoors in all weather. He used to insist on walks no matter how cold or rainy the day, and this dragging me away from my books, from my lethargy, into the open, into the country, made me begin to breathe. If breath is life, then I was beginning to be full of it because of him. I was filling my lungs with it, walking on the beach, resting on the pier beside him while he fished, rowing with him in the calm bay, walking through fields and woods—a new experience entirely for me, one which brought me to life, and filled me with joy.

I had been passing through some years of fret and strife, beauty and ugliness—even some weeks of sadness and despair. There had been periods of intense joy but seldom had there been the quiet beauty and happiness I had now. I had thought all those years that I had freedom, but now I felt that I had never known real freedom nor even had knowledge of what freedom meant.

Now, just as in my childhood, I was enchained, tied to one spot, unable to pick up and travel from one part of the country to another, from one job to another. I was tied down because I was going to have a baby. No matter how much I might sometimes wish to flee from my quiet existence, I could not, nor would I be able to for several years. I had to accept my quiet and stillness, and accepting it, I rejoiced in it.

For a long time I had thought I could not bear a child, and the longing in my heart for a baby had been growing. My home, I felt, was not a home without one. The simple joys of the kitchen and garden and beach brought sadness with them because I felt myself unfruitful, barren. No matter how much one was loved or one loved, that love was lonely without a child. It was incomplete.

I will never forget my blissful joy when I was first sure that I was pregnant—I had wanted a baby all the first year we were together. When I was finally sure, it was a beautiful June day and we were going on a picnic to Tottenville to see a circus, Malcolm and Peggy, Forster and I. It was a circus in a tent, and it was Peggy who insisted on going. We brought dandelion wine and pickled eels and good home-made bread and butter. A fantastic lunch, but I remember enjoying the root beer and popcorn later, and feeling so much in love, so settled, so secure that now I had found what I was looking for.

It did not last all through my pregnancy, that happiness. There were conflicts because Forster did not believe in bringing children into such a world as we lived in. He still was obsessed by the war. His fear of responsibility, his dislike of having the control of others, his extreme individualism made him feel that he of all men should not be a father.

Our child was born in March at the end of a harsh winter. In December I had come in from the country and taken an apartment in town. My sister came to stay with me, to help me over the last hard months. It was good to be there, close to friends, close to a church where I could pray. I read the *Imitation of Christ* a great deal during those months. I knew that I was going to have my child baptized, cost what it may. I knew that I was not going to have her floundering through many years as I had done, doubting and hesitating, undisciplined and amoral. I felt it was the greatest thing I could do for my child. For myself, I prayed for the gift of faith. I was sure, yet not sure. I postponed the day of decision.

A woman does not want to be alone at such a time. Even the most hardened, the most irreverent, is awed by the stupendous fact of creation. Becoming a Catholic would mean facing life alone and I clung to family life. It was hard to contemplate giving up a mate in order that my child and I could become members of the Church. Forster would have nothing to do with religion or with me if I embraced it. So I waited.

Those last months of waiting I was too happy to know the unrest of indecision. The days were slow in passing, but week by week the time came nearer. I spent some time in writing, but for the most part I felt a great stillness. I was incapable of going to meetings, of seeing many people, of taking up the threads of my past life.

When the little one was born, my joy was so great that I sat up in bed in the hospital and wrote an article for the *New Masses* about my child, wanting to share my joy with the world. I was glad to write this joy for a workers' magazine because it was a joy all women knew, no matter what their grief at poverty, unemployment and class war. The article so appealed to my Marxist friends that the account was reprinted all over the world in workers' papers. Diego Rivera, when I met him some four years afterward in Mexico, greeted me as the author of it. And Mike Gold, who was at that time editor of the *New Masses,* said it had been printed in many Soviet newspapers and that I had rubles awaiting me in Moscow.

When Tamar Teresa—for that is what I named her—was six weeks old, we went back to the beach. It was April and, though it was still cold, it was definitely spring.

Every morning while she napped on the sunny porch, well swathed in soft woolen blankets, I went down to the beach and with the help of Lefty brought up driftwood, enough to last until next morning. Forster was home only week ends and then he chopped enough wood to last a few days. But when the wind was high and piercing it penetrated the house so that much wood was needed, and it was a pleasure to tramp up and down the beach in the bright sun and collect wood which smelled of seaweed, brine and tar. It was warmer outside than it was in the house, and on the porch Teresa was nicely sheltered. Sometimes in the afternoon I put her in her carriage and went out along the woods, watching, almost feeling the buds bursting through their warm coats. Song sparrows, woodpeckers, hawks, crows, robins, nuthatches and of course laughing gulls made the air gay with their clamor. Starlings chattered in the branches of the old pine in front of the porch. We collected azalea buds, dogwood, sassafras and apple-tree branches to decorate the room. Best of all there were skunk cabbages, gleaming mottled-green, dark red, and yellow, small enough to make a most decorative centerpiece, propped up with stones. They were never so colorful as they were that year, and spring after spring since I have watched for them thrusting up vigorously in marshy places. Skunk cabbages and the spring peepers—these tiny frogs—mean that the winter is over and gone.

There was arbutus still buried under the leaves so that one had to look carefully for it like buried treasure. There were spring beauties and adder's-tongue and dandelion greens. The year before I had been planting radishes on March first but this year gardening gave way to more delightful tasks.

Supper always was early and the baby comfortably tucked away before it was dark. Then, tired with all the activities that so rejoiced and filled my days, I sat in the dusk in a stupor of contentment.

Yet always those deep moments of happiness gave way to a feeling of struggle, of a long silent fight still to be gone through. There had been the physical struggle, the mortal combat almost, of giving birth to a child, and now there was coming the struggle for my own soul. Tamar would be baptized, and I knew the rending it would cause in human relations around me. I was to be torn and agonized again, and I was all for putting off the hard day.

Love Overflows

"THOU shalt love the Lord thy God with thy whole heart and with thy whole soul and with thy whole mind." This is the first Commandment.

The problem is, how to love God? We are only too conscious of the hardness of our hearts, and in spite of all that religious writers tell us about *feeling* not being necessary, we do want to feel and so know that we love God.

"Thou wouldst not seek Him if thou hadst not already found Him," Pascal says, and it is true too that you love God if you want to love Him. One of the disconcerting facts about the spiritual life is that God takes you at your word. Sooner or later one is given a chance to prove his love. The very word "diligo," the Latin word used for "love," means "I prefer." It was all very well to love God in His works, in the beauty of His creation which was crowned for me by the birth of my child. Forster had made the physical world come alive for me and had awakened in my heart a flood of gratitude. The final object of this love and gratitude was God. No human creature could receive or contain so vast a flood of love and joy as I often felt after the birth of my child. With this came the need to worship, to adore. I had heard many say that they wanted to worship God in their own way and did not need a Church in which to praise Him, nor a body of people with whom to associate themselves. But I did not agree to this. My very experience as a radical, my whole make-up, led me to want to associate myself with others, with the masses, in loving and praising God. Without even looking into the claims of the Catholic Church, I was willing to admit that for me she was the one true Church. She had come down through the centuries since the time of Peter, and far from being dead, she claimed and held the allegiance of the masses of people in all the cities where I had lived. They poured in and out of her doors on Sundays and holy days, for novenas and missions. What if they were compelled to come in by the law of the Church, which said they were guilty of mortal sin if they did not go to Mass every Sunday? They obeyed that law. They were given a chance to show their preference. They accepted the Church. It may have been an unthinking, unquestioning faith, and yet the chance certainly came, again and again, "Do I prefer the Church to my own will," even if it was only the small matter of sitting at home on a Sunday morning with the papers? And the choice was the Church.

There was the legislation of the Church in regard to marriage, a stumbling block to many. That was where I began to be troubled, to be afraid. To become a Catholic meant for me to give up a mate with whom I was much in love. It got to the point where it was the simple question of whether I chose God or man. I had known enough of love to know that a good healthy family life was as near to heaven as one could get in this life.

There was another sample of heaven, of the enjoyment of God. The very sexual act itself was used again and again in Scripture as a figure of the beatific vision. It was not because I was tired of sex, satiated, disillusioned, that I turned to God. Radical friends used to insinuate this. It was because through a whole love, both physical and spiritual, I came to know God.

From the time Tamar Teresa was born I was intent on having her baptized. There had been that young Catholic girl in the bed next to me at the hospital who gave me a medal of St. Thérèse of Lisieux.

"I don't believe in these things," I told her, and it was another example of people saying what they do not mean.

"If you love someone you like to have something around which reminds you of them," she told me.

It was so obvious a truth that I was shamed. Reading William James' *Varieties of Religious Experience* had acquainted me with the saints, and I had read the life of St. Teresa of Avila and fallen in love with her. She was a mystic and a practical woman, a recluse and a traveler, a cloistered nun and yet most active. She liked to read novels when she was a young girl, and she wore a bright red dress when she entered the convent. Once when she was traveling from one part of Spain to another with some other nuns and a priest to start a convent, and their way took them over a stream, she was thrown from her donkey. The story goes that our Lord said to her, "That is how I treat my friends." And she replied, "And that is why You have so few of them." She called life a "night spent at an uncomfortable inn." Once when she was trying to avoid that recreation hour which is set aside in convents for nuns to be together, the others insisted on her joining them, and she took castanets and danced. When some older nuns professed themselves shocked, she retorted, "One must do things sometimes to make life more bearable." After she was a superior she gave directions when the nuns became melancholy, "to feed them steak," and there were other delightful little touches to the story of her life which made me love her and feel close to her. I have since heard a priest friend of ours remark gloomily that one could go to hell imitating the imperfections of the saints, but these little incidents brought out in her biography made her delightfully near to me. So I decided to name my daughter after her. That is why my neighbor offered me a medal of St. Thérèse of Lisieux, who is called the little Teresa.

Her other name came from Sasha's sister Liza. She had named her daughter Tamar, which in Hebrew means "little palm tree," and knowing nothing of the unhappy story of the two Tamars in the Old Testament, I named my child Tamar also. Tamar is one of the forebears of our Lord, listed in the first chapter of Matthew, and not only Jews and Russians, but also New Englanders used the name.

What a driving power joy is! When I was unhappy and repentant in the past I turned to God, but it was my joy at having given birth to a child that made me do something definite. I wanted Tamar to have a way of life and instruction. We all crave order, and in the Book of Job, hell is described as a place where no order is. I felt that "belonging" to a Church would bring that order into her life which I felt my own had lacked. If I could have felt that communism was the answer to my desire for a cause, a motive, a way to walk in, I would have remained as I was. But I felt that only faith in Christ could give the answer. The Sermon on the Mount answered all the questions as to how to love God and one's brother. I knew little about the Sacraments, and yet here I was believing, knowing that without them Tamar would not be a Catholic.

I did not know any Catholics to speak to. The grocer, the hardware storekeeper, my neighbors down the road were Catholics, yet I could not bring myself to speak to them about religion. I was full of the reserves I noted in my own family. But I could speak to a nun. So when I saw a nun walking down the road near St. Joseph's-by-the-Sea, I went up to her breathlessly and asked her how I could have my child baptized. She was not at all reticent about asking questions and not at all surprised at my desires. She was a simple old sister who had taught grade school all her life. She was now taking care of babies in a huge home on the bay which had belonged to Charles Schwab, who had given it to the Sisters of Charity. They used it for summer retreats for the Sisters and to take care of orphans and unmarried mothers and their babies.

Sister Aloysia had had none of the university summer courses that most Sisters must take nowadays. She never talked to me about the social encyclicals of the Popes. She gave me a catechism and brought me old copies of the *Messenger of the Sacred Heart,* a magazine which, along with the Kathleen Norris type of success story, had some good solid articles about the teachings of the Church. I read them all; I studied my catechism; I learned to say the Rosary; I went to Mass in the chapl by the sea; I walked the beach and I prayed; I read the *Imitation of Christ,* and St. Augustine, and the New Testament. Dostoevski, Huysmans (what different men!) had given me desire and background. Huysmans had made me at home in the Church.

"How can your daughter be brought up a Catholic unless you become one yourself?" Sister Aloysia kept saying to me. But she went resolutely ahead in making arrangements for the baptism of Tamar Teresa.

"You must be a Catholic yourself," she kept telling me. She had no reticence. She speculated rather volubly at times on the various reasons why she thought I was holding back. She brought me pious literature to read, saccharine stories of virtue, emasculated lives of saints young and old, back numbers of pious magazines. William James, agnostic as he was, was more help. He had introduced me to St. Teresa of Avila and St. John of the Cross.

Isolated as I was in the country, knowing no Catholics except my neighbors, who seldom read anything except newspapers and secular magazines, there was not much chance of being introduced to the good Catholic literature of the present day. I was in a state of dull content—not in a state to be mentally stimulated. I was too happy with my child. What faith I had I held on to stubbornly. The need for patience emphasized in the writings of the saints consoled me on the slow road I was traveling. I would put all my affairs in the hands of God and wait.

Three times a week Sister Aloysia came to give me a catechism lesson, which I dutifully tried to learn. But she insisted that I recite word for word, with the repetition of the question that was in the book. If I had not learned my lesson, she rebuked me, "And you think you are intelligent!" she would say witheringly. "What is the definition of grace—actual grace and sanctifying grace? My fourth-grade pupils know more than you do!"

I hadn't a doubt but that they did. I struggled on day by day, learning without question. I was in an agreeable and lethargic, almost bovine state of mind, filled with an animal content, not wishing to inquire into or question the dogmas I was learning. I made up my mind to accept what I did not understand, trusting light to come, as it sometimes did, in a blinding flash of exultation and realization.

She criticized my housekeeping. "Here you sit at your typewriter at ten o'clock and none of your dishes done yet. Supper and breakfast dishes besides. . . . And why don't you calcimine your ceiling? It's all dirty from wood smoke."

She brought me vegetables from the garden of the home, and I gave her fish and clams. Once I gave her stamps and a dollar to send a present to a little niece and she was touchingly grateful. It made me suddenly realize that, in spite of Charlie Schwab and his estate, the Sisters lived in complete poverty, owning nothing, holding all things in common.

I had to have godparents for Tamar, and I thought of Aunt Jenny, my mother's sister, the only member of our family I knew who had become a Catholic. She had married a Catholic and had one living child, Grace. I did not see them very often but I looked them up now and asked Grace and her husband if they would be godparents to my baby. Tamar was baptized in July. We went down to Tottenville, the little town at the south end of the island; there in the Church of Our Lady, Help of Christians, the seed of life was implanted in her and she was made a child of God.

We came back to the beach house to a delightful lunch of boiled lobsters and salad. Forster had caught the lobsters in his traps for the feast and then did not remain to partake of it. He left, not returning for several days. It was his protest against my yearnings toward the life of the spirit, which he considered a morbid escapism. He exulted in his materialism. He well knew the dignity of man. Heathen philosophers, says Matthias Scheeben, a great modern theologian, have called man a miracle, the marrow and the heart of the world, the most beautiful being, the king of all creatures. Forster saw man in the light of reason and not in the light of faith. He had thought of the baptism only as a mumbo jumbo, the fuss and flurry peculiar to woman. At first he had been indulgent and had brought in the lobsters for the feast. And then he had become angry with some sense of the end to which all this portended. Jealousy set in and he left me.

As a matter of fact, he left me quite a number of times that coming winter and following summer, as he felt my increasing absorption in religion. The tension between us was terrible. Teresa had become a member of the Mystical Body of Christ. I didn't know anything of the Mystical Body or I might have felt disturbed at being separated from her.

But I clutched her close to me and all the time I nursed her and bent over that tiny round face at my breast, I was filled with a deep happiness that nothing could spoil. But the obstacles to my becoming a Catholic were there, shadows in the background of my life.

I had become convinced that I would become a Catholic; yet I felt I was betraying the class to which I belonged, the workers, the poor of the world, with whom Christ spent His life. I wrote a few articles for the *New Masses* but did no other work at that time. My life was crowded in summer because friends came and stayed with me, and some of them left their children. Two little boys, four and eight years old, joined the family for a few months and my days were full, caring for three children and cooking meals for a half-dozen persons three times a day.

Sometimes when I could leave the baby in trusted hands I could get to the village for Mass on Sunday. But usually the gloom that descended on the household, the scarcely voiced opposition, kept me from Mass. There were some feast days when I could slip off during the week and go to the little chapel on the Sisters' grounds. There were "visits" I could make, unknown to others. I was committed, by the advice of a priest I consulted, to the plan of waiting, and trying to hold together the family. But I felt all along that when I took the irrevocable step it would mean that Tamar and I would be alone, and I did not want to be alone. I did not want to give up human love when it was dearest and tenderest.

During the month of August many of my friends, including my sister, went to Boston to picket in protest against the execution of Sacco and Vanzetti, which was drawing near. They were all arrested again and again. Throughout the nation and the world the papers featured the struggle for the lives of these two men. Radicals from all over the country gathered in Boston, and articles describing those last days were published, poems were written. It was an epic struggle, a tragedy. One felt a sense of impending doom. These men were Catholics, inasmuch as they were Italians. Catholics by tradition, but they had rejected the Church. . . .

The day they died, the papers had headlines as large as those which proclaimed the outbreak of war. All the nation mourned. All the nation, I mean, that is made up of the poor, the worker, the trade unionist—those who felt most keenly the sense of solidarity—that very sense of solidarity which made me gradually understand the doctrine of the Mystical Body of Christ whereby we are the members one of another.

Forster was stricken over the tragedy. He had always been more an anarchist than anything else in his philosophy, and so was closer to these two men than to Communist friends. He did not eat for days. He sat around the house in a stupor of misery, sickened by the cruelty of life and men. He had always taken refuge in nature as being more kindly, more beautiful and peaceful than the world of men. Now he could not even escape through nature, as he tried to escape so many problems in life.

During the time he was home he spent days and even nights out in his boat fishing, so that for weeks I saw little of him. He stupefied himself in his passion for the water, sitting out on the bay in his boat. When he began to recover he submerged himself in maritime biology, collecting, reading only scientific books, and paying no attention to what went on around him. Only the baby interested him. She was his delight. Which made it, of course, the harder to contemplate the cruel blow I was going to strike him when I became a Catholic. We both suffered in body as well as in soul and mind. He would not talk about the faith and relapsed into a complete silence if I tried to bring up the subject. The point of my bringing it up was that I could not become a Catholic and continue living with him, because he was averse to any ceremony before officials of either Church or state. He was an anarchist and an atheist, and he did not intend to be a liar or a hypocrite. He was a creature of utter sincerity, and however illogical and bad-tempered about it all, I loved him. It was killing me to think of leaving him.

Fall nights we read a great deal. Sometimes he went out to dig bait if there were a low tide and the moon was up. He stayed out late on the pier fishing, and came in smelling of seaweed and salt air; getting into bed, cold with the chill November air, he held me close to him in silence. I loved him in every way, as a wife, as a mother even. I loved him for all he knew and pitied him for all he didn't know. I loved him for the odds and ends I had to fish out of his sweater pockets and for the sand and shells he brought in with his fishing. I loved his lean cold body as he got into bed smelling of the sea, and I loved his integrity and stubborn pride.

It ended by my being ill the next summer. I became so oppressed I could not breathe and I awoke in the night choking. I was weak and listless and one doctor told me my trouble was probably thyroid. I went to the Cornell clinic for a metabolism test and they said my condition was a nervous one. By winter the tension had become so great that an explosion occurred and we separated again. When he returned, as he always had, I would not let him in the house; my heart was breaking with my own determination to make an end, once and for all, to the torture we were undergoing.

The next day I went to Tottenville alone, leaving Tamar with my sister, and there with Sister Aloysia as my godparent, I too was baptized conditionally, since I had already been baptized in the Episcopal Church. I made my first confession right afterward, and looked forward the next morning to receiving communion.

I had no particular joy in partaking of these three sacraments, Baptism, Penance and Holy Eucharist. I proceeded about my own active participation in them grimly, coldly, making acts of faith, and certainly with no consolation whatever. One part of my mind stood at one side and kept saying, "What are you doing? Are you sure of yourself? What kind of an affectation is this? What act is this you are going through? Are you trying to induce emotion, induce faith, partake of an opiate, the opiate of the people?" I felt like a hypocrite if I got down on my knees, and shuddered at the thought of anyone seeing me.

At my first communion I went up to the communion rail at the *Sanctus* bell instead of at the *Domine, non sum dignus,* and had to kneel there all alone through the consecration, through the *Pater Noster,* through the *Agnus Dei*—and I had thought I knew the Mass so well! But I felt it fitting that I be humiliated by this ignorance, by this precipitance.

I speak of the misery of leaving one love. But there was another love too, the life I had led in the radical movement. That very winter I was writing a series of articles, interviews with the workers, with the unemployed. I was working with the Anti-Imperialist League, a Communist affiliate, that was bringing aid and comfort to the enemy, General Sandino's forces in Nicaragua. I was just as much against capitalism and imperialism as ever, and here I was going over to the opposition, because of course the Church was lined up with property, with the wealthy, with the state, with capitalism, with all the forces of reaction. This I had been taught to think and this I still think to a great extent. "Too often," Cardinal Mundelein said, "has the Church lined up on the wrong side." "Christianity," Bakunin said, "is precisely the religion par excellence, because it exhibits, and manifests, to the fullest extent, the very nature and essence of every religious system, which is the impoverishment, enslavement, and annihilation of humanity for the benefit of divinity."

I certainly believed this, but I wanted to be poor, chaste and obedient. I wanted to die in order to live, to put off the old man and put on Christ. I loved, in other words, and like all women in love, I wanted to be united to my love. Why should not Forster be jealous? Any man who did not participate in this love would, of course, realize my infidelity, my adultery. In the eyes of God, any turning toward creatures to the exclusion of Him is adultery and so it is termed over and over again in Scripture.

I loved the Church for Christ made visible. Not for itself, because it was so often a scandal to me. Romano Guardini said the Church is the Cross on which Christ was crucified; one could not separate Christ from His Cross, and one must live in a state of permanent dissatisfaction with the Church. . . .

It was an age-old battle, the war of the classes, that stirred in me when I thought of the Sacco-Vanzetti case in Boston. Where were the Catholic voices crying out for these men? How I longed to make a synthesis reconciling body and soul, this world and the next, the teachings of Prince Peter Kropotkin and Prince Demetrius Gallitzin, who had become a missionary priest in rural Pennsylvania.

Where had been the priests to go out to such men as Francisco Ferrer in Spain, pursuing them as the Good Shepherd did His lost sheep, leaving the ninety and nine of their good parishioners, to seek out that which was lost, bind up that which was bruised. No wonder there was such a strong conflict going on in my mind and heart.

Vietnamese guide at a bombed provincial hospital, North Vietnam (*Courtesy of Denise Levertov*)

Denise Levertov, 1923–

"Advent 1966"; "In Thai Binh (Peace) Province"; "With the Seabrook Natural Guard in Washington" (1978)

Susan Sontag, 1933–

Trip to Hanoi (1969)

The war in Vietnam became for many Americans much more than a terrible political error—it was a constant presence with which they lived as they would with a malignancy, hating and fearing it, feeling impotent in the face of its brutality and destructiveness. Anger and futility at the waste of lives demanded a response beyond those appropriate to merely political events: the evils of war became personal, and individuals sought to assume and expiate the collective guilt as their own. As descendants of the British imperialists—like Madeline Slade—had gone to India, so many Americans went to North Vietnam in the hope that personal reconciliation and personal sorrow could offer some compensation for the attacks of the giant, America, on the small nation of Vietnam.

The contrast of large and small, translated into moral terms, runs through many of the accounts of such journeys: "All three of us feel huge all the time that we are in Vietnam," Denise Levertov wrote, and Susan Sontag's account frequently makes the same point. Gawky, awkward, too big, embarrassed—these adolescent characteristics of the visitors accentuated the gentleness of the Vietnamese hosts and the cold ferocity of the loud, streaking, power-laden bombers sent by the American government. Going to Hanoi was a risk, because of the chance of prosecution for violating the State Department ban against travel to North Vietnam, and because of the real physical danger from the bombs. To take risks in opposition to the war—through acts of civil disobedience at home or through such forbidden journeys—was felt to be necessary, however, if the war was ever to be stopped.

As in the years before World War I, women were active leaders in the movement against the war. The protest against World War I coincided with the movement for woman's rights; in the 1960's the antiwar movement helped to create the consciousness of women's potential for political effectiveness that led to the feminism of the 1970's. The women who went to Vietnam—in 1966, Barbara Deming and Patricia Griffiths, Susan Sontag in 1968, Denise Levertov, Muriel Rukeyser, and Jane Hart in 1972—and others as well, were themselves striking figures, writers and intellectuals, often with long histories of political engagement, invited because of their known opposition to the United States' continuation of the war. Invariably they were thrown off balance by the actual experience of Hanoi, its Oriental serenity punctuated by the screams of bombers and the pockmarks of shelters. "My life is flying to your life," Muriel Rukeyser says in "Flying to Hanoi"; that desire to personalize the war appears in other women's accounts, too, but none oversimplifies the difficulties involved in bridging cultures, languages, and expectations of each other. Their freedom, as American women, from being called to fight imposed a responsibility to make peace, and to restore the distinction between ideology and human beings that war destroys.

Because their imaginations could encompass the ambiguities of being at once penitents for and symbols of America, the women's accounts of their journeys have become valuable documents of an American consciousness in a critical time. Their journeys—as well as those of such men as David Dellinger and Daniel Berrigan—are different from the earlier journeys of American intellectuals to the Soviet Union after the 1917 Revolution. The travellers to Russia had gone in search of utopia; the travellers to Vietnam went seeking forgiveness.

Susan Sontag and Denise Levertov came to Hanoi from very different personal and political histories. Denise Levertov grew up in London, the daughter of a Welsh schoolteacher, Beatrice Spooner-Jones Levertoff, who gave her a "love of Nature and my ability to read aloud well" and the inheritance of the Welsh mystic, Angel Jones of Mold. Her father, Paul Levertoff, was an Hasidic Jew who became an Anglican priest. A scholar, he wrote in several languages and took as his particular mission the reconciliation of Christians and Jews. Denise Levertov never went to school, learning from her parents and from the visitors and books that crowded the house. In 1947, she married the American writer Mitchell Goodman and came to the United States. Her poetry responded to the new stimulus of the American culture and language and she became, as Richard Howard has said, "not merely an agent but an origin of that language." Her first involvement in the peace movement in the United States came during the Cold War, when she demonstrated against compulsory air-raid drills and against nuclear proliferation. In 1965 she was prominent in the founding of the Writers' and Artists' Protest Against the War in Vietnam; and throughout the sixties she travelled extensively to join protests and demonstrations against the war, becoming more deeply committed to resistance. As the brutal war continued and protests were mounted and resisted with growing antagonism on both sides, the assurance that lay at the center of her poetry—that "there is a form in all things (and in our experience) which the poet can discover and reveal"—was challenged by the overwhelming, all-consuming irrationality of the struggle in Vietnam. In *The Sorrow Dance* (1967), and increasingly in *Relearning the Alphabet* (1970) and *To Stay Alive* (1971), her poetry responded to the chaos of war that attackèd her "poet's caressive sight" and obscured, even denied the order of the world. As anger mounted the poems became angrier and harsher, although never formless, never the "vomit-it-all-out" poetry that she deplored ("A Testament and a Postscript," in *The Poet of the World,* p. 4). "There comes a time when only anger is love," she came to believe, when tolerance becomes criminal, and the only choice is "revolution or death. . . . Of course I choose/ revolution" ("From a Notebook").

In the fall of 1972, Denise Levertov was invited to Vietnam with the poet Muriel Rukeyser and Jane Hart, the wife of Senator Philip Hart and a leader in antiwar protests in Washington. There she met poets and artists and saw the grotesque devastation of a still beautiful land and a cultured people. In an earlier poem, "What Were They Like," she had imagined the total destruction of this old civilization; what she saw in Vietnam confirmed her sense both of the richness of the culture and of the risk of its annihilation.

In the years since the end of the war in Vietnam, Levertov's poetry has been freed to speak of matters other than the political, but she has continued to protest against the power that led to war and in the 1970's to the expansion of nuclear technology. Renewing her commitment to pacifism and nonviolence, she has been several times arrested in antinuclear protests, such as that of the Seabrook Natural Guard in Washington, the occasion of the comparison of protest in the 1960's with that of the 1970's, included here.

For Susan Sontag, the trip to Hanoi was not an outgrowth of long-standing participation in political protest movements. It was, instead, the means to a major reversal in her intellectual career, ending her skepticism about the validity of such protest and about herself as a political activist.

By 1968, Susan Sontag was established as one of the most original thinkers of her time. Her early life seems to have been dominated by precocity and privilege: she graduated from North Hollywood High School at 15, from the University of Chicago at 18, already married (in 1950 to sociologist Philip Rieff), and bore a child before she was twenty. She spoke several languages and while in high school was highly political, read the left-wing New York paper *PM,* and campaigned for Henry Wallace. Her family considered the way she lived to be her own affair, and her combination of intelligence and striking beauty made it no surprise that she passed through the life styles of more ordinary people early and went on to more esoteric and exotic interests. She left her husband in 1957 (they were divorced in 1958) and spent some time in France, forming the habit of passing part of every year in Paris. Much of her subsequent work has been concerned with transmitting to America the ideas of French philosophers and critics such as Sartre, Antonin Artaud, and Roland Barthes. One consequence of her study of speculative philosophy was a growing irony about her own earlier politicism and an alienation from the critical portion of the American intelligentsia as well as from its conformist portion.

Although as a "veteran signer of petitions" she had given her name to printed protests against the war, she found it impossible to speak with a political vocabulary or to convert agreement with those who opposed the war into action. She accepted the invitation to Hanoi determined not to write about it on her return. As a "stubbornly unspecialized writer, who [had] so far been unable to incorporate into either novels or essays my evolving radical political convictions and sense of moral dilemma at being a citizen of the American Empire," she believed nothing she wrote could add to the "already eloquent opposition to the war." Her decision to publish her journal is testimony to the significance of the journey as marking the end of her alienation from political action. After it, she turned her mind to modes of protest and engagement she had long neglected.

"Trip to Hanoi," first published in *Esquire* magazine and later included in *Styles of Radical Will,* presents in diary form Sontag's encounter with the reality of a country and cause which had existed for her only as idea. Intensely self-aware, she shifts her focus from the personal to the communal, and from the aesthetic to the political, as she comes to identify herself with the grossness and blunders of America. Committed to authenticity as a moral imperative, she finds that in her encounter with the Vietnamese it is impossible to seem authentic. What she has become, how she thinks, her criteria of moral and social value do not apply, and, as the selection here suggests, she is thrown initially into confusion, irritation, and self-deprecation. In the later sections of "Trip to Hanoi," Sontag moves forward from these crises; the dilemmas and their resolution make her journal a significant document in the intellectual history of our times.

EDITIONS USED:

"Advent 1966" from Denise Levertov, *To Stay Alive.* New York: New Directions, 1971.
"In Thai Binh (Peace) Province" from Denise Levertov, *The Freeing of the Dust.* New York: New Directions, 1975.
"Trip to Hanoi" from Susan Sontag, *Styles of Radical Will.* New York: Farrar, Straus and Giroux, 1969.

SUGGESTED READINGS:

Berrigan, Daniel. *Night Flight to Hanoi.* New York: Grossman, 1974.
Deming, Barbara. *We Cannot Live Without Our Lives.* New York: Grossman, 1974.
Levertov, Denise. *The Poet in the World.* New York: New Directions, 1973.
Mersmann, James. *Out of the Vietnam Vortex: A Study of Poets and Poetry Against the War.* Lawrence: University Press of Kansas, 1974.
Rukeyser, Muriel. *Breaking Open.* New York: Random House, 1973.
Sontag, Susan. *Against Interpretation.* New York: Farrar, Straus and Giroux, 1966.
_____. *I, Etcetera.* New York: Farrar, Straus and Giroux, 1978.
_____. *On Photography.* New York: Farrar, Straus and Giroux, 1977.

Advent 1966

Because in Vietnam the vision of a Burning Babe
is multiplied, multiplied,
              the flesh on fire
not Christ's, as Southwell saw it, prefiguring
the Passion upon the Eve of Christmas,

but wholly human and repeated, repeated,
infant after infant, their names forgotten,
their sex unknown in the ashes,
set alight, flaming but not vanishing,
not vanishing as his vision but lingering,

cinders upon the earth or living on
moaning and stinking in hospitals three abed;

because of this my strong sight,
my clear caressive sight, my poet's sight I was given
that it might stir me to song,
is blurred.
          There is a cataract filming over
my inner eyes. Or else a monstrous insect
has entered my head, and looks out
from my sockets with multiple vision,

seeing not the unique Holy Infant
burning sublimely, an imagination of redemption,
furnace in which souls are wrought into new life,
but, as off a beltline, more, more senseless figures aflame.

And this insect (who is not there—
it is my own eyes do my seeing, the insect

is not there, what I see is there)
will not permit me to look elsewhere,

or if I look, to see except dulled and unfocused
the delicate, firm, whole flesh of the still unburned.

In Thai Binh (Peace) Province

for Muriel and Jane

I've used up all my film on bombed hospitals,
bombed village schools, the scattered
lemon-yellow cocoons at the bombed silk-factory,

and for the moment all my tears too
are used up, having seen today
yet another child with its feet blown off,
        a girl, this one, eleven years old,
patient and bewildered in her home, a fragile
small house of mud bricks among rice fields.

So I'll use my dry burning eyes
to photograph within me
dark sails of the river boats,
warm slant of afternoon light
apricot on the brown, swift, wide river,
village towers—church and pagoda—on the far shore,
and a boy and small bird both
perched, relaxed, on a quietly grazing
buffalo.   Peace within the
        long war.

It is that life, unhurried, sure, persistent,
I must bring home when I try to bring
the war home.
        Child, river, light.

Here the future, fabled bird
that has migrated away from America,
nests, and breeds, and sings.

common as any sparrow.

With the Seabrook Natural Guard in Washington

*** Two hundred people spent over 56 (fifty six) hours living on a piece of sidewalk in front of the NRC building—eating, sleeping, holding meetings, chanting, singing, or simply sitting. (Dan Ellsberg quoted Ghandi to us at the rally which preceded the sit-in: "Sitting is good. But it does make a difference *where* you sit.") For those of us who also spent long hours on the excruciating steel cots in the holding cells Thursday night the last day was particularly uncomfortable; speaking for myself, my 54-year-old body seemed to develop aching knobs and knots all over, and I couldn't sit, lie, or stand with comfort. Yet we all, including me, kept getting another wind. . . .

****Throughout the action, no one smoked dope or drank liquor or beer or offered provocation to the police or others or trashed anything. And we left our sidewalk home as clean, or cleaner, than we found it. This was not because anyone came and harangued us or gave us pep talks. Discipline came from within individuals and their affinity groups. How different an atmosphere from the fierce, bitching, trashing, "off the pig"-shouting demonstrations of the late 60's, early 70's! I then got caught up in that behavior myself, but I see the present mode of confrontation as having a far more effective potential. Besides, I've come back to my original belief that, for anything of value to evolve, the means must be consonant with the end, as far as is humanly possible. Of course, the disillusion that followed the assassinations of Dr. King and Malcom X, our seeming impotence to stop the napalming and bombing in SE Asia, the Kent State killings, the hunting down of the Panthers—that disillusion and the nihilistic rage that ensued, could occur again. But the sense of inner, individual change and growth that characterises the nonviolence of the antinuclear movement does seem to me to promise more staying power. Most of the people involved had no first-hand experience of the violent, frustrated style of the early 70's, and it would seem very alien to them—offensively so. Most of them come from the environmental movement; many have Earth Days and backpacking trips as memories from high school years. They've evolved a gentle, unpretentious, civilized style of daily life, and they seem to me more mature than the people of the same average age—early 20's—that I knew and acted with nine or ten years ago. A lot of them are only beginning to perceive political interconnections; but they are fast learners. The people in my Seabrook affinity group are all connected to Tufts, where the university's South African investments and its acceptance of a million dollars from the infamous Marcos, dictator of the Philippines, have been strongly protested during the past year, and where such issues as the J.P. Stevens Boycott have drawn support. Most of us have been involved in some or all of these causes as well as in the Mobilization for Survival Teach-in and Environmental Action's follow-up to it last fall. Clams and Natural Guards are neither Flower Children nor Maoists nor any of the stereotypes in between. They distrust authority, but are generous listeners to the convictions, or the thinking-out-loud doubts, of others; they are skeptical of presumptuous or pretentious opinion, but open to persuasion if they feel it is coming from a sincere source. I feel I have much to learn from these brothers and sisters.

Denise Levertov and Jane Hart with Vietnamese guides at the remains of a
provincial hospital, North Vietnam (*Courtesy of Denise Levertov*)

Trip to Hanoi

May 6

Of course, I'm not sorry to have come. Being in Hanoi is at the very least a duty, for me an important act of personal and political affirmation. What I'm not yet reconciled to is that it's also a piece of political theatre. They are playing their roles, we (I) must play ours (mine). The heaviness of it all comes from the fact that the script is written entirely by them; and they're directing the play, too. Though this is how it has to be—it's their country, their life-and-death struggle, while we are volunteers, extras, figurants who retain the option of getting off the stage and sitting safely in the audience—it makes my acts here appear to me largely dutiful, and the whole performance a little sad.

We have a role: American friends of the Vietnamese struggle. (About forty Americans in some way connected with the anti-war movement in the States have made this trip before us.) The trip to Hanoi is a kind of reward or patronage. We are being given a treat, being thanked for our unsolicited efforts; and then we are to return home with a reinforced sense of solidarity, to continue our separate ways of opposing the current American policy.

There is, of course, an exquisite politeness in this corporate identity. We are not asked, separately or collectively, to say why we merit this trip. Our being recommended (by Americans who were invited earlier and retain the confidence of the Vietnamese) and our willingness to come (all this way, at our own expense, and facing the risk of prosecution when we return to the States) seem to put Bob's, Andy's, and my efforts on the same level. Nobody here poses questions about what we specifically do for the anti-war movement, or asks us to justify the quality of our activities; it seems to be assumed that we each do what we can. Though our Vietnamese hosts evidently know we are not Communists, and indeed seem to have no illusions about the American Communist Party—"We know our Communist friends in the United States are not in great number," a government official remarked dryly—nobody inquires into our political beliefs. We are *cac ban* all.

Everybody says, "We know the American people are our friends. Only the present American government is our enemy." A journalist we met commended our efforts to "safeguard the freedom and prestige of the United States." Though I honor the nobility of this attitude, I'm exasperated by their naïveté. Do they really believe what they're saying? Don't they understand anything about America? Part of me can't help regarding them as children—beautiful, patient, heroic, martyred, stubborn children. And I know that I'm not a child, though the theatre of this visit requires that I play the role of one. The same shy, tender smile appears on the face of the soldier we pass in the park, the elderly Buddhist scholar,, and the waitress in the hotel dining room as on the faces of the children lined up to greet us at the evacuated primary school we visited today just outside Hanoi; and we're smiling at them like that, too. We get little presents and souvenirs wherever we go, and at the end of each visit Bob distributes a handful of anti-war buttons (how lucky that he thought to bring a bagful of them). The most impressive of his random collection are the jumbo blue and white buttons from last October's March on the Pentagon, which we save for special occasions. How could we not be moved at the moment we are pinning on their tiny red and gold badges while they are adorning themselves with our big anti-war buttons? How could we not also be in bad faith?

The root of my bad faith: that I long for the three-dimensional, textured, "adult" world in which I live in America—even as I go about my (their) business in this two-dimensional world of the ethical fairy tale where I am paying a visit, and in which I do believe.

Part of the role (theirs and mine) is the stylizing of language: speaking mostly in simple declarative sentences, making all discourse either expository or interrogative. Everything is on one level here. All the words belong to the same vocabulary: struggle, bombings, friend, aggressor, imperialist, patriot, victory, brother, freedom, unity, peace. Though my strong impulse is to resist their flattening out of language, I've realized that I must talk this way—with moderation—if I'm to say anything that's useful to them. That even includes using the more loaded local epithets like "the puppet troops" (for the forces of the Saigon government) and "the American movement" (they mean *us!*). Luckily, I'm already comfortable with some of the key words. Within the last year, back in the States, I had started saying "the Front" (instead of Viet Cong) and "black people" (instead of Negroes) and "liberated zones" (for territory controlled by the National Liberation Front). But I'm far from getting it right, from their point of view. I notice that when I say "Marxism," it's usually rendered by our translator as "Marxism-Leninism." And while they may speak of "the socialist camp," it's hardly possible for me to say anything other than "Communist countries."

It's not that I judge their words to be false. For once, I think, the political and moral reality is as simple as the Communist rhetoric would have it. The French *were* "the French colonialists"; the Americans *are* "imperialist agressors"; the Thieu-Ky regime *is* a "puppet government." Then what finicky private standard or bad vibrations make me balk? Is it just the old conviction of the inadequacy of that language, to which I was first introduced during my precociously political childhood when I read *PM* and Corliss Lamont and the Webbs on Russia, and later, by the time I was a junior at North Hollywood High School, worked in the Wallace campaign and attended screenings of Eisenstein films at the American-Soviet Friendship Society? But surely neither the philistine fraud of the American CP nor the special pathos of fellow-traveling in the 1940's is relevant here: North Vietnam, spring 1968. Yet how difficult it is, once words have been betrayed, to take them seriously again. Only within the last two years (and that very much because of the impact of the Vietnam war) have I been able to pronounce the words "capitalism" and "imperialism" again. For more than fifteen years, though capitalism and imperialism hardly ceased to be facts in the world, the words themselves had seemed to me simply unusable, dead, dishonest (because a tool in the hands of dishonest people). A great deal is involved in these recent linguistic decisions: a new connection with my historical memory, my aesthetic sensibility, my very idea of the future. That I've begun to use some elements of Marxist or neo-Marxist language again seems almost a miracle, an unexpected remission of historical muteness, a new chance to address problems that I'd renounced ever understanding.

Still, when I hear these tag words here, spoken by the Vietnamese, I can't help experiencing them as elements of an *official* language, and they become again an alien way of talking. I'm not referring now to the truth of this language (the realities that the words point to), which I do acknowledge, but to the context and range of sensibility it presupposes. What's painfully exposed for me, by the way the Vietnamese talk, is the gap between ethics and aesthetics. As far as I can tell, the Vietnamese possess— even within the terribly austere and materially deprived existence they are forced to lead now—a lively, even passionate aesthetic sense. More than once, for instance, people have quite unaffectedly expressed their indignation and sadness at the disfigurement of the *beauty* of the Vietnamese countryside by the American bombing. Someone even commented on the "many beautiful names," like Cedar Falls and Junction City, that the Americans have given their "savage operations in the south." But the leading way of thinking and speaking in Vietnam is unreservedly moralistic. (I suspect this is quite natural to the Vietnamese, a cultural trait that precedes any grafting on of the moralizing framework of Communist language.) And perhaps it's the general tendency of aesthetic consciousness, when developed, to make judgments more complex and more highly qualified, while it's in the very nature of moral consciousness to be simplifying, even simplistic, and to sound—in translation at least—stiff and old-fashioned. There's a committee here (someone had left a piece of stationery in the hotel lobby) for maintaining contact with South Vietnamese intellectuals, called "Committee of Struggle Against U.S. Imperialists and Henchmen's Persecution of Intellectuals in South Vietnam." Henchmen! But aren't they? In today's Vietnam News Agency bulletin the American soldiers are called "cruel thugs." Although again the quaintness of phrase makes me smile, that is just what they are—from the vantage point of helpless peasants being napalmed by swooping diving metal birds. Still, quite apart from the quaintness of particular words, such language does make me uncomfortable. Whether because I am laggard or maybe just dissociated, I both assent to the unreserved moral judgment and shy away from it, too. I believe they are right. At the same time, nothing here can make me forget that events are much more complicated than the Vietnamese represent them. But exactly what complexities would I have them acknowledge? Isn't it enough that their struggle is, objectively, just? Can they ever afford subtleties when they need to mobilize every bit of energy to continue standing up to the American Goliath? . . . Whatever I conclude, it seems to me I end up patronizing them.

Perhaps all I'm expressing is the difference between being an actor (them) and being a spectator (me). But that's a big difference, and I don't see how I can bridge it. My sense of solidarity with the Vietnamese, however genuine and felt, is a moral abstraction developed (and meant to be lived out) at a great distance from them. Since my arrival in Hanoi, I must maintain that sense of solidarity alongside new unexpected feelings which indicate that, unhappily, it will always remain a moral abstraction. For me—a spectator?—it's monochromatic here, and I feel oppressed by that.